Study Guide

for use with

Sociology

Tenth Edition

Richard T. Schaefer
DePaul University

Prepared by

Richard T. Schaefer
DePaul University

Rebecca Matthews, Ph.D., Sociology
Cornell University

McGraw Hill

Boston   Burr Ridge, IL   Dubuque, IA   Madison, WI   New York   San Francisco   St. Louis
Bangkok   Bogotá   Caracas   Kuala Lumpur   Lisbon   London   Madrid   Mexico City
Milan   Montreal   New Delhi   Santiago   Seoul   Singapore   Sydney   Taipei   Toronto

The McGraw·Hill Companies

McGraw-Hill Higher Education

Study Guide for use with
SOCIOLOGY
Richard T. Schaefer

Published by McGraw-Hill, an imprint of The McGraw-Hill Companies, Inc., 1221 Avenue of the Americas, New York, NY 10020. Copyright © 2007, 2005 by The McGraw-Hill Companies, Inc. All rights reserved. No part of this publication may be reproduced or distributed in any form or by any means, or stored in a database or retrieval system, without the prior written consent of The McGraw-Hill Companies, Inc., including, but not limited to, in any network or other electronic storage or transmission, or broadcast for distance learning.

1 2 3 4 5 6 7 8 9 0 CUS/CUS 0 9 8 7 6 5

ISBN-13: 978-0-07-312576-3
ISBN-10:   0-07-312576-8

www.mhhe.com

CONTENTS

Introduction v

Chapter 1 1
Chapter 2 15
Chapter 3 31
Chapter 4 47
Chapter 5 61
Chapter 6 77
Chapter 7 93
Chapter 8 107
Chapter 9 123
Chapter 10 139
Chapter 11 153
Chapter 12 169
Chapter 13 183
Chapter 14 197
Chapter 15 213
Chapter 16 227
Chapter 17 241
Chapter 18 255
Chapter 19 269
Chapter 20 283
Chapter 21 297
Chapter 22 311
Chapter 23 325

INTRODUCTION

This study guide is designed to enhance your understanding of the discipline of sociology and to help you prepare for examinations covering *Sociology*, 10th Edition, by Richard T. Schaefer. Careful use of this supplement will assist you in reviewing discussions of sociological theory, important research findings, and social policy sections.

The study guide has been developed specifically to provide you with a clearer understanding of the assigned material. The organization is identical to that of the textbook: each chapter in the study guide corresponds directly to one of the 23 chapters in *Sociology: A Brief Introduction*, 10th Edition. Within each chapter of the study guide, the material is presented in the same sequence as in the textbook and is keyed to page numbers in the text. Consequently, if you have problems with a particular subject or study guide exercise, you can return to the relevant pages in the text for further study.

You may find some sections of the study guide more helpful than others, but you should probably use all sections for the first few chapters until you learn what works best for you. Regardless of which sections you use, the study guide will be most valuable if you have read the textbook first. The purpose of the study guide is to assist you in reviewing the material after you have read an entire chapter of the text. We recommend waiting for a day *after* reading a chapter before turning to the study guide.

A *chapter outline* begins each chapter of the study guide; it presents the major topics of the chapter in the same order in which they appear in the text. If you review this outline, and immediately recognize certain areas in which your comprehension is weak, you should probably return to the text before continuing your work with the study guide.

After the chapter outline there is a section of *key points*. In this section, 7 to 15 short excerpts from the chapter are summarized in paragraph form, with glossary items highlighted and page references provided. These key points summarize the most important themes and concepts discussed in the chapter; they should be studied carefully before you proceed to later exercises in the study guide.

A list of *key terms* is included in each chapter of the study guide; each glossary item is presented in the order in which it appears in the textbook. Space is provided so that you can test yourself by filling in the definition of each term. Although these key terms appear in boldface in the text, this section of the study guide offers another opportunity to reinforce your understanding of the basic concepts used by sociologists. You may be tempted to check them off as you think to yourself, "I remember that," but it is important to write out the answers in the study guide. The very act of writing them out will reinforce your mastery of these terms. Once you have finished, you can check your answers against the correct definitions, which are included in the same study guide chapter.

The *self-test* for each chapter allows you to examine your understanding of the text material. Each self-test includes 15 *modified true/false questions*, 15 *multiple-choice questions*, and 15 *fill-in questions*. Page references and correct answers are provided for all sections of the self-test. Students will often ask, "Are the practice questions similar to the 'real' test questions?" The publisher materials for this course have been created in an integrated team approach. Therefore, if your instructor is using test material that is part of this package, there should be a high level of consistency between your Study Guide questions and the questions that you see on your tests.

To gain the greatest benefits from the self-test sections, do not use them after a hurried initial skimming of the chapter. Instead, use the self-test as a practice examination only after you have thoroughly studied the textbook material. As you take the test, note your weak areas; keep track of the questions on which you find yourself guessing. Recognize how you may be misreading or misinterpreting certain types of questions. After you check your answers, return to and reread the textbook passages where your comprehension was weak. Even if your instructor uses broad short-answer questions or essay questions on examinations, you will find the exercises in the self-test helpful in improving your understanding of the material in the textbook.

For each of the chapters in the textbook that ends with a social policy section, there is a corresponding exercise on *understanding social policy* in the study guide. These exercises ask questions about the social policy material in the text. Space is provided for your responses, and correct answers are included later in the study guide chapter.

In addition to this study guide, the *Reel Society Interactive Movie CD-ROM* included with your textbook and the Online Learning Center (the text's companion website) are valuable tools to help you study and master the material in the textbook. The CD-ROM features an interactive movie that demonstrates the sociological imagination through the use of actors and scenarios involving campus life. The program allows you to interact with the concepts described in the textbook in a relevant and meaningful context. A wide variety of issues and perspectives are addressed in order to relate major sociological concepts and theories to your everyday life. The Online Learning Center, located at www.mhhe.com/schaefer10, offers interactive quizzes and maps, social policy exercises, Census updates, chapter glossaries, vocabulary flashcards, and additional resources.

Effective use of the *Reel Society Interactive Movie CD-ROM*, the Online Learning Center Website, and this study guide, along with effective study habits, will ensure that your introduction to the discipline of sociology will be both meaningful and enjoyable.

Rebecca Matthews

CHAPTER 1
UNDERSTANDING SOCIOLOGY

What Is Sociology?
   The Sociological Imagination
   Sociology and the Social Sciences
   Sociology and Common Sense

What Is Sociological Theory?

The Development of Sociology
   Early Thinkers
   Émile Durkheim
   Max Weber
   Karl Marx
   Modern Developments

Major Theoretical Perspectives
   Functionalist Perspective
   Conflict Perspective
   Interactionist Perspective
   The Sociological Approach

Developing a Sociological Imagination
   Theory in Practice
   Research in Action
   Thinking Globally
   The Significance of Social Inequality
   Speaking across Race, Gender, and National Boundaries
   Social Policy throughout the World

Appendix: Careers in Sociology

BOXES
SOCIOLOGY IN THE GLOBAL COMMUNITY: *The Global Response to the 2004 Tsunami*
RESEARCH IN ACTION: *Looking at Sports from Three Theoretical Perspectives*

KEY POINTS

Sociology as a Field of Study: **Sociology** is the scientific study of social behavior and human groups. It focuses on social relationships, how those relationships influence people's behavior, and how societies develop and change. (5)

The Sociological Imagination: In attempting to understand social behavior, sociologists rely on an unusual type of creative thinking. C. Wright Mills described such thinking as the **sociological imagination:** an awareness of the relationship between an individual and the wider society. A key element in the sociological imagination is the ability to view one's own society as an outsider would, rather than only from the limited perspective of personal experiences and cultural biases. (5)

Sociology as a Science: The term **science** refers to the body of knowledge obtained by methods based upon systematic observation. Just like other scientific disciplines, sociology engages in organized, systematic study of phenomena (in this case, human behavior) in order to enhance understanding. In contrast to other social sciences, sociology emphasizes the influence that society has on people's attitudes and behavior and examines the ways in which people interact and shape society. (8)

Sociological Theory: Within sociology, a **theory** is a set of statements that seeks to explain problems, actions, or behavior. An effective theory may have both explanatory and predictive power. That is, it can help us to see the relationships among seemingly isolated phenomena, and to understand how one type of change in an environment leads to other changes. (9–10)

Early Thinkers—Comte, Martineau, and Spencer: Auguste Comte (1798–1857) coined the term sociology to apply to the science of human behavior. He believed that a theoretical science of society and systematic investigation of behavior were needed to improve society. Harriet Martineau (1820–1876) offered insightful observations of the customs and social practices of both her native Britain and the United States. Herbert Spencer (1820–1903) adapted Charles Darwin's evolutionary view of the "survival of the fittest" by arguing that it is "natural" that some people are rich while others are poor. (10–11)

Émile Durkheim: Émile Durkheim (1858–1917) was appointed as one of the first professors of sociology in France. Above all, Durkheim will be remembered for his insistence that behavior must be understood within a larger social context, not just in individualistic terms. Durkheim concluded that, like other forms of group behavior, religion reinforces a group's solidarity. Another of Durkheim's main interests was the consequences of work in modern societies. (11)

Max Weber: Max Weber (1864–1920), a German sociologist, taught his students that they should employ *Verstehen*, the German word for "understanding" or "insight," in their intellectual work. To fully comprehend behavior, we must learn the subjective meanings people attach to their actions; how they themselves view and explain their own behavior. We also owe credit to Weber for a key conceptual tool: the ideal type. In his own works, Weber identified various characteristics of bureaucracy as ideal types. (11–12)

Karl Marx: In the analysis of Karl Marx (1818–1883), society was fundamentally divided between classes who clash in pursuit of their own class interests. When Marx examined the industrial societies of his time, he saw the factory as the center of conflict between the exploiters (the owners of the means of production) and the exploited (the workers). In *The Communist Manifesto*, which first appeared in 1848, Marx and Friedrich Engels (1820–1895) argued that the masses of people (whom they referred to as the *proletariat*) with no resources other than their labor should unite to fight for the overthrow of capitalist societies. (13)

Charles Horton Cooley: Charles Horton Cooley (1864–1929) preferred to use the sociological perspective to look at smaller units of people; intimate, face-to-face groups, such as families, gangs, and friendship networks. He saw these groups as the seedbeds of society, in the sense that they shape people's ideals, beliefs, values, and social nature. Cooley's work increased our understanding of groups of relatively small size. (13)

Functionalist Perspective: In the view of functionalists, society is like a living organism in which each part of the organism contributes to its survival. Therefore, the **functionalist perspective** emphasizes the way that parts of a society are structured to maintain its stability. For over four decades, Harvard University sociologist Talcott Parsons (1902–1979) dominated sociology in the United States with his advocacy of functionalism. Parsons saw any society as a vast network of connected parts, each of which contributes to the maintenance of the system as a whole. (14)

Conflict Perspective: Where functionalists see stability and consensus, conflict sociologists see a social world in continual struggle. The **conflict perspective** assumes that social behavior is best understood in terms of conflict or tension between competing groups. Expanding on Marx's work, conflict theorists are interested in how society's institutions—including the family, government, religion, education, and the media—may help to maintain the privileges of some groups and keep others in a subservient position. (15)

Conflict Perspective—An African American View: One important contribution of conflict theory is that it has encouraged sociologists to view society through the eyes of those segments of the population that rarely influence decision-making. Early black sociologists, such as W.E.B. Du Bois (1868–1963), conducted research that they hoped would assist the struggle for a racially egalitarian society. (16)

The Feminist View: The **feminist view** sees inequity in gender as central to all behavior and organization. Because it clearly focuses on one aspect of inequality, the feminist view is often allied with the conflict perspective. Those who hold to the feminist perspective tend to focus on the macro-level relationships of everyday life, just as conflict theorists do. Drawing on the work of Marx and Engels, contemporary feminist theorists often view women's subordination as inherent in capitalist societies. (16)

Interactionist Perspective: The **interactionist perspective** generalizes about everyday forms of social interaction in order to understand society as a whole. It is a sociological framework for viewing human beings as living in a world of meaningful objects. These "objects" may include material things, actions, other people, relationships, and even symbols. George Herbert Mead (1863–1931) is widely regarded as the founder of the interactionist perspective. (17)

Thinking Globally: Sociologists recognize that social behavior must be viewed in a global context. Today, developments outside a country are as likely to influence people's lives as changes at home. Some observers see globalization and its effects as the natural result of advances in communications technology, particularly the Internet and satellite transmission of the mass media. Others view it more critically, as a process that allows multinational corporations to expand unchecked. (19–20)

Applied and Clinical Sociology: **Applied sociology** is the use of the discipline with the specific intent of yielding practical applications for human behavior and organizations. Often, the goal of such work is to assist in resolving a social problem. The growing popularity of applied sociology has led to the rise of the specialty of **clinical sociology**, which is dedicated to facilitating change by altering social relationships or restructuring social institutions. Applied and clinical sociology can be contrasted with **basic** (or pure) **sociology**, which seeks a more profound knowledge of the fundamental aspects of social phenomena. (21–22)

KEY TERMS

Briefly define or identify the following terms in the spaces provided below. The definitions of these terms can be found later in this chapter of the study guide.

Sociology	Science
Sociological imagination	Natural science

Social science	Conflict perspective
Theory	Feminist view
Anomie	Interactionist perspective
Verstehen	Nonverbal communication
Ideal type	Dramaturgical approach
Macrosociology	Globalization
Microsociology	Social inequality
Functionalist perspective	Applied sociology
Manifest function	Clinical sociology
Latent function	Basic sociology
Dysfunction	

SELF-TEST

MODIFIED TRUE/FALSE QUESTIONS: If the statement below is true, write "true" in the space provided. If the statement is false, briefly correct the error.

1. Sociology is concerned only with how major social institutions like the government, religion, and the economy affect us.

2. In the aftermath of natural disasters, a community's social organization and structure tend to collapse.

3. Émile Durkheim concluded that the suicide rates of a society reflected the extent to which people were or were not integrated into the group life of the society.

4. French theorist Émile Durkheim coined the term *sociology*.

5. The sociologist Harriet Martineau applied Charles Darwin's evolutionary concepts to societies.

6. When Max Weber discussed the ideal bureaucracy, he was focusing on the best type of organization that was possible.

7. Karl Marx argued that the working class needed to overthrow the existing class system.

8. Émile Durkheim was a modern-day sociologist who focused on small groups.

9. George Herbert Mead emphasized that sociology should strive to bring together the "macro-level" and "micro-level" approaches to the study of society.

10. Microsociology concentrates on large-scale phenomena or entire civilizations.

11. Talcott Parsons dominated sociology in the United States for over four decades with his advocacy of the interactionist perspective.

12. Ida Wells-Barnett used her analysis of society as a means of resisting oppression. In her case, she researched what it meant to be African American, a woman in the United States, and an African American woman in the United States.

13. Interactionists see symbols as an especially important part of human communication.

14. George Herbert Mead is widely regarded as the founder of the interactionist perspective.

15. A study at DePaul University examining the impact of a Motorola cellular phone plant on the community of Harvard, Illinois, is an example of basic sociology.

MULTIPLE-CHOICE QUESTIONS: In each of the following, select the phrase that best completes the statement.

1. Sociology is concerned with
   a. social behavior and human groups.
   b. the behavior of an individual.
   c. random human actions.
   d. all of the above

2. Which of the following is most closely associated with the concept of the sociological imagination?
   a. Émile Durkheim
   b. Max Weber
   c. Karl Marx
   d. C. Wright Mills

3. In his study of suicide, Émile Durkheim was primarily concerned with
   a. suicide rates and how they varied from country to country.
   b. personalities of individual suicide victims.
   c. means people used to take their own lives.
   d. effects of suicide on the families of victims.

4. 4. In *Society in America*, which early sociologist gave special attention to social class distinctions and to such factors as gender and race?
   a. Émile Durkheim
   b. Max Weber
   c. Auguste Comte
   d. Harriet Martineau

5. Which one of the following concepts did Max Weber introduce to the field of sociology?
   a. dramaturgy
   b. the ideal type
   c. functionalism
   d. macrosociology

6. *The Communist Manifesto* was written by
    a. Karl Marx and Georg Hegel.
    b. George Herbert Mead and Jane Addams.
    c. Friedrich Engels and Karl Marx.
    d. Talcott Parsons and Robert Merton.

7. Which sociologist cofounded the famous Chicago settlement house called Hull House?
    a. Charles Horton Cooley
    b. Jane Addams
    c. George Herbert Mead
    d. C. Wright Mills

8. Robert Merton's contributions to sociology include
    a. successfully combining theory and research.
    b. an analysis of deviant behavior that focuses on societal goals and means.
    c. an attempt to bring "macro-level" and "micro-level" analyses together.
    d. all of the above

9. Which sociological perspective views society as a network of connected parts, each of which contributes to the maintenance of the system as a whole?
    a. the functionalist perspective
    b. the conflict perspective
    c. the interactionist perspective
    d. the dramaturgical perspective

10. A university that serves as a meeting ground for people seeking marital partners is performing
    a. a manifest function.
    b. a latent function.
    c. a dysfunction.
    d. a manifest dysfunction.

11. Karl Marx's view of the struggle between social classes inspired the contemporary
    a. functionalist perspective.
    b. conflict perspective.
    c. interactionist perspective.
    d. dramaturgical approach.

12. Which of the following was an early Black sociologist, active in the struggle for a racially egalitarian society, who was critical of theorists who seemed content with the status quo?
    a. Harriet Martineau
    b. Herbert Spencer
    c. Booker T. Washington
    d. W. E. B. Du Bois

13. Sports perpetuate the false idea that success can be achieved simply through hard work, while failure should be blamed on the individual alone (rather than on injustices in the larger social system). This statement would most accurately represent which perspective?
    a. the functionalist perspective
    b. the conflict perspective
    c. the interactionist perspective
    d. the feminist perspective

14. Which sociological perspective examines sports on the micro level by focusing on how day-to-day social behavior is shaped by the distinctive norms, values, and demands of the world of sports?
    a. the functionalist perspective
    b. the conflict perspective
    c. the interactionist perspective
    d. the psychological perspective

15. 15. Perhaps the major theme of analysis in sociology today is _____—a condition in which members of society have differing amounts of wealth, prestige, or power.
    a. macrosociology
    b. the dramaturgical approach
    c. *Verstehen*
    d. social inequality

FILL-IN QUESTIONS: Fill in the blank spaces in the sentences below with the correct words. Where two or more words are required, there will be a corresponding number of blank spaces.

1. Sociology focuses primarily on the influence of _____ _____ on people's behavior and on how societies develop and change.

2. While the findings of sociologists may at times seem like common sense, they have been _____ by researchers.

3. _____ _____ noted that while suicide is a solitary act, it is related to group life, and that Protestants, unmarried individuals, and soldiers were more likely to commit suicide than Catholics, married individuals, and civilians.

4. In *Society in America*, originally published in 1837, English scholar _____ _____ examined religion, politics, child rearing, and immigration in the young nation.

5. _____ _____ adapted Charles Darwin's evolutionary view of the "survival of the fittest" by arguing that it is "natural" that some people are rich while others are poor.

6. _____ _____ concern for a value-free, objective sociology was a direct response to Marx's deeply held convictions.

7. _____ _____ pioneering work has led contemporary sociologists to focus on how membership in a particular gender classification, age group, racial group, or economic class affects a person's attitudes and behavior.

8. In the early 1900s, sociologist _____ _____ saw smaller groups as the seedbeds of society.

9. Examinations of international crime rates, Émile Durkheim's cross-cultural study of suicide, stereotypes of Asian Americans as a "model minority," and population patterns of Islamic countries are all examples of _____. By contrast, research in which small groups are studied in laboratories is an example of _____.

10. _____ _____ saw society as a vast network of connected parts, each of which helps to maintain the system as a whole.

11. The university's role in certifying academic competence and excellence is an example of a _____ function.

12. In contrast to functionalists' emphasis on stability and consensus, _____ theorists see the social world in continuous struggle.

13. The _____ _____ draws on the work of Marx and Engels in that it often views women's subordination as inherent in capitalist societies.

14. _____ scholars have argued for a gender-balanced study of society in which women's experiences and contributions are as visible as those of men.

15. The _____ perspective would note that participation in sports might promote friendship networks that permeate everyday life.

DEFINITIONS OF KEY TERMS

Sociology: The scientific study of social behavior and human groups. (5)

Sociological imagination: An awareness of the relationship between an individual and the wider society. (5)

Science: The body of knowledge obtained by methods based on systematic observation. (8)

Natural science: The study of the physical features of nature and the ways in which they interact and change. (8)

Social science: The study of the social features of humans and the ways in which they interact and change. (8)

Theory: In sociology, a set of statements that seeks to explain problems, actions, or behavior. (9)

Anomie: The loss of direction felt in a society when social control of individual behavior has become ineffective. (11)

Verstehen: The German word for "understanding" or "insight"; used to stress the need for sociologists to take into account the subjective meanings people attach to their actions. (12)

Ideal type: A construct or model for evaluating specific cases. (12)

Macrosociology: Sociological investigation that concentrates on large-scale phenomena or entire civilizations. (14)

Microsociology: Sociological investigation that stresses the study of small groups, often through experimental means. (14)

Functionalist perspective: A sociological approach that emphasizes the way in which the parts of a society are structured to maintain its stability. (14)

Manifest function: An open, stated, and conscious function. (15)

Latent function: An unconscious or unintended function that may reflect hidden purposes. (15)

Dysfunction: An element or a process of a society that may disrupt the social system or reduce its stability. (15)

Conflict perspective: A sociological approach that assumes that social behavior is best understood in terms of conflict or tension between competing groups. (15)

Feminist view: A sociological approach that views inequity in gender as central to all behavior and organization. (16)

Interactionist perspective: A sociological approach that generalizes about everyday forms of social interaction in order to explain society as a whole. (17)

Nonverbal communication: The sending of messages through the use of gestures, facial expressions, and postures. (17)

Dramaturgical approach: A view of social interaction in which people are seen as theatrical performers. (17)

Globalization: The worldwide integration of government policies, cultures, social movements, and financial markets through trade and the exchange of ideas. (19)

Social inequality: A condition in which members of society have differing amounts of wealth, prestige, or power. (20)

Applied sociology: The use of the discipline of sociology with the specific intent of yielding practical applications for human behavior and organizations. (21)

Clinical sociology: The use of the discipline of sociology with the specific intent of altering social relationships or restructuring social institutions. (22)

Basic sociology: Sociological inquiry conducted with the objective of gaining a more profound knowledge of the fundamental aspects of social phenomena. Also known as *pure sociology*. (22)

ANSWERS TO SELF-TEST

Modified True/False Questions
1. Sociology is a very broad field of study. Sociologists are concerned with how major social institutions affect us, but they also study how other people influence our behavior, and how we ourselves affect other individuals, groups, and organizations. (5)
2. In the aftermath of natural disasters, greater social organization and structure emerge to deal with a community's problems. (9)
3. True (10)
4. The term *sociology* was coined by Auguste Comte. (10)
5. Herbert Spencer applied Charles Darwin's evolutionary concepts to societies. (11)
6. When Max Weber discussed the ideal bureaucracy, he was providing a useful standard for measuring how bureaucratic an actual organization was. (12)
7. True (12–13)
8. Charles Horton Cooley was a modern-day sociologist who focused on small groups. (13)
9. Robert Merton emphasized that sociology should strive to bring together the "macro-level" and "micro-level" approaches to the study of society. (14)
10. Macrosociology concentrates on large-scale phenomena or entire civilizations. Microsociology stresses study of small groups. (14)

11. Talcott Parsons dominated sociology in the United States for over four decades with his advocacy of the functionalist perspective. (14)
12. True (16)
13. True (17)
14. True (17)
15. The study at DePaul University examining the impact of a Motorola cellular phone plant on the community of Harvard, Illinois, is an example of applied sociology. (21)

Multiple-Choice Questions

1. a (5)
2. d (5)
3. a (10)
4. d (10–11)
5. b (12)
6. c (12)
7. b (13)
8. d (14)
9. a (14)
10. b (15)
11. b (15)
12. d (16)
13. b (19)
14. c (19)
15. d (20)

Fill-In Questions

1. social relationships (5)
2. tested (9)
3. Émile Durkheim (10)
4. Harriet Martineau (10)
5. Herbert Spencer (11)
6. Max Weber's (12)
7. Karl Marx's (13)
8. Charles (Horton) Cooley (13)
9. macrosociology; microsociology (14)
10. Talcott Parsons (14)
11. manifest (15)
12. conflict (15)
13. feminist view (16)
14. feminist (16)
15. interactionist (17)

CHAPTER 2
SOCIOLOGICAL RESEARCH

What Is the Scientific Method?
   Defining the Problem
   Reviewing the Literature
   Formulating the Hypothesis
   Collecting and Analyzing Data
   Developing the Conclusion
   In Summary: The Scientific Method

Major Research Designs
   Surveys
   Observation
   Experiments
   Use of Existing Sources

Ethics of Research
   Confidentiality
   Research Funding
   Value Neutrality

Technology and Sociological Research

Social Policy and Sociological Research: Studying Human Sexuality
   The Issue
   The Setting
   Sociological Insights
   Policy Initiatives

Appendix I: Using Statistics, Tables, and Graphs

Appendix II: Writing a Research Report

BOXES
   RESEARCH IN ACTION: *Polling in Baghdad*
   SOCIAL INEQUALITY: *Researching Privilege and Discrimination in Employment*
   SOCIOLOGY ON CAMPUS: *Does Hard Work Lead to Better Grades?*
   TAKING SOCIOLOGY TO WORK: *Dave Eberbach, Research Coordinator, United Way of Central Iowa*

KEY POINTS

The Scientific Method: The **scientific method** is a systematic, organized series of steps that ensures maximum objectivity and consistency in researching a problem. There are five basic steps in the scientific method: defining the problem, reviewing the literature, formulating the hypothesis, selecting the research design and then collecting and analyzing data, and developing the conclusion. (29)

Defining the Problem: The first step in any research project is to state as clearly as possible what you hope to investigate. An **operational definition** is an explanation of an abstract concept that is specific enough to allow a researcher to assess the concept. (30)

Formulating the Hypothesis: After reviewing earlier research and drawing on the contributions of sociological theorists, the researchers formulate the **hypothesis**: a speculative statement about the relationship between two or more factors known as variables. A **variable** is a measurable trait or characteristic that is subject to change under different conditions. The variable hypothesized to cause or influence another is called the **independent variable**. The second variable is termed the **dependent variable** because its action "depends" on the influence of the independent variable. (30)

Collecting and Analyzing Data: In most studies, social scientists must carefully select what is known as a **sample**. A sample is a selection from a larger population that is statistically representative of that population. The most frequently used sample is a **random sample** in which every member of the entire population being studied has the same chance of being selected. (31)

Validity and Reliability: The scientific method requires that research results be both valid and reliable. **Validity** refers to the degree to which a measure or scale truly reflects the phenomenon under study. **Reliability** refers to the extent to which a measure provides consistent results. (32)

Surveys: A **survey** is a study, generally in the form of an interview or questionnaire, which provides sociologists with information about how people think and act. Among the best-known surveys of opinion in the United States are the Gallup poll and the Harris poll. Surveys can be indispensable sources of information, but only if the sampling is done properly and the questions are worded accurately and without bias. (35)

Observation: Investigators who collect information through direct participation and/or closely watching a group or community are engaged in **observation**. This method allows sociologists to examine certain behaviors and communities that could not be investigated through other research techniques. In some cases, the sociologist actually joins a group for a period of time to gain an accurate sense of how it operates. This is called *participant observation*. (35–36)

Experiments: When sociologists want to study a possible cause-and-effect relationship, they may conduct experiments. An **experiment** is an artificially created situation that allows the researcher to manipulate variables. In the classic method of conducting an experiment, two groups of people are selected and matched for similar characteristics, such as age or education. The **experimental group** is exposed to an independent variable; the **control group** is not. (36)

Use of Existing Sources: Sociologists do not necessarily need to collect new data in order to conduct research and test hypotheses. The term **secondary analysis** refers to a variety of research techniques that make use of previously collected and publicly accessible information and data. Many social scientists find it useful to study cultural, economic, and political documents including newspapers, periodicals, radio and television, tapes, the Internet, scripts, diaries, songs, folklore, and legal papers. In examining these sources, researchers employ a technique known as **content analysis**, which is the systematic coding and objective recording of data, guided by some rationale. (37–38)

Ethics of Research: The American Sociological Association (ASA), the professional society of the discipline, first published the Code of Ethics in 1971. It includes the following basic principles: maintain objectivity and integrity in research, respect the subject's right to privacy and dignity, protect subjects from personal harm, preserve confidentiality, seek informed consent from research participants, acknowledge research collaboration and assistance, and disclose all sources of financial support. (39)

Research Funding: Sometimes disclosing all the sources of funding for a study is not a sufficient guarantee of ethical conduct. Accepting funds from a private organization or even a government agency that stands to benefit from a study's results can call into question a researcher's objectivity and integrity. (40)

Value Neutrality: Max Weber believed that sociologists must practice **value neutrality** in their research. In his view, researchers cannot allow their personal feelings to influence the interpretation of data. Investigators have an obligation to accept research findings, even when the data run contrary to their own personal views, to theoretically based explanations, or to widely accepted beliefs. The issue of value neutrality does not mean that sociologists can't have opinions, but it does mean that they must work to overcome any biases, however unintentional, that they may bring to their research. (40–41)

Technology and Sociological Research: The increased speed and capacity of computers are enabling sociologists to handle larger and larger sets of data. Anyone with a desktop computer and a modem can access information and learn more about social behavior. The Internet is an inexpensive way to reach large numbers of potential respondents, and get a quick response. However, there are some obvious dilemmas: How do you protect a respondent's anonymity? How do you define the potential audience? (41–42)

Studying Human Sexuality: The controversy surrounding research on human sexual behavior raises the issue of value neutrality, which becomes especially delicate when one considers the relationship of sociology to the government. The federal government has become the major source of funding for sociological research. In 1991, the U.S. Senate voted to forbid funding any survey on adult sexual practices. Nevertheless, a group of researchers was able to raise $1.6 million in private funding to develop the National Health and Social Life Survey (NHSLS). The NHSLS researchers argue that using data from their survey allows us to more easily address public policy issues such as AIDS, sexual harassment, welfare reform, sex discrimination, abortion, teenage pregnancy, and family planning. (43–44)

KEY TERMS

Briefly define or identify the following terms in the spaces provided below. The definitions of these terms can be found later in this chapter of the study guide.

Scientific method	Correlation
Operational definition	Sample
Hypothesis	Random sample
Variable	Validity
Independent variable	Reliability
Dependent variable	Control variable
Causal logic	Research design

Survey	Hawthorne effect
Interview	Secondary analysis
Questionnaire	Content analysis
Quantitative research	Code of ethics
Qualitative research	Value neutrality
Observation	Percentage
Ethnography	Mean
Experiment	Mode
Experimental group	Median
Control group	Cross-tabulation

SELF-TEST

MODIFIED TRUE/FALSE QUESTIONS: If the statement below is true, write "true" in the space provided. If the statement is false, briefly correct the error.

1. The second step in the scientific method is formulating the hypothesis.

2. The dependent variable in a hypothesis is thought to cause or influence the independent variable.

3. Television viewers and radio listeners who e-mail their views on news headlines or on political contests are participating in a random sample.

4. After collecting and analyzing data, the researchers come to the final step in the scientific method: creating a theory.

5. Sociologists classify the Gallup poll and the Harris poll as examples of observation research.

6. There are two main types of samples: the interview and the questionnaire.

7. In William F. Whyte's *Street Corner Society*, he revealed his identity to the men he was studying and joined in their conversations, bowled with them, and participated in other leisure-time activities.

8. The control group is exposed to an independent variable; the experimental group is not.

9. Worker productivity in the Hawthorne studies diminished when researchers observed them, because the employees became self-conscious.

10. The most frequently used existing sources in sociological research are census data, crime statistics, newspapers, and periodicals.

11. The American Sociological Association's (ASA) Code of Ethics requires sociologists to maintain objectivity, preserve confidentiality, report all illegal behavior to appropriate authorities, and acknowledge research collaboration and assistance.

12. Rick Scarce, a doctoral candidate in sociology, agreed to testify before a grand jury in 1993 and share with them research findings on his study of environmental protestors.

13. Following the *Valdez* disaster, Exxon approached sociologists to do research on jury deliberations.

14. Émile Durkheim's assertion that suicide was the result of social forces rather than supernatural forces was an illustration of a sociologist maintaining value neutrality.

15. The development of computer technology has had little effect on sociological research.

MULTIPLE-CHOICE QUESTIONS: In each of the following, select the phrase that best completes the statement.

1. The first step in any sociological research project is to
    a. collect data.
    b. define the problem.
    c. review previous research.
    d. formulate a hypothesis.

2. Formulating the hypothesis is the _____ step in the scientific method.
    a. first
    b. second
    c. third
    d. fourth

3. Suppose that how well a student does on a test is determined by how much the student studies for it. In this example, studying for an exam is a(n)
    a. correlation.
    b. independent variable.
    c. dependent variable.
    d. sample.

4. Through which type of research technique does a sociologist ensure that data are statistically representative of the population being studied?
    a. sampling
    b. experiments
    c. validity
    d. control variables

5. In order to obtain a random sample, a researcher might
    a. administer a questionnaire to every fifth woman who enters a business office.
    b. examine the attitudes of residents of a city by interviewing every twentieth name in the city's telephone book.
    c. study the attitudes of registered Democratic voters by choosing every tenth name found on a city's list of registered Democrats.
    d. do all of the above

6. A detailed plan or method for obtaining data scientifically is called a(n)
    a. sample.
    b. experiment.
    c. research design.
    d. scientific method.

7. A researcher can obtain a higher response rate by using which type of survey?
    a. interviews
    b. questionnaires
    c. representative samples
    d. observation techniques

8. One reason that face-to-face interviews in the home are appropriate for social research in Baghdad is that
    a. they help respondents to feel at ease.
    b. they allow women to participate.
    c. they are less expensive than written surveys.
    d. a and b

9. William F. Whyte's study of a low-income Italian neighborhood in Boston was a classic example of
    a. participant observation research.
    b. a survey.
    c. content analysis.
    d. an experiment.

10. Which one of the following is exposed to an independent variable?
    a. the control group
    b. the representative group
    c. the experimental group
    d. none of the above

11. An instructor wants to determine if giving essay tests increases student learning. In one class that the instructor teaches, she continues to test as she has always done. In another class, she gives the students essay questions. She then measures the differences in learning, if any, between the two classes. The class that is given essay questions is the
    a. control group.
    b. representative group.
    c. experimental group.
    d. correlation group.

12. A researcher examines the literature written by Black novelists during the "Negro Renaissance" (1913–1935) to see if they reflect the political movements going on in the Black community in the United States at that time. What type of research methodology is being used in this example?
    a. secondary analysis
    b. interviews
    c. observation
    d. content analysis

13. Which one of the following statements is not part of the Code of Ethics developed by the American Sociological Association?
    a. Acknowledge research collaboration and assistance.
    b. Preserve confidentiality.
    c. Protect subjects from personal harm.
    d. Make all research notes available for public scrutiny.

14. Max Weber
    a. recognized that it is impossible for scholars to prevent their personal values from influencing the questions that they select for research.
    b. stressed that researchers had to maintain the confidentiality of their subjects.
    c. emphasized that under no conditions could a researcher allow his or her personal feelings to influence the interpretation of data.
    d. both a and c

15. Which one of the following is a finding of the National Health and Social Life Survey?
    a. Well-educated and affluent women are more likely to have abortions than poor teens.
    b. Adults in the United States have sex 2-3 times per week.
    c. Forty-seven percent of all women reported that they had been coerced into a sexual encounter at some time.
    d. Eleven percent of men and nine percent of women stated that they were homosexual or bisexual.

FILL-IN QUESTIONS: Fill in the blank spaces in the sentences below with the correct words. Where two or more words are required, there will be a corresponding number of blank spaces.

1. Unlike the typical citizen, the sociologist has a commitment to the use of the _____ method in studying society.

2. The scientific method includes the following steps: defining the problem, reviewing the _____, formulating the hypothesis, selecting the research design and then collecting and analyzing data, and developing the conclusion.

3. A hypothesis is a speculative statement about the relationship between two or more factors known as _____.

4.
4. In formulating a _____, researchers generally must suggest how one aspect of human behavior influences or affects another.

5. Consider this hypothesis: The more an individual eats, the more he or she weighs. In this hypothesis, how much a person eats is a(n) _____ variable.

6. In order to obtain data scientifically, researchers need to select a research _____.

7. A _____ is a study, generally in the form of an interview or questionnaire, which provides sociologists with information concerning how people think and act.

8. If scientists were testing a new type of toothpaste in an experimental setting, they would administer the toothpaste to a(n) _____ group, but not to a(n) _____ group.

9. A researcher using census data in a way that was unintended by the initial collectors of that information would be an example of _____ _____.

10. Researchers can avoid the _____ effect by conducting secondary analysis.

11. Using content analysis, _____ _____ conducted a pioneering exploration of how advertisements in 1979 portrayed women as inferior to men.

12. The American Sociological Association's Code of _____ requires sociologists to maintain objectivity and integrity in research and to preserve the confidentiality of their subjects.

13. Examining efforts of the Exxon corporation to solicit social science research on jury deliberations allows us to explore _____ issues in research.

14. As part of their commitment to _____ neutrality, investigators have an ethical obligation to accept research findings even when the data run counter to their own personal views or widely accepted beliefs.

15. In her book *The Death of White Sociology*, _____ _____ called attention to the tendency of mainstream sociology to treat the lives of African Americans as a social problem.

UNDERSTANDING SOCIAL POLICY: All of the following questions are based on material that appears in the social policy section on Studying Human Sexuality. Write a brief answer to each question in the space provided below.

1. What research has been done in regard to studying human sexuality?

2. How does the issue of value neutrality relate to studying human sexuality?

3. What attempts have been made to administer a national survey and how did the government respond?

DEFINITIONS OF KEY TERMS

Scientific method: A systematic, organized series of steps that ensures maximum objectivity and consistency in researching a problem. (29)

Operational definition: An explanation of an abstract concept that is specific enough to allow a researcher to assess the concept. (30)

Hypothesis: A speculative statement about the relationship between two or more variables. (30)

Variable: A measurable trait or characteristic that is subject to change under different conditions. (30)

Independent variable: The variable in a causal relationship that causes or influences a change in a second variable. (30)

Dependent variable: The variable in a causal relationship that is subject to the influence of another variable. (30)

Causal logic: The relationship between a condition or variable and a particular consequence, with one event leading to the other. (30)

Correlation: A relationship between two variables in which a change in one coincides with a change in the other. (31)

Sample: A selection from a larger population that is statistically representative of that population. (31)

Random sample: A sample for which every member of an entire population has the same chance of being selected. (33)

Validity: The degree to which a measure or scale truly reflects the phenomenon under study. (32)

Reliability: The extent to which a measure produces consistent results. (32)

Control variable: A factor that is held constant to test the relative impact of an independent variable. (33)

Research design: A detailed plan or method for obtaining data scientifically. (35)

Survey: A study, generally in the form of an interview or questionnaire, that provides researchers with information about how people think and act. (35)

Interview: A face-to-face or telephone questioning of a respondent to obtain desired information. (35)

Questionnaire: A printed or written form used to obtain information from a respondent. (35)

Quantitative research: Research that collects and reports data primarily in numerical form. (35)

Qualitative research: Research that relies on what is seen in field or naturalistic settings more than on statistical data. (35)

Observation: A research technique in which an investigator collects information through direct participation and/or closely watching a group or community. (35)

Ethnography: The study of an entire social setting through extended systematic observation. (35)

Experiment: An artificially created situation that allows a researcher to manipulate variables. (36)

Experimental group: The subjects in an experiment who are exposed to an independent variable introduced by a researcher. (36)

Control group: The subjects in an experiment who are not introduced to the independent variable by the researcher. (36)

Hawthorne effect: The unintended influence that observers of experiments can have on their subjects. (37)

Secondary analysis: A variety of research techniques that make use of previously collected and publicly accessible information and data. (37–38)

Content analysis: The systematic coding and objective recording of data, guided by some rationale. (38)

Code of ethics: The standards of acceptable behavior developed by and for members of a profession. (39)

Value neutrality: Max Weber's term for objectivity of sociologists in the interpretation of data. (41)

Percentage: A portion of 100. (47)

Mean: A number calculated by adding a series of values and then dividing by the number of values. (47)

Mode: The single most common value in a series of values. (47)

Median: The midpoint or number that divides a series of values into two groups of equal numbers of values. (47)

Cross-tabulation: A tables that shows the relationship between two or more variables. (48)

ANSWERS TO SELF-TEST

Modified True/False Questions

1. The second step in the scientific method is reviewing the literature. Formulating the hypothesis is the third step in the process. (29)
2. The variable hypothesized to cause or influence another is called the independent variable. The dependent variable "depends" on the influence of the independent variable. (30)

3. The results of such polls reflect nothing more than the views of those who happened to see the television program or hear the radio broadcast and took the time, perhaps at some cost, to register their opinions. (32)
4. After collecting and analyzing data, the researchers come to the final step in the scientific method: they develop the conclusion. (32)
5. The Gallup poll and the Harris poll are among the best-known surveys of opinions in the United States. (35)
6. There are two main types of *surveys*: the interview and the questionnaire. (35)
7. True (36)
8. The experimental group is exposed to an independent variable; the control group is not. (36)
9. In the Hawthorne study, worker productivity increased because of the greater attention being paid to them and the novelty of being subjects in an experiment. (37)
10. The most frequently used existing sources in sociological research are census data; crime statistics; and birth, death, marriage, divorce, and health statistics. (38)
11. The Code of Ethics does not expect researchers to report all illegal behavior to appropriate authorities. This would be a violation of confidentiality, and would destroy the relationship the researcher has with the subject(s). (39)
12. Rick Scarce declined to tell a federal grand jury what he knew, or even whether he knew anything, about a 1991 raid on a university research library. He was jailed for contempt of court and served 159 days in jail. (40)
13. True (40)
14. True (41)
15. The development of computer technology has had a significant impact on sociological research. For example, sociologists can now handle larger and larger data sets. (41)

Multiple-Choice Questions

1. b (29)
2. c (29)
3. b (30)
4. a (31)
5. c (31)
6. c (35)
7. a (35)
8. d (34)
9. a (36)
10. c (36)
11. c (36)
12. d (38)
13. d (39)
14. d (40–41)
15. a (44)

Fill-In Questions

1. scientific (29)
2. literature (29)
3. variables (30)
4. hypothesis (30)
5. independent (30)
6. design (35)
7. survey (35)
8. experimental; control (36)
9. secondary analysis (37–38)
10. Hawthorne (38)
11. Erving Goffman (38)
12. Ethics (39)

13. ethical (40)
14. value (41)
15. Joyce Ladner (41)

Understanding Social Policy: Studying Human Sexuality

1. Sociologists have little reliable data on patterns of sexual behavior in the United States. Until recently, the only comprehensive study of sexual behavior was the famous two-volume Kinsey Report prepared in the 1940s. The volunteers interviewed for the report were not representative of the nation's adult population. In part, we lack reliable data on patterns of sexual behavior because it is difficult for researchers to obtain accurate information about this sensitive subject. Moreover, until AIDS emerged in the 1980s, there was little scientific demand for data on sexual behavior, except for specific concerns such as contraception. (43)

2. The controversy surrounding research on human sexual behavior raises the issue of value neutrality, which becomes especially delicate when one considers the relationship of sociology to the government. The federal government has become the major source of funding for sociological research. Yet Max Weber urged that sociology remain an autonomous discipline, and not become unduly influenced by any one segment of society. (43)

3. In 1987, the National Institute of Child Health and Human Development sought proposals for a national survey of sexual behavior. However, in 1991, the U.S. Senate voted to forbid funding any survey on adult sexual practices. (43)

CHAPTER 3: CULTURE

Culture and Society

Development of Culture around the World
    Cultural Universals
    Innovation
    Globalization, Diffusion and Technology
    Sociobiology

Elements of Culture
    Language
    Norms
    Sanctions
    Values

Culture and the Dominant Ideology

Cultural Variation
    Aspects of Cultural Variation
    Attitudes toward Cultural Variation

Social Policy and Culture: Bilingualism
    The Issue
    The Setting
    Sociological Insights
    Policy Initiatives

BOXES
    SOCIOLOGY IN THE GLOBAL COMMUNITY: *Life in the Global Village*
    SOCIOLOGY ON CAMPUS: *A Culture of Cheating?*

KEY POINTS

Culture and Society: **Culture** is the totality of learned, socially transmitted customs, knowledge, material objects, and behavior. It includes the ideas, values, and artifacts (for example, DVDs, comic books, and birth control devices) of groups of people. A large number of people are said to constitute a **society** when they live in the same territory, are relatively independent of people outside their area, and participate in a common culture. Members of a society generally share a common language, which facilitates day-to-day exchanges with others. (53)

Cultural Universals: Despite their differences, all societies have developed certain common practices and beliefs, known as **cultural universals**. Anthropologist George Murdock compiled a list of cultural universals, including athletic sports, cooking, funeral ceremonies, medicine, marriage, and sexual restrictions. The cultural practices Murdock listed may be universal, but the manner in which they are expressed varies from culture to culture. (53–54)

Material and Nonmaterial Culture: Sociologist William F. Ogburn made a useful distinction between the elements of material and nonmaterial culture. **Material culture** refers to the physical or technological aspects of our daily lives, including food, houses, factories, and raw materials. **Nonmaterial culture** refers to ways of using material objects and to customs, beliefs, philosophies, governments, and patterns of communication. Generally, the nonmaterial culture is more resistant to change than the material culture. (58)

Sociobiology: **Sociobiology** is the systematic study of how biology affects human social behavior. Sociobiologists apply Charles Darwin's principle of natural selection to the study of human behavior. In its extreme form, sociobiology suggests that *all* behavior is the result of genetic or biological factors and that social interactions play no role in shaping people's conduct. (58)

Language: **Language** is an abstract system of word meanings and symbols for all aspects of culture. It includes speech, written characters, numerals, symbols, and gestures and expressions of nonverbal communication. While language is a cultural universal, striking differences in the way different cultures use language. (59)

Norms: **Norms** are the established standards of behavior maintained by a society. **Formal norms** generally have been written down and specify strict punishments for violators. By contrast, **informal norms** are generally understood, but are not precisely recorded. **Mores** are norms deemed highly necessary to the welfare of a society, often because they embody the most cherished principles of a people. **Folkways** are norms governing everyday behavior. Society is less likely to formalize folkways than mores, and their violation raises comparatively little concern. (61)

Sanctions: **Sanctions** are penalties and rewards for conduct concerning a social norm. Conformity to a norm can lead to positive sanctions such as a pay raise, a medal, a word of gratitude, or a pat on the back. Negative sanctions include fines, threats, imprisonment, and stares of contempt. (62)

Values: **Values** are collective conceptions of what is considered good, desirable, and proper—or bad, undesirable, and improper—in a culture. Values influence people's behavior and serve as criteria for evaluating the actions of others. The values, norms, and sanctions of a culture are often directly related. (63)

Culture and the Dominant Ideology: Functionalists maintain that stability requires a consensus and the support of society's members; strong central values and common norms provide that support. Conflict theorists agree that a common culture may exist, but they argue that it serves to maintain the privileges of some groups rather than others. The term **dominant ideology** describes the set of cultural beliefs and practices that help to maintain powerful social, economic, and political interests. From a conflict perspective, the dominant ideology has major social significance. Not only do a society's most powerful groups and institutions control wealth and property; more importantly, they control the means of producing beliefs about reality through religion, education, and the media. (64–65)

Subcultures: A **subculture** is a segment of society that shares a distinctive pattern of mores, folkways, and values that differs from the patterns of the larger society. The existence of many subcultures is characteristic of complex societies such as the United States. Members of a subculture participate in the dominant culture while at the same time engaging in their unique and distinctive forms of behavior. Frequently, a subculture will develop an **argot**, or specialized language, that distinguishes it from the wider society. (65)

Culture Shock: Anyone who feels disoriented, uncertain, out of place, even fearful, when immersed in an unfamiliar culture may be experiencing **culture shock**. All of us, to some extent, take for granted the cultural practices of our society. As a result, it can be surprising and even disturbing to realize that other cultures do not follow our way of life. (66)

Ethnocentrism: Sociologist William Graham Sumner coined the term **ethnocentrism** to refer to the tendency to assume that one's own culture and way of life represent the norm or are superior to all others. The ethnocentric person sees his or her own group as the center or defining point of culture and views all other cultures as deviations from what is "normal." Conflict theorists point out that ethnocentric value judgments serve to devalue groups and to deny equal opportunities. Functionalists note that ethnocentrism serves to maintain a sense of solidarity by promoting group pride. (67)

Cultural Relativism: While ethnocentrism evaluates foreign cultures using the familiar culture of the observer as a standard of correct behavior, **cultural relativism** views people's behavior from the perspective of their own culture. It places a priority on understanding other cultures, rather than dismissing them as "strange" or "exotic." Unlike ethnocentrism, cultural relativism employs the kind of value neutrality in scientific study that Max Weber saw as so important. (67)

Bilingualism: Bilingualism refers to the use of two or more languages in a particular setting, such as the workplace or schoolroom. This issue has prompted a great deal of debate among educators and policymakers. For a long time, people in the United States demanded conformity to a single language. Recent decades have seen challenges to this pattern of forced obedience to the dominant ideology. Beginning in the 1960s, active movements for Black pride and ethnic pride insisted that people regard the traditions of all race and ethnic subcultures as legitimate and important. (68)

KEY TERMS

Briefly define or identify the following terms in the spaces provided below. The definitions of these terms can be found later in this chapter of the study guide.

Culture	Diffusion
Society	Technology
Cultural universal	Material culture
Innovation	Nonmaterial culture
Discovery	Culture lag
Invention	Sociobiology

Language	Value
Sapir-Whorf hypothesis	Dominant ideology
Norm	Subculture
Formal norm	Argot
Law	Counterculture
Informal norm	Culture shock
Mores	Ethnocentrism
Folkway	Cultural relativism
Sanction	Bilingualism

SELF-TEST

MODIFIED TRUE/FALSE QUESTIONS: If the statement below is true, write "true" in the space provided. If the statement is false, briefly correct the error.

1. In the view of sociologists, a portrait by Rembrandt is an aspect of culture; the work of graffiti artists is not.

2. Some of the examples of cultural universals noted in your text are athletic sports, funerals, medicine, and war.

3. There are two forms of innovation: discovery and diffusion.

4. Material culture is more resistant to change than nonmaterial culture.

5. A sociobiologist would argue that cultural similarities across societies are probably coincidental.

6. The Sapir-Whorf hypothesis holds that language is a "given."

7. The requirements for a college major and the rules of a card game are considered informal norms.

8. Society is more likely to formalize mores than folkways.

9. Even on clotheslines, mores in parts of Southeast Asia dictate male dominance in that women's attire is hung lower than that of men.

10. Conformity to a norm can lead to positive sanctions.

11. The values, norms, and sanctions of a culture are often directly related.

12. From a functionalist perspective, the dominant ideology has major social significance. Not only do a society's most powerful groups and institutions control wealth and property; more importantly, they control the means of producing beliefs about reality through religion, education, and the family.

13. Feminists would argue that the dominant ideology in the United States will help to control women and keep them in a subordinate position.

14. Sociologist Robert Merton coined the term *ethnocentrism* to refer to the tendency to assume that one's own culture and way of life constitute the norm or are superior to all others.

15. Cultural relativism requires that we accept without question every form of behavior characteristic of a culture.

MULTIPLE-CHOICE QUESTIONS: In each of the following, select the phrase that best completes the statement.

1. Which of the following is an aspect of culture?
    a. a comic book
    b. patriotic attachment to the flag of the United States
    c. slang words
    d. all of the above

2. A list of cultural universals was compiled by anthropologist
   a. Max Weber.
   b. George Murdock.
   c. Margaret Mead.
   d. William F. Ogburn.

3. 3. The identification of a new moon of Saturn was an act of
   a. invention.
   b. discovery.
   c. diffusion.
   d. cultural integration.

4. The distinction between elements of material and nonmaterial culture was made by sociologist
   a. Max Weber.
   b. George Murdock.
   c. Margaret Mead.
   d. William F. Ogburn.

5. Which of the following is an example of language?
   a. hand gestures
   b. frowns and smiles
   c. written characters
   d. all of the above

6. In the United States, we often formalize norms into
   a. folkways.
   b. mores.
   c. values.
   d. laws.

7. Which of the following statements about norms is correct?
   a. People do not follow norms in all situations. In some cases, they evade a norm because they know it is weakly enforced.
   b. In some instances, behavior that appears to violate society's norms may actually represent adherence to the norms of a particular group.
   c. Norms are violated in some instances because one norm conflicts with another.
   d. all of the above

8. Which of the following statements about values is correct?
    a. Values never change.
    b. The values of a culture may change, but most remain relatively stable during any one person's lifetime.
    c. Values are constantly changing; sociologists view them as being very unstable.
    d. all of the above

9. Which sociological perspective argues that a common culture serves to maintain the privileges of some groups while keeping others in a subservient position?
    a. the functionalist perspective
    b. the conflict perspective
    c. the interactionist perspective
    d. all of the above

10. Which of the following argued that a capitalist society has a dominant ideology that serves the interests of the ruling class?
    a. Max Weber
    b. Talcott Parsons
    c. Karl Marx
    d. Margaret Mead

11. Residents of a retirement community, workers in an offshore oil rig, and rodeo riders, are all examples of what sociologists refer to as
    a. subcultures.
    b. countercultures.
    c. cultural universals.
    d. argot.

12. While vacationing in Great Britain, you discover that the British drive on the "wrong" side of the road, are critical of your American accent, and will not accept dollars in stores. You feel disoriented and out of place. You are experiencing
    a. xenocentrism.
    b. the Hawthorne effect.
    c. the Sapir-Whorf hypothesis.
    d. culture shock.

13. The term *ethnocentrism* was coined by sociologist
    a. William F. Ogburn.
    b. William Graham Sumner.
    c. George Murdock.
    d. Max Weber.

14. Which sociological perspective emphasizes that ethnocentrism serves to maintain a sense of solidarity by promoting group pride?
    a. the functionalist perspective
    b. the conflict perspective
    c. the interactionist perspective
    d. the dramaturgical perspective

15. As of 2004, how many states in the U.S. had declared English to be their official language?
    a. none
    b. 12
    c. 27.
    d. 50

FILL-IN QUESTIONS: Fill in the blank spaces in the sentences below with the correct words. Where two or more words are required, there will be a corresponding number of blank spaces.

1. A _____ is the largest form of human group.

2. The bow and arrow, the automobile, and the television are all examples of _____.

3. The emergence of Starbucks in China is an example of _____.

4. Sociobiology is founded on the ideas of _____.

5. Language does more than describe reality; it also serves to _____ the reality of a culture.

6. "Put on some clean clothes for dinner," and "thou shalt not kill" are both examples of _____ found in our culture.

7. The United States has strong _____ against murder, treason, and child abuse that have been institutionalized into formal norms.

8. As security searches in contemporary Iraq demonstrate, the sudden violation of long-standing cultural _____ can upset an entire population.

9. During the 1980s and 1990s, there was growing support for values having to do with _____, power, and status.

10. From a _____ perspective, the dominant ideology has major social significance. Not only do a society's most powerful groups and institutions control wealth and property; more importantly, they control the means of producing beliefs about reality through religion, education, and the media.

11. Sociologists associated with the _____ perspective emphasize that language and symbols offer a powerful way for a subculture to maintain its identity.

12. Hippies can be viewed as an example of a _____.

13. Countercultures are typically popular among the _____, who have the least investment in the existing culture.

14. The _____ approach to social behavior points out that ethnocentric value judgments serve to devalue groups and contribute to denial of equal opportunities.

15. Cultural relativism places a priority on _____ other cultures rather than dismissing them as "strange" or "exotic."

UNDERSTANDING SOCIAL POLICY: All of the following questions are based on material that appears in the social policy section on bilingualism. Write a brief answer to each question in the space provided below.

1. What is bilingualism?

2. What is the functionalist view of bilingualism and what is the problem with this approach?

3. What is the conflict view of bilingualism?

4. What are the two major areas in which bilingualism has policy implications?

DEFINITIONS OF KEY TERMS

Culture: The totality of learned, socially transmitted customs, knowledge, material objects, and behavior. (53)

Society: A fairly large number of people who live in the same territory, are relatively independent of people outside it, and participate in a common culture. (53)

Cultural universal: A common practice or belief found in every culture. (53)

Innovation: The process of introducing a new idea or object into a culture through discovery or invention. (56)

Discovery: The process of making known or sharing the existence of an aspect of reality. (56)

Invention: The combination of existing cultural items into a form that did not exist before. (56)

Diffusion: The process by which a cultural item spreads from group to group or society to society. (56)

Technology: Cultural information about how to use the material resources of the environment to satisfy human needs and desires. (57)

Material culture: The physical or technological aspects of our daily lives. (58)

Nonmaterial culture: Ways of using material objects, as well as customs, beliefs, philosophies, governments, and patterns of communication. (58)

Culture lag: A period of maladjustment when the nonmaterial culture is still struggling to adapt to new material conditions. (58)

Sociobiology: The systematic study of how biology affects human social behavior. (58)

Language: An abstract system of word meanings and symbols for all aspects of culture; includes gestures and other nonverbal communication. (59)

Sapir-Whorf hypothesis: A hypothesis concerning the role of language in shaping our interpretation of reality. It holds that language is culturally determined. (59)

Norm: An established standard of behavior maintained by a society. (61)

Formal norm: A norm that has been written down and that specifies strict punishments for violators. (61)

Law: Governmental social control. (61)

Informal norm: A norm that is generally understood but not precisely recorded. (61)

Mores: Norms deemed highly necessary to the welfare of a society. (61)

Folkway: A norm governing everyday behavior whose violation raises comparatively little concern. (61)

Sanction: A penalty or reward for conduct concerning a social norm. (62)

Value: A collective conception of what is considered good, desirable, and proper—or bad, undesirable, and improper—in a culture. (63)

Dominant ideology: A set of cultural beliefs and practices that helps to maintain powerful social, economic, and political interests. (65)

Subculture: A segment of society that shares a distinctive pattern of mores, folkways, and values that differs from the pattern of the larger society. (65)

Argot: Specialized language used by members of a group or subculture. (65)

Counterculture: A subculture that deliberately opposes certain aspects of the larger culture. (66)

Culture shock: The feeling of surprise and disorientation that people experience when they encounter cultural practices that are different from their own. (66)

Ethnocentrism: The tendency to assume that one's culture and way of life represent the norm or are superior to all others. (67)

Cultural relativism: The viewing of people's behavior from the perspective of their own culture. (67)

Bilingualism: The use of two or more languages in a particular setting, such as the workplace or schoolroom, treating each language as equally legitimate. (68)

ANSWERS TO SELF-TEST

Modified True/False Questions
1. Sociologists consider both a portrait by Rembrandt and the work of graffiti artists to be aspects of culture. (53)
2. Athletic sports, funerals, and medicine are on the list of cultural universals developed by George Murdock, but war is not. (53)
3. There are two forms of innovation: discovery and invention. (56)
4. Generally, nonmaterial culture is more resistant to change than is material culture. (58)
5. A sociobiologist would argue that many cultural similarities are rooted in a common human genetic make-up. (58)
6. The Sapir-Whorf hypothesis holds that language is not a "given." Rather, it is culturally determined. (59)
7. The requirements for a college major and the rules of a card game are considered formal norms. (61)
8. True (61)

9. Even on clotheslines in parts of Southeast Asia, *folkways* dictate male dominance: women's attire is hung lower than that of men. (61–62)
10. True (62)
11. True (63)
12. From a conflict perspective, the dominant ideology has major social significance. Not only do a society's most powerful groups and institutions control wealth and property; even more important, they control the means of producing beliefs about reality through religion, education, and the media. (65)
13. True (65)
14. Sociologist William Graham Sumner coined the term *ethnocentrism* to refer to the tendency to assume that one's own culture and way of life constitute the norm or are superior to all others. (67)
15. While cultural relativism does not suggest that we must accept without question every form of behavior characteristic of a culture, it does require a serious and unbiased effort to evaluate norms, values, and customs in light of the distinctive culture of which they are a part. (67)

Multiple-Choice Questions
1. d (53)
2. b (53)
3. b (56)
4. d (58)
5. d (59)
6. d (61)
7. d (62)
8. b (63)
9. b (65)
10. c (65)
11. a (65)
12. d (66)
13. b (67)
14. a (67)
15. c (69)

Fill-In Questions
1. society (53)
2. inventions (56)
3. globalization (56)
4. Charles Darwin (58)
5. shape (59)
6. norms (61)
7. mores (61)
8. norms (62)
9. money (63)
10. conflict (65)
11. interactionist (65–66)
12. counterculture (66)
13. young (66)
14. conflict (67)
15. understanding (67)

Understanding Social Policy: Bilingualism
1. Bilingualism refers to the use of two or more languages in a particular setting, such as the workplace or schoolroom, treating each language as equally legitimate. Thus, a teacher of bilingual education may instruct children in their native language while gradually introducing them to the language of the host society. If the curriculum is also bicultural, it will teach children about the mores and folkways of both the dominant culture and the subculture. (68)

2. For a long time, people in the United States demanded conformity to a single language. This demand coincides with the functionalist view that language serves to unify members of a society. In some cases, immigrant children were actually forbidden to speak their native languages on school grounds. There was little respect granted to immigrants' cultural traditions. (68)
3. Conflict theory helps us to understand some of the attacks on bilingual programs. Many of the attacks stem from an ethnocentric point of view, which holds that any deviation from the majority is bad. This attitude tends to be expressed by those who wish to stamp out foreign influence wherever it occurs, especially in our schools. (68)
4. Bilingualism has policy implications largely in two areas: efforts to maintain language purity and programs to enhance bilingual education. Nations vary dramatically in their tolerance for a variety of languages. Policymakers in the United States have been somewhat ambivalent in dealing with the issue of bilingualism. In 1965, the Elementary and Secondary Education Act (ESEA) provided for bilingual, bicultural education. Then, in the 1970s, the federal government took an active role in establishing the proper form for bilingual programs. However, more recently, federal policy has been less supportive of bilingualism and local school districts have been forced to provide an increased share of funding for their bilingual programs. (69)

CHAPTER 4
SOCIALIZATION

The Role of Socialization
   Social Environment: The Impact of Isolation
   The Influence of Heredity

The Self and Socialization
   Sociological Approaches to the Self
   Psychological Approaches to the Self

Socialization and the Life Course
   The Life Course
   Anticipatory Socialization and Resocialization

Agents of Socialization
   Family
   School
   Peer Group
   Mass Media and Technology
   Workplace
   Religion and the State

Social Policy and Socialization: Child Care around the World
   The Issue
   The Setting
   Sociological Insights
   Policy Initiatives

BOXES
   SOCIOLOGY ON CAMPUS: *Impression Management by Students*
   SOCIOLOGY IN THE GLOBAL COMMUNITY: *Raising Amish Children*

KEY POINTS

Socialization: **Socialization** is the process in which people learn the attitudes, values, and actions appropriate for members of a particular culture. From a microsociological perspective, socialization helps us discover how to behave "properly" and what to expect from others if we follow (or challenge) society's norms and values. From a macrosociological perspective, socialization provides for the transmission of a culture from one generation to the next, and thereby for the long-term continuance of a society. (74–75)

Nature versus Nurture: Researchers have traditionally clashed over the relative importance of biological inheritance and environmental factors in human development; a conflict called the *nature versus nurture* (or *heredity versus environment*) debate. Today, most social scientists have moved beyond this debate, acknowledging instead the interaction of these variables in shaping human development. (75)

Cooley and the Looking-Glass Self: In the early 1900s, Charles Horton Cooley advanced the belief that we learn who we are by interacting with others. Cooley used the phrase **looking-glass self** to emphasize that the self is the product of our social interactions with other people. A subtle but critical aspect of Cooley's looking-glass self is that the self results from an individual's "imagination" of how others view him or her. (77)

Mead—Stages of the Self: George Herbert Mead continued Cooley's exploration of interactionist theory. Mead developed a useful model of the process by which the self emerges, defined by three distinct stages. During the preparatory stage, children merely imitate the people around them, especially family members with whom they continually interact. During the play stage, they begin to pretend to be other people. Just as an actor "becomes" a character, a child becomes a doctor, parent, superhero, or ship captain. Finally, in the game stage, the child of about eight or nine years old no longer just plays roles, but begins to consider several actual tasks and relationships simultaneously. (77–78)

Goffman—Presentation of the Self: Early in life, the individual learns to slant his or her presentation of the self in order to create distinctive appearances and to satisfy particular audiences. Erving Goffman referred to this altering of the presentation of the self as **impression management**. He makes so many explicit parallels to the theater that his view has been termed the **dramaturgical approach**. According to this perspective, people resemble performers in action. (79)

Anticipatory Socialization and Resocialization: **Anticipatory socialization** refers to the processes of socialization in which a person "rehearses" for future positions, occupations, and social relationships. Occasionally, assuming a new social or occupational position requires us to unlearn a previous orientation. **Resocialization** refers to the process of discarding former behavior patterns and accepting new ones as part of a transition in one's life. (83)

Total Institutions: Erving Goffman coined the term **total institutions** to refer to institutions, such as prisons, the military, mental hospitals, and convents that regulate all aspects of a person's life under a single authority. Because the total institution is generally cut off from the rest of society, it provides for all the needs of its members. People often lose their individuality within total institutions. (83)

The Family as an Agent of Socialization: The family is the most important agent of socialization in the United States, especially for children. The lifelong process of socialization begins shortly after birth. Newborns are constantly orienting themselves to the outside world, and family members constitute an important part of their social environment. As the primary agents of socialization, parents play a critical role in guiding children into those gender roles deemed appropriate in a society. (84–85)

Schools as an Agent of Socialization: Like the family, schools have an explicit mandate to socialize people in the United States—and especially children—into the norms and values of our culture. Functionalists point out that schools, as agents of socialization, fulfill the function of teaching the values and customs of the larger society. Conflict theorists agree, but add that schools can reinforce the divisive aspects of society, especially those of social class. (85–86)

Mass Media and Technology as Agents of Socialization: In the last 80 years, media innovations—radio, motion pictures, recorded music, television, and the Internet—have become important agents of socialization. Television, and increasingly the Internet, are critical forces in the socialization of children in the United States. In a national survey done in 2000, 47 percent of parents reported that at least one of their children had a television in his or her bedroom. A third of youths ages 10 to 17 use the Internet every day. (87)

The Workplace as an Agent of Socialization: Learning to behave appropriately within an occupation is a fundamental aspect of human socialization. More and more young people work today. Some observers feel that the increasing number of teenagers working earlier in life and for longer hours are now finding the workplace almost as important an agent of socialization as school. Socialization in the workplace changes when it involves a more permanent shift from an after-school job to full-time employment. (88)

The State and Religion as Agents of Socialization: Increasingly, social scientists are recognizing the importance of both government and religion as agents of socialization, because of their impact on the life course. Traditionally, family members have served as the primary caregivers in our culture, but in the 20th century, the family's protective function was steadily transferred to outside agencies such as hospitals, mental health clinics, and insurance companies. Both government and organized religion have impacted the life course by reinstituting some of the rites of passage once observed in agricultural communities and early industrial societies. (88)

Child Care around the World: Day care centers have become the functional equivalent of the nuclear family, performing some of the nurturing and socialization functions previously handled only by family members. Researchers have found that high-quality child care centers do not adversely affect the socialization of children; in fact, good day care benefits children. Viewed from a conflict perspective, child care costs are an especially serious burden for lower class families. Feminists suggest that high-quality child care receives little governmental support because it is regarded as "merely a way to let women work." (89)

KEY TERMS

Briefly define or identify the following terms in the spaces provided below. The definitions of these terms can be found later in this chapter of the study guide.

Socialization	Significant other
Personality	Impression management
Self	Dramaturgical approach
Looking-glass self	Face-work
Symbol	Cognitive theory of development
Role taking	Rite of passage
Generalized other	Life course approach

Anticipatory socialization	Degradation ceremony
Resocialization	Gender role
Total institution	

SELF-TEST

MODIFIED TRUE/FALSE QUESTIONS: If the statement below is true, write "true" in the space provided. If the statement is false, briefly correct the error.

1. Harry Harlow's study of Isabelle, who was raised in social isolation, supports the importance of socialization on development.

2. The self is a distinct identity that forms early in life and remains relatively unchanged as we age.

3. Charles Horton Cooley developed the concept of the looking-glass self.

4. Margaret Mead theorized about the development of the self in the early years of one's life.

5. During the preparatory stage identified by George Herbert Mead, children become skilled in role taking.

6. There appear to be striking differences in whom African Americans and whites from similar economic backgrounds regard as their significant others.

7. Sociologists Daniel Albas and Cheryl Albas found that students' impression management strategies are constrained by society's informal norms regarding modesty and consideration for less successful peers.

8. The life course approach is distinctive because of its emphasis on events in infancy and early childhood.

9. Upon entering prison to begin "doing time," a person may experience the humiliation of a degradation ceremony as he or she is stripped of clothing, jewelry, and other personal possessions.

10. The Amish way of life has changed very little since this group began arriving in the United States during the eighteenth and nineteenth centuries.

11. Although schools are making progress toward equitable treatment of boys and girls, girls still lag behind boys in technological training, which is currently much in demand in the labor force.

12. Television is always a negative socializing influence.

13. Researchers are finding that families are socialized into multitasking as the social norm; devoting one's full attention to one task—even eating or driving—is less common on a typical day.

14. Some observers feel that the increasing number of teenagers who are working earlier in life and for longer hours are now finding the workplace almost as important an agent of socialization as school.

15. The state and religion have had a noteworthy impact on the life course by abolishing traditional rites of passage.

MULTIPLE-CHOICE QUESTIONS: In each of the following, select the phrase that best completes the statement.

1. Isabelle was
   a. reared in an interracial family.
   b. kept in almost total seclusion for the first six years of her life.
   c. subjected to mistreatment in a mental institution.
   d. a child whose language skills were of genius caliber.

2. Harry Harlow conducted a study of
   a. Isabelle and the impact of social isolation on the socialization process.
   b. Nell and the impact of social isolation on the socialization process.
   c. rhesus monkeys that had been raised away from their mothers.
   d. nature versus nurture that focused on sociobiology.

3. Which of the following used the phrase looking-glass self to emphasize that the self is the product of our social interactions with other people?
   a. George Herbert Mead
   b. Charles Horton Cooley
   c. Erving Goffman
   d. Harry Harlow

4. Which sociologist distinguished between significant others and generalized others?
   a. George Herbert Mead
   b. Charles Horton Cooley
   c. Erving Goffman
   d. W. I. Thomas

5. A person does poorly on a college chemistry test and later tells a friend, "The exam wasn't fair! There were trick questions and it covered material that we weren't assigned!" This is an example of
    a. reverse socialization.
    b. face-work.
    c. studied nonobservance.
    d. anticipatory socialization.

6. In studying the strategies that college students employ to create desired appearances after grades have been awarded, sociologists Daniel Albas and Cheryl Albas drew upon the concept of impression management developed by
    a. George Herbert Mead.
    b. Charles Horton Cooley.
    c. Erving Goffman.
    d. Jean Piaget.

7. Jean Piaget found that although newborns have no self in the sense of a looking-glass image, they are quite
    a. ethnocentric.
    b. self-centered.
    c. other-directed.
    d. deterministic.

8. Which of the following is an example of a rite of passage?
    a. school graduation
    b. marriage
    c. retirement
    d. all of the above

9. Which of the following is considered a total institution?
    a. a university
    b. a mental hospital
    c. a factory
    d. all of the above

10. On the first day of basic training in the army, a recruit has his civilian clothes replaced with army "greens," has his hair shaved off, loses his privacy, and finds that he must use a communal bathroom. All of these humiliating activities are part of
    a. a significant other.
    b. impression management.
    c. a degradation ceremony.
    d. face-work.

11. The institution most closely associated with the process of socialization is the
    a. family.
    b. peer group.
    c. school.
    d. state.

12. The term gender role refers to
    a. the biological fact that we are male or female.
    b. a role that is given to us by a teacher.
    c. a role that is given to us in a play.
    d. expectations regarding the proper behavior, attitudes and activities of males and females.

13. Which sociological perspective emphasizes that schools in the United States foster competition through built-in systems of reward and punishment?
    a. the functionalist perspective
    b. the conflict perspective
    c. the interactionist perspective
    d. the psychological perspective

14. In the twentieth century, the family's protective function was increasingly transferred to outside agencies, such as
    a. hospitals.
    b. mental health clinics.
    c. insurance companies.
    d. all of the above

56 | *Sociology*

15. The state has had a noteworthy impact on the life course by reinstituting the rites of passage that had disappeared in agricultural societies and in periods of early industrialization. An example of this is
    a. the driving age.
    b. the legal drinking age.
    c. age at which one can marry without parental permission.
    d. all of the above

FILL-IN QUESTIONS: Fill in the blank spaces in the sentences below with the correct words. Where two or more words are required, there will be a corresponding number of blank spaces.

1. _____ provides for intergenerational transmission of culture, and it shapes the image that we hold of ourselves.

2. Studies of twins raised apart suggest that both _____ and _____ influence human development.

3. Those people who play a major role in shaping a person's identity, such as parents, friends, coworkers, coaches, and teachers, are _____ others.

4. A clerk may try to appear busier than he or she actually is if a supervisor happens to be watching. Sociologist _____ _____ examined such behavior using the dramaturgical approach.

5. Early work in _____, such as that of Sigmund Freud, stressed the role of inborn drives—among them the drive for sexual gratification—in channeling human behavior.

6. The first stage in Jean Piaget's well-known cognitive theory of development is the _____ stage, when children first discover that their hands are actually part of themselves.

7. Preparation for many aspects of adult life begins with _____ socialization during childhood and adolescence, and continues throughout our lives as we prepare for new responsibilities.

8. Resocialization is particularly effective when it occurs within a(n) _____ institution.

9. Amish youth often go through a period of discovery called _____, a term that means "running around."

10. Traditional _____ roles include men being "tough" and women being "tender."

11. The _____ perspective reminds us that socialization concerning not only masculinity and femininity, but also marriage and parenthood, begins in childhood as a part of family life.

12. The _____ perspective of sociology emphasizes the role of schools in teaching the values and customs of the larger society.

13. As children grow older, the family becomes less important in social development, while _____ _____ become more important.

14. Among media innovations, television and the _____ are critical forces in the socialization of children.

15. Both the government and organized religion have impacted the life course by reinstituting some of the _____ _____ _____ once observed in agricultural communities and early industrial societies.

UNDERSTANDING SOCIAL POLICY: All the following questions are based on material that appears in the social policy section on Child Care around the World. Write a brief answer to each question in the space provided below.

1. According to studies, what is the effect of day care on children?

2. What are the conflict and feminist concerns about day care?

3. Why is the turnover of teaching personnel so high in day care centers?

DEFINITIONS OF KEY TERMS

Socialization: The lifelong process in which people learn the attitudes, values, and behaviors appropriate for members of a particular culture. (74)

Personality: A person's typical patterns of attitudes, needs, characteristics, and behavior. (75)

Self: A distinct identity that sets us apart from others. (77)

Looking-glass self: A concept that emphasizes the self as the product of our social interactions with others. (77)

Symbol: A gesture, object, or word that forms the basis of human communication. (77)

Role taking: The process of mentally assuming the perspective of another and responding from that imagined viewpoint. (78)

Generalized other: The attitudes, viewpoints, and expectations of society as a whole that a child takes into account in his or her behavior. (78)

Significant other: An individual who is most important in the development of the self, such a parent, friend, or teacher. (79)

Impression management: The altering of the presentation of the self in order to create distinctive appearances and satisfy particular audiences. (79)

Dramaturgical approach: A view of social interaction in which people are seen as theatrical performers. (79)

Face-work: The efforts people make to maintain the proper image and avoid public embarrassment. (79)

Cognitive theory of development: The theory that children's thought progresses through four stages of development. (80)

Rite of passage: A ritual marking the symbolic transition from one social position to another. (81)

Life course approach: A research orientation in which sociologists and other social scientists look closely at the social factors that influence people throughout their lives, from birth to death. (82)

Anticipatory socialization: Processes of socialization in which a person "rehearses" for future positions, occupations, and social relationships. (83)

Resocialization: The process of discarding former behavior patterns and accepting new ones as part of a transition in one's life. (83)

Total institution: An institution that regulates all aspects of a person's life under a single authority, such as a prison, the military, a mental hospital, or a convent. (83)

Degradation ceremony: An aspect of the socialization process within some total institutions, in which people are subjected to humiliating rituals. (83)

Gender role: Expectations regarding the proper behavior, attitudes, and activities of males and females. (85)

ANSWERS TO SELF-TEST

Modified True/False Questions
1. Harry Harlow studied social isolation using rhesus monkeys. (76)
2. The self continues to develop and change throughout our lives. (77)
3. True (77)
4. George Herbert Mead (no relation to Margaret Mead) theorized about the development of the self in the early years of one's life. (77)
5. During the preparatory stage identified by George Herbert Mead, children merely imitate the people around them. Role taking occurs during the play stage. (77–78)
6. There appears to be little difference in whom African Americans and Whites from similar backgrounds regard as their significant others. (79)
7. True (80)
8. Social scientists who take a life course approach look at social factors that influence people throughout their lives. (82)
9. True (83)
10. True (84)
11. True (86)
12. Television can be a positive socializing influence. It can introduce children to unfamiliar lifestyles and cultures. (87)
13. True (88)
14. True (88)
15. Both the government and organized religion have had a noteworthy impact on the life course by reinstituting the rites of passage that had disappeared in agricultural societies and in periods of early industrialization. (88)

Multiple-Choice Questions

1. b (75)	6. c (80)	11. a (83)
2. c (76)	7. b (80)	12. d (85)
3. b (77)	8. d (81)	13. b (85)
4. a (78–79)	9. b (83)	14. d (88)
5. b (79)	10. c (83)	15. d (88)

Fill-In Questions
1. Socialization (74)
2. heredity; environment (75)
3. significant (79)
4. Erving Goffman (79)
5. psychology (79)
6. sensorimotor (80)
7. anticipatory (83)
8. total (83)
9. rumspringe (84)
10. gender (85)

11. interactionist (85)
12. functionalist (86)
13. peer groups (86)
14. Internet (87)
15. rites of passage (90)

Understanding Social Policy: Child Care around the World

1. Studies indicate that the socialization of children placed in high-quality day care centers is not adversely affected by such experiences; in fact, good day care benefits children. It is difficult, however, to generalize about child care, since there is so much variability among day care providers. (89)

2. Conflict theorists and feminists are concerned that parents in wealthy neighborhoods have an easier time finding day care than those in poor or working class communities, that day care costs are an especially serious burden for lower-class families, and that nearly all day care workers are women who often find themselves in low-status, minimum wage jobs. (91)

3. Nearly all child care workers are women; many find themselves in low-status, minimum wage jobs. Most child care workers earn less than $8.00 per hour, which is typically less than food servers, messengers, and gas station attendants make. (91)

CHAPTER 5
SOCIAL INTERACTION AND SOCIAL STRUCTURE

Social Interaction and Reality

Elements of Social Structure
  Statuses
  Social Roles
  Groups
  Social Networks and Technology
  Social Institutions

Social Structure in Global Perspective
  Durkheim's Mechanical and
    Organic Solidarity
  Tönnies's Gemeinschaft and
    Gesellschaft
  Lenski's Sociocultural Evolution
    Approach

Social Policy and Social Structure: The AIDS Crisis
  The Issue
  The Setting
  Sociological Insights
  Policy Initiatives

BOXES
  SOCIAL INEQUALITY: Disability as a Master Status
  RESEARCH IN ACTION: Adolescent Sexual Networks

KEY POINTS

Social Interaction and Social Structure: Sociologists use the term **social interaction** to refer to the ways in which people respond to one another. **Social structure** refers to the way in which a society is organized into predictable relationships. These concepts are central to sociological study. (94)

Social Interaction and Reality: According to Herbert Blumer, reality is shaped by our perceptions, evaluations, and definitions. The ability to define social reality reflects a group's power within a society. Indeed, one of the most crucial aspects of the relationship between dominant and subordinate groups is the ability of the dominant or majority group to define a society's values. (95)

Statuses: We normally think of a person's "status" as having to do with influence, wealth, and fame. However, sociologists use the term **status** to refer to any of the full range of socially defined positions within a large group or society, from the lowest to the highest position. Clearly, a person can hold a number of statuses at the same time. (96)

Ascribed and Achieved Status: An **ascribed status** is assigned to a person by society without regard to that person's unique talents or characteristics. Generally, this assignment takes place at birth; thus, a person's racial background, gender, and age are all considered ascribed statuses. Unlike ascribed statuses, an **achieved status** comes to us largely through our own efforts. We must do something, such as going to school, learning a skill, establishing a friendship, or inventing a new product, in order to acquire an achieved status. (96–97)

Social Roles: A **social role** is a set of expectations for people who occupy a given social position or status. With each distinctive social status—whether ascribed or achieved—come particular role expectations. Roles are a significant component of social structure. Viewed from a functionalist perspective, roles contribute to a society's stability by enabling members to anticipate the behavior of others and to pattern their own actions accordingly. Yet, social roles can also be dysfunctional if they restrict people's interaction and relationships. (97)

Groups: In sociological terms, a **group** is any number of people with similar norms, values, and expectations who interact with one another on a regular basis. Groups play a vital part in a society's social structure. Much of our social interaction takes place within groups and is influenced by their norms and sanctions. (102)

Social Institutions: The mass media, the government, the economy, the family, and the health care system are all examples of social institutions found in our society. **Social institutions** are organized patterns of beliefs and behavior centered on basic social needs, such as replacing personnel (the family) and preserving order (the government). (104)

Functionalist View of Social Institutions: One way to understand social institutions can be to see how they fulfill essential functions. Social scientists have identified five major tasks, or functional prerequisites, that a society or relatively permanent group must accomplish if it is to survive. These are (1) replacing personnel, (2) teaching new recruits, (3) producing and distributing goods and services, (4) preserving order, and (5) providing and maintaining a sense of purpose. (104–105)

Conflict View of Social Institutions: While both the functionalist and the conflict perspectives agree that social institutions are organized to meet basic social needs, conflict theorists object to the implication inherent in the functionalist view that the outcome is necessarily efficient and desirable. From a conflict perspective, major institutions help maintain the privileges of the most powerful individuals and groups within a society, while contributing to the powerlessness of others. Conflict theorists, as well as feminists and interactionists, have pointed out that social institutions also operate in gendered or racist environments. In schools, offices, and government institutions, assumptions that are made about what people can do, reflect the sexism and racism of the larger society. (105)

Interactionist View of Social Institutions: Interactionist theorists emphasize that our social behavior is conditioned by the roles and statuses that we accept, the groups to which we belong, and the institutions within which we function. (106)

Durkheim's Mechanical and Organic Solidarity: Émile Durkheim argued that social structure depends on the division of labor in a society. In a society in which there is a minimal division of labor, a collective consciousness develops that emphasizes group solidarity. Durkheim called this **mechanical solidarity**. As societies become more advanced technologically, a greater division of labor takes place. These societies are characterized by **organic solidarity**, a collective consciousness that rests on mutual interdependence. (106–107)

Tönnies's *Gemeinschaft* and *Gesellschaft*: According to sociologist Ferdinand Tönnies, the *Gemeinschaft* community is typical of rural life. It is a small community in which people have similar backgrounds and life experiences. In contrast, the *Gesellschaft* is an ideal community that is characteristic of modern urban life. In this community, most people are strangers who feel little in common with other community residents. Self-interest dominates, and there is little consensus concerning values or commitment to the group. (107–108)

Lenski's Sociocultural Evolution Approach: Sociologist Gerhard Lenski sees human societies as undergoing a process of change according to a dominant pattern, known as **sociocultural evolution**. In Lenski's view, a society's level of technology is critical to the way it is organized. There are three types of preindustrial societies, which are categorized according to the way in which the economy is organized: (1) the hunting-and-gathering society, (2) the horticultural society, and (3) the agrarian society. As the industrial revolution proceeded, a new form of social structure emerged. An **industrial society** is a society that depends on mechanization to produce its goods and services. Industrial societies rely on new inventions that facilitated agricultural and industrial production, and on new sources of energy, such as steam. (108–109)

The AIDS Crisis: AIDS caught major social institutions—particularly the government, the health care system, and the economy—by surprise when it initially was noticed by medical practitioners in the 1970s. As functionalists would predict, new social networks have emerged for dealing with the AIDS crisis. Self-help groups, especially in the gay communities of major cities, have been established to care for the sick, educate the healthy, and lobby for public policies that are more responsive. The label of "person with AIDS" or "HIV positive" often functions as a master status that stigmatizes those so labeled. (111)

KEY TERMS

Briefly define or identify the following terms in the spaces provided below. The definitions of these terms can be found later in this chapter of the study guide.

Social interaction	Social role
Social structure	Role conflict
Status	Role strain
Ascribed status	Role exit
Achieved status	Group
Master status	Social network

Social institution	Hunting-and-gathering society
Mechanical solidarity	Horticultural society
Organic solidarity	Agrarian society
Gemeinschaft	Industrial society
Gesellschaft	Postindustrial society
Sociocultural evolution	Postmodern society
Technology	

SELF-TEST

MODIFIED TRUE/FALSE QUESTIONS: If the statement below is true, write "true" in the space provided. If the statement is false, briefly correct the error.

1. Friends talking over the telephone and co-workers communicating over a computer are engaged in social interaction.

2. The social structure of Zimbardo's mock prison influenced the interactions between the guards and the prisoners.

3. The four basic elements of social structure are functions, behaviors, statuses, and social roles.

4. William I. Thomas noted that people respond only to the objective features of a person or situation.

5. Each person can hold only one status.

6. It is relatively easy to change an ascribed status.

7. Many people with disabilities find that their status as "disabled" functions as a master status that overshadows their actual ability to perform successfully in meaningful employment.

8. With each distinctive social role, whether ascribed or achieved, come particular status expectations. However, actual performance varies from individual to individual.

9. Social roles can be dysfunctional by restricting people's relationships with each other.

10. The last stage of role exit involves the creation of a new identity.

11. Through a study of adolescent sexual networks, sociologists Bearman, Moody, and Stovel found that today's teenagers face little risk of contracting sexually transmitted diseases.

12. According to Talcott Parsons and Robert Merton, the five major tasks or functional prerequisites that a society or relatively permanent group must accomplish if it is to survive are replacing personnel, teaching new recruits, producing and distributing goods and services, preserving order, and providing and maintaining a sense of purpose.

13. Interactionist theorists emphasize that our social behavior is conditioned by the roles and statuses that we accept, the groups to which we belong, and the institutions within which we function.

14. Organic solidarity implies a group orientation in the community.

15. Social change is an important aspect of life in the *Gemeinschaft*; it can be strikingly evident even within a single generation.

MULTIPLE-CHOICE QUESTIONS: In each of the following, select the phrase that best completes the statement.

1. In Zimbardo's mock prison experiment at Stanford University
    a. the social interactions between the prisoners and the guards influenced the social structure of the prison.
    b. the social structure of the prison influenced the social interactions between the prisoners and the guards.
    c. there was no relationship between social interaction and social structure.
    d. Zimbardo believed that social structure and social interaction influence each other.

2. Which sociologist saw that the "definition of the situation" could mold the thinking and personality of the individual?
   a. Philip Zimbardo
   b. Herbert Blumer
   c. William I. Thomas
   d. Erving Goffman

3. Which of the following is an ascribed status?
   a. daughter
   b. long-distance runner
   c. doctor
   d. all of the above

4. 4. Which of the following is an achieved status?
   a. senior citizen
   b. member of the female sex
   c. bank robber
   d. Native American

5. Arthur Ashe was a retired tennis star, an author, a political activist, and a person with AIDS. If he is remembered mainly as a well-known personality with AIDS, then this is his
   a. master status.
   b. self-fulfilling prophecy.
   c. ascribed status.
   d. social role.

6. During World War II, Christians living in Nazi Germany had to choose between trying to protect Jewish friends and associates, and turning them in to the authorities. This is an example of
   a. cultural universalism.
   b. role strain.
   c. functional prerequisites.
   d. role conflict.

7. You are a student at XYZ College, and you have your sociology and history final exams on the same morning. You know that preparing for both exams at the same time is going to lead to lower grades in one or both of the exams. The conflict that you are experiencing as you try to fulfill both of your responsibilities at the college is an example of
    a. role conflict.
    b. role exit.
    c. role strain.
    d. role dissonance.

8. Which of the following would experience role exit?
    a. a retired person
    b. a recovering alcoholic
    c. a nun who leaves her religious order
    d. all of the above

9. 9. In sociological terms, which of the following constitutes a group?
    a. members of a hospital's business office
    b. all residents of the state of Vermont
    c. women in the United States 50 years-old and over
    d. all of the above

10. One finding from the study of adolescent sexual networks (Bearman, et al.) is that
    a. Most adolescents are not sexually active.
    b. Most sexually-active adolescents have a single, steady partner.
    c. Most high school students have at least one sexually transmitted disease.
    d. Most respondents had been sexually active sometime during the past eighteen months.

11. Which sociological perspective has identified five major tasks that a society must accomplish if it is to survive?
    a. the functionalist perspective
    b. the conflict perspective
    c. the interactionist perspective
    d. the clinical perspective

70 | Sociology

12. The native people of Tasmania, a large island just south of Australia, are now extinct because they failed to
    a. teach new recruits.
    b. preserve order.
    c. replace personnel.
    d. provide and maintain a sense of purpose.

13. Which sociological perspective emphasizes that the outcome of major social institutions is not necessarily efficient and desirable?
    a. the functionalist perspective
    b. the conflict perspective
    c. the interactionist perspective
    d. all of the above

14. In studying the social behavior of word processors in a Chicago law firm, sociologist Mitchell Duneier drew on the
    a. functionalist perspective.
    b. conflict perspective.
    c. interactionist perspective.
    d. macrosociological perspective.

15. 15, In Gerhard Lenski's theory of sociocultural evolution, a society's level of _____ is critical to the way it is organized.
    a. agriculture
    b. health care
    c. technology
    d. all of the above

FILL-IN QUESTIONS: Fill in the blank spaces in the sentences below with the correct words. Where two or more words are required, there will be a corresponding number of blank spaces.

1. According to Herbert Blumer, our response to someone's behavior is based on the_____ we attach to his or her actions.

2. _____ theorists are especially interested in ascribed statuses, since these statuses often confer privileges or reflect a person's membership in a subordinate group.

3. The African American activist Malcolm X wrote in his autobiography that his position as a Black man (_____ status) was an obstacle to his dream of becoming a lawyer (_____ status).

4. Contemporary sociologists have suggested that society has attached a _____ to many forms of disability and that this leads to prejudicial treatment.

5. With each distinctive social status come particular _____ expectations.

6. Sociologist Helen Rose Fuchs Ebaugh developed the term _____ _____ to describe the process of disengagement from a role that is central to one's self-identity, and reestablishment of an identity in a new role.

7. The mass media, the government, the economy, the family, and the health care system are all examples of _____ _____ found in the United States.

8. Teaching of new recruits can take place formally within schools (where learning is a _____ function) or informally through interaction in peer groups (where instruction is a _____ function).

9. Viewed from a _____ perspective, major social institutions help maintain the privileges of the most powerful individuals and groups in a society, while contributing to the powerlessness of others.

10. According to Durkheim, societies with a minimal division of labor are characterized by _____ _____, while societies with a complex division of labor are characterized by _____ _____.

11. The concepts of *Gemeinschaft* and *Gesellschaft* were developed by German sociologist _____ _____.

12. The theory of sociocultural evolution was developed by _____ _____.

13. _____ societies relied on new inventions that facilitated agricultural and industrial production, and on new sources of energy such as steam.

14. Daniel Bell views the transition from industrial to postindustrial society as a positive development. He sees a rise in interest groups concerned with such

national issues as health, education, and the environment. Bell's outlook is _____ because he portrays postindustrial society as basically consensual.

15. _____ theorists take a global perspective and note the ways that aspects of culture cross national boundaries.

UNDERSTANDING SOCIAL POLICY: All of the following questions are based on material that appears in the social policy section on The AIDS Crisis. Write a brief answer to each question in the space provided below.

1. Why is there such a strong stigma attached to infection with the HIV virus and to AIDS?

2. Regarding the micro level of social interaction, what did sociologists predict about the AIDS crisis?

3. What are the two concerns that interactionists have with AIDS that are outlined in the text?

DEFINITIONS OF KEY TERMS

Social interaction: The ways in which people respond to one another. (94)

Social structure: The way in which a society is organized into predictable relationships. (94)

Status: A term used by sociologists to refer to any of the full range of socially defined positions within a large group or society. (96)

Ascribed status: A social position that is assigned to a person by society without regard for the person's unique talents or characteristics. (96)

Achieved status: A social position a person attains largely through his or her own efforts. (97)

Master status: A status that dominates others and thereby determines a person's general position in society. (97)

Social role: A set of expectations for people who occupy a given social position or status. (97)

Role conflict: The situation that occurs when incompatible expectations arise from two or more social positions held by the same person. (98)

Role strain: The difficulty that arises when the same social position imposes conflicting demands and expectations. (99)

Role exit: The process of disengagement from a role that is central to one's self-identity in order to establish a new role and identity. (99)

Group: Any number of people with similar norms, values, and expectations who interact with one another on a regular basis. (102)

Social network: A series of social relationships that links a person directly to others and through them indirectly to still more people. (102)

Social institution: An organized pattern of beliefs and behavior centered on basic social needs. (104)

Mechanical solidarity: A collective consciousness that emphasizes group solidarity, characteristic of societies with minimal division of labor. (106)

Organic solidarity: A collective consciousness that rests on mutual interdependence, characteristic of societies with a complex division of labor. (107)

Gemeinschaft: A close-knit community, often found in rural areas, in which strong personal bonds unite members. (107)

Gesellschaft: A community, often urban, that is large and impersonal, with little commitment to the group or consensus on values. (108)

Sociocultural evolution: The process of change and development in human societies that results from cumulative growth in their stores of cultural information. (108)

Technology: Cultural information about how to use the material resources of the environment to satisfy human needs and desires. (108)

Hunting-and-gathering society: A preindustrial society in which people rely on whatever foods and fibers are readily available in order to survive. (109)

Horticultural society: A preindustrial society in which people plant seeds and crops rather than merely subsist on available foods. (109)

Agrarian society: The most technologically advanced form of preindustrial society. Members are engaged primarily in the production of food, but increase their crop yields through technological innovations such as the plow. (109)

Industrial society: A society that depends on mechanization to produce its goods and services. (120)

Postindustrial society: A society whose economic system is engaged primarily in the processing and control of information. (110)

Postmodern society: A technologically sophisticated society that is preoccupied with consumer goods and media images. (110)

ANSWERS TO SELF-TEST

Modified True/False Questions
1. True (94)
2. True (94)
3. The five basic elements of social structure are statuses, social roles, groups, social networks, and social institutions. (95)
4. William I. Thomas observed that people respond not only to the objective features of a person or situation, but also to the meaning that the person or situation has for them. (95)
5. A person can hold more than one status simultaneously. (96)
6. In many cases, there is little that people can do to change an ascribed status. (96)
7. True (97)
8. With each distinctive social status, whether ascribed or achieved, come particular role expectations. (97)
9. True (97)
10. True (102)
11. Bearman et al. found that, because many are involved in a free flowing network of sexual partners, adolescent risk of being exposed to sexually transmitted diseases is relatively high. (103)
12. The five major tasks or functional prerequisites were developed by David F. Aberle, Raymond Mack, and Calvin Bradford. (104)
13. True (106)
14. Mechanical solidarity implies group orientation. (106)
15. Social change is an important aspect of life in the *Gesellschaft*; it can be strikingly evident within a single generation. (108)

Multiple-Choice Questions
1. b (94)
2. c (94)
3. a (95)
4. c (96)
5. a (97)
6. d (98)
7. c (99)
8. d (99)
9. a (102)
10. d (103)
11. a (104)
12. b (105)
13. b (105)
14. c (106)
15. c (108)

Fill-In Questions
1. meaning (95)
2. Conflict (96)
3. ascribed; achieved (97)
4. stigma (97)
5. role (97)
6. role exit (99)
7. social institutions (104)
8. manifest; latent (104–105)

9. conflict (105)
10. mechanical solidarity; organic solidarity (106–107)
11. Ferdinand Tönnies (107)
12. Gerhard Lenski (108)
13. Industrial (109)
14. functionalist (110)
15. Postmodern (110)

Understanding Social Policy: The AIDS Crisis

1. People who have AIDS or who are infected with the HIV virus actually face a powerful dual stigma. Not only are they associated with a lethal and contagious disease, but they also have a disease that disproportionately afflicts already stigmatized groups, such as gay males and drug users. (111)

2. Viewed from a conflict perspective, policymakers were slow to respond to the AIDS crisis because those in high-risk groups—gay men and IV drug users—were comparatively powerless. This linkage with stigmatized groups delayed recognition of the severity of the AIDS epidemic; the media took little interest in the disease until it seemed to be spreading beyond the gay community. (111)

3. On the micro level of social interaction, observers widely forecast that AIDS would lead to a more conservative sexual climate—among both homosexuals and heterosexuals—in which people would be much more cautious about becoming involved with new partners. (111)

CHAPTER 6: GROUPS AND ORGANIZATIONS

Understanding Groups
    Types of Groups
    Studying Small Groups

Understanding Organizations
    Formal Organizations and Bureaucracies
    Characteristics of a Bureaucracy
    Bureaucracy and Organizational Culture
    Voluntary Associations

Case Study: Bureaucracy and the Space Shuttle Columbia

The Changing Workplace
    Organizational Restructuring
    Telecommuting
    Electronic Communication

Social Policy and Organizations: The State of the Unions
    The Issue
    The Setting
    Sociological Insights
    Policy Initiatives

BOXES
    RESEARCH IN ACTION: *Pizza Delivery Employees as a Secondary Group*
    SOCIOLOGY IN THE GLOBAL COMMUNITY: *Amway the Chinese Way*

KEY POINTS

Understanding Groups: A **group** is any number of people with similar norms, values, and expectations who interact with one another on a regular basis. College sororities and fraternities, dance companies, tenants' associations, and chess clubs are all considered examples of groups. The study of groups has become an important part of sociological investigation because they play such a key role in the transmission of culture. (119)

Primary and Secondary Groups: Sociologist Charles Horton Cooley coined the term **primary group** to refer to a small group characterized by intimate, face-to-face association and cooperation. When we find ourselves identifying closely with a group, it is probably a primary group. However, we also participate in many groups that are not characterized by close bonds of friendship, such as large classes and business associations. The term **secondary group** refers to a formal, impersonal group in which there is little social intimacy or mutual understanding. (119)

In-Groups, Out-Groups, and Reference Groups: An **in-group** is a group or category to which people feel they belong, and an **out-group** is a group or category to which people feel they do not belong. Sociologists use the term **reference group** when speaking of any group that individuals use as a standard for evaluating themselves and their own behavior. Reference groups have two basic purposes: (1) they serve a normative function by setting and enforcing standards of conduct and belief; (2) they also perform a comparison function by serving as a standard against which people can measure themselves and others. (120–121)

Studying Small Groups: The term **small group** refers to a group small enough for all members to interact simultaneously; that is, to talk with one another, or at least be well acquainted. We may think of small groups as being informal and unpatterned; yet, as interactionist researchers have revealed, there are distinct and predictable processes at work in the functioning of small groups. (121)

Formal Organizations: As contemporary societies have shifted to more advanced forms of technology and their social structures have become more complex, our lives have become increasingly dominated by large secondary groups referred to as **formal organizations**. A formal organization is a group designed for a special purpose and structured for maximum efficiency. The U.S. Postal Service, the Boston Pops orchestra, and the college you attend are all examples of formal organizations. In our society, formal organizations fulfill an enormous variety of personal and societal needs and shape the lives of every one of us. (123)

Characteristics of a Bureaucracy: A **bureaucracy** is a component of formal organization that uses rules and hierarchical ranking to achieve efficiency. Elements of bureaucracy enter into almost every occupation in an industrial society. Max Weber first directed researchers to the significance of bureaucratic structure. For analytical purposes, he developed an ideal type of bureaucracy that would reflect the most characteristic aspects of all human organizations. He argued that the ideal bureaucracy will have five basic characteristics: division of labor, hierarchy of authority, written rules and regulations, impersonality, and employment based on technical qualifications. (123–125)

Bureaucratization as a Process: Sociologists have used the term bureaucratization to refer to the process by which a group, organization, or social movement becomes increasingly bureaucratic. Normally, we think of bureaucratization in terms of large organizations. But bureaucratization also takes place within small-group settings. (125)

The Iron Law of Oligarchy: German sociologist Robert Michels studied socialist parties and labor unions in Europe before World War I and found that such organizations were becoming increasingly bureaucratic. Michels originated the idea of the **iron law of oligarchy**, under which a democratic organization will eventually develop into a bureaucracy ruled by a few. Michels argued that members of an oligarchy are strongly motivated to maintain their leadership roles, privileges, and power. (125–126)

Bureaucracy and Organizational Culture: How does bureaucratization affect the average individual who works in an organization? According to the **classical theory** of formal organizations, also known as the **scientific management approach**, workers are motivated almost entirely by economic rewards. The **human relations approach** emphasizes the role of people, communication, and participation within a bureaucracy. (126)

Voluntary Associations: **Voluntary associations** are organizations based on a common interest, whose members volunteer or even pay to participate. The Girl Scouts of America, the American Jewish Congress, the Kiwanis Club, and the League of Women Voters are all considered voluntary associations. Voluntary associations in the United States are largely segregated by gender. (127–128)

The Changing Workplace: Besides the far-reaching impact of technological advances such as computerization, workers must cope with organizational restructuring. Increasingly, workers are turning into telecommuters in many industrial countries. **Telecommuters** are employees who work full-time or part-time at home rather than in an outside office, and who are linked to their supervisors and colleagues through computer terminals, phone lines, and fax machines. (129)

The State of the Unions: **Labor unions** consist of organized workers who share either the same skill or the same employer. In 1954, unions represented 39 percent of workers in the private sector of the U.S. economy; in 2004, they represented only 12.5 percent. There are several arguments about the reasons for this decline: changes in the type of industry (manufacturing replaced by service industries); growth in part-time jobs; changes in the legal system; globalization; employer offensive; and union rigidity and bureaucratization. (130–131)

KEY TERMS

Briefly define or identify the following terms in the spaces provided below. The definitions of most of these terms can be found later in this chapter of the study guide.

McDonaldization	Coalition
Group	Groupthink
Primary group	Formal organization
Secondary group	Bureaucracy
In-group	Ideal type
Out-group	Alienation
Reference group	Trained incapacity
Small group	Goal displacement
Dyad	Peter principle
Triad	Bureaucratization

Iron law of oligarchy	Voluntary association
Classical theory	Telecommuter
Scientific management approach	Labor union
Human relations approach	

SELF-TEST

MODIFIED TRUE/FALSE QUESTIONS: If the statement below is true, write "true" in the space provided. If the statement is false, briefly correct the error.

1. People who are flying on the same airplane from New York City to London are members of a group.

2. Members of a primary group, such as neighbors, close friends, and especially kinfolk can play a vital role in assisting people with complicated schedules for taking prescription medicines.

3. Patrick Kinkade and Michael Katovich used the functionalist perspective to explore the social relationships that developed among urban pizza delivery drivers as they socialized during work while waiting for orders, and after work in bars.

4. Each of the following statements implies the existence of reference groups: "Our generation does not have those sexual hang-ups," "We Christians go to church every week," and "We Southerners have to stick together."

5. Only one reference group can influence an individual at a given time.

6. Charles Horton Cooley is credited as the first sociologist to emphasize the importance of interaction processes within groups and note how they change as the group's size changes.

7. Adding an additional member to a dyad always serves a unifying role.

8. The term groupthink was coined by William H. Whyte.

9. Elements of bureaucracy are found in about one-third of the occupations in an industrial society such as the United States.

10. The five characteristics of bureaucracies that Weber discussed include division of labor, hierarchy of authority, written rules and regulations, dysfunctions, and impersonality.

11. Although division of labor has certainly been beneficial in the performance of many complex bureaucracies, in some cases it can lead to the Peter principle in which workers become so specialized that they develop blind spots and fail to notice obvious problems.

12. 12. Max Weber used the term goal displacement to refer to overzealous conformity to official regulations.

13. Normally, we think of bureaucratization in terms of large organizations. But bureaucratization also takes place within small-group settings.

14. The iron law of oligarchy describes how even a democratic organization will develop into a bureaucracy ruled by a few (the oligarchy).

15. It was not until workers organized unions, and forced management to recognize that they were not objects, that theorists of formal organizations began to revise the classical approach.

MULTIPLE-CHOICE QUESTIONS: In each of the following, select the phrase that best completes the statement.

1. All of the redheaded people in the United States are an example of a(n)
    a. group.
    b. aggregate.
    c. category.
    d. formal organization.

2. Close friends who have known each other since childhood would be an example of a(n)
    a. primary group.
    b. secondary group.
    c. out-group.
    d. formal organization.

3. 3. _____ groups often emerge in the workplace among those who share special understandings about their occupation.
    a. Primary
    b. Secondary
    c. Out-
    d. Formal

4. The purpose of a reference group is to serve a(n)
   a. normative function by enforcing standards of conduct and belief.
   b. comparison function by serving as a standard against which people can measure themselves and others.
   c. elimination function by dissolving groups that no longer have a social purpose.
   d. both a and b

5. Which of the following statements about small groups is correct?
   a. All small groups are primary groups.
   b. All small groups are secondary groups.
   c. Many small groups differ from primary groups in that they do not necessarily offer the intimate personal relationships characteristic of primary groups.
   d. both b and c

6. In larger groups each person has
   a. less time to speak.
   b. more points of view to absorb.
   c. a more elaborate structure within which to function.
   d. all of the above

7. 7. Which pioneer of sociology first directed researchers to the significance of bureaucratic structure?
   a. Émile Durkheim
   b. Max Weber
   c. Karl Marx
   d. Ferdinand Tönnies

8. The President of the United States need not be a good typist; a surgeon need not be able to fill a cavity. This is because of the bureaucratic characteristic of
   a. division of labor.
   b. impersonality.
   c. employment based on technical qualifications.
   d. written rules and regulations.

9. Steve is the star of the college football team. He takes a history course and fails all of the exams in that course. Nevertheless, the instructor gives Steve an "A" in the course. This would violate which component of bureaucracies?
    a. division of labor
    b. written rules and regulations
    c. employment based on technical qualifications
    d. impersonality

10. Claude is in a major automobile accident and is severely injured. When he is brought by ambulance to the hospital, he is refused admission because he cannot find his health insurance card. This situation would illustrate
    a. the Peter principle.
    b. trained incapacity.
    c. goal displacement.
    d. division of labor.

11. When workers organized unions and forced management to recognize that they were not objects, theorists of formal organizations began to revise the
    a. classical theory.
    b. scientific management approach.
    c. human relations approach.
    d. both a and b

12. The space shuttle *Columbia* disaster illustrates some of the possible problems when
    a. safety concerns are not fully addressed.
    b. organizations are bureaucratized.
    c. an organization tries to dismantle its hierarchy.
    d. both a and c

13. 13. Minimal hierarchy involves
    a. a traditional bureaucracy.
    b. a lack of rules in the workplace.
    c. a flatter organizational structure.
    d. an absence of traditional job titles.

14. What are the social implications of a shift toward the virtual office—the increasing number of telecommuters?
    a. Supervisors will find that performance goals must be defined more clearly, which may lead to further bureaucratization.
    b. It should increase autonomy and job satisfaction for many employees.
    c. It will lead to greater worker privacy and job security.
    d. both a and b

15. Which of the following have expressed particular concern about the longevity of union leaders who are not always responsive to the needs and demands of membership?
    a. functionalists
    b. conflict theorists
    c. interactionists
    d. classical theorists

FILL-IN QUESTIONS: Fill in the blank spaces in the sentences below with the correct words. Where two or more words are required, there will be a corresponding number of blank spaces.

1. People who happen to be in the same place at the same time, such as members of a Broadway theatre audience, are a(n) _____.

2. The theorist who coined the term primary group was _____ _____.

3. When we find ourselves identifying closely with a group, it is probably a _____ group.

4. William Graham Sumner distinguished between _____ and _____.

5. In many cases, people model their behavior after groups to which they may not belong. These groups are called _____ groups.

6. A group with two members is called a(n) _____, a group with three members is called a(n) _____, and both of these are examples of a(n) _____ group.

7. A third member of a group may try to gain control by having the other two members become rivals. This is known as the _____-_____-_____ strategy.

8. Formal organizations have a(n) _____ form of organization.

9. Max Weber developed a(n) _____ _____ of bureaucracy, which reflects the most characteristic aspects of all human organizations.

10. Trained incapacity, goal displacement, and the Peter principle are all examples of bureaucratic _____.

11. The division of labor in a bureaucracy can sometimes cause workers to become so specialized that they develop blind spots, and fail to notice obvious problems. This problem is called _____ _____.

12. Every person who walks into a fast food restaurant is greeted with a smile and the statement, "May I take your order, please?" This standardized treatment, characteristic of all bureaucracies, is known as _____.

13. The iron law of oligarchy was developed by German sociologist _____ _____.

14. Robert Michels argues that the rank and file of a movement or organization look to leaders for direction, and thereby reinforce the process of rule by a _____.

15. _____ are employees of business or government agencies who work full-time or part-time at home rather than in an outside office, and who are linked to their supervisors and colleagues through computer terminals, phone lines, and fax machines.

UNDERSTANDING SOCIAL POLICY: All of the following questions are based on material that appears in the social policy section on The State of the Unions. Write a brief answer to each question in the space provided below.

1. What is the definition of a labor union?

2. Give six reasons that account for the decline of labor unions, and explain each.

3. What do conflict theorists and functionalist theorists have in common in the discussion of labor unions?

4. Describe the right to work law. How many states have this law, and how does it affect labor unions?

DEFINITIONS OF KEY TERMS

McDonaldization: The process by which the principles of the fast-food restaurant are coming to dominate more and more sectors of American society as well as the rest of the world. (118)

Group: Any number of people with similar norms, values, and expectations who interact with one another on a regular basis. (119)

Primary group: A small group characterized by intimate, face-to-face association and cooperation. (119)

Secondary group: A formal, impersonal group in which there is little social intimacy or mutual understanding. (119)

In-group: Any group or category to which people feel they belong. (120)

Out-group: A group or category to which people feel they do not belong. (120)

Reference group: Any group that individuals use as a standard for evaluating themselves and their own behavior. (121)

Small group: A group small enough for all members to interact simultaneously—that is, to talk with one another, or at least be well acquainted. (121)

Dyad: A two-member group. (122)

Triad: A three-member group. (122)

Coalition: A temporary or permanent alliance geared toward a common goal. (122)

Groupthink: Uncritical acceptance of or conformity to the prevailing viewpoint. (122)

Formal organization: A group designed for a special purpose and structured for maximum efficiency. (123)

Bureaucracy: A component of formal organization that uses rules and hierarchical ranking to achieve efficiency. (123)

Ideal type: A construct or model for evaluating specific cases. (123)

Alienation: A condition of estrangement or dissociation from the surrounding society. (124)

Trained incapacity: The tendency of workers in a bureaucracy to become so specialized that they develop blind spots and fail to notice obvious problems. (124)

Goal displacement: Overzealous conformity to official regulations of a bureaucracy. (125)

Peter principle: A principle of organizational life according to which every employee within a hierarchy tends to rise to his or her incompetence. (125)

Bureaucratization: The process by which a group, organization, or social movement becomes increasingly bureaucratic. (125)

Iron law of oligarchy: A principle of organizational life under which even a democratic organization will develop into a bureaucracy ruled by a few individuals. (126)

Classical theory: An approach to the study of formal organizations that views workers as being motivated almost entirely by economic rewards. (126)

Scientific management approach: Another name for the classical theory of formal organizations. (126)

Human relations approach: An approach to the study of formal organizations that emphasizes the role of people, communication, and participation in a bureaucracy and tends to focus on the informal structure of the organization. (126)

Voluntary association: An organization based on a common interest, whose members volunteer or even pay to participate. (127)

Telecommuter: An employee who works full-time or part-time at home rather than in an outside office, and who is linked to supervisor and colleagues through computer terminals, phone lines, and fax machines. (129)

Labor union: Organized workers who share either the same skill or the same employer. (130)

ANSWERS TO SELF-TEST

Modified True/False Questions

1. People who are flying on the same airplane happen to be in the same place at the same time and are an aggregate, not a group. (119)
2. True (119)
3. Kinkade and Katovich use interactionism in the study of pizza delivery employees. (120)
4. Each of the phrases implies the existence of in-groups and out-groups—groups to which we feel that we belong or do not belong. (120)
5. It is not uncommon for two or more reference groups to influence us at the same time. (121)

6. Georg Simmel was the first sociologist to emphasize the importance of interaction processes within groups and note how they change as the group's size changes. (122)
7. Adding an additional person to a dyad may serve a unifying role, a mediating role, or may lead to a divide-and-rule strategy. (122)
8. True (122)
9. Elements of bureaucracy enter into almost every occupation in an industrial society. (123)
10. Dysfunctions are not one of the five characteristics of bureaucracy discussed by Max Weber. Employment based on technical qualifications should be added to the list. (124)
11. When workers become so specialized that they develop blind spots and fail to notice obvious problems, it is called trained incapacity. (124)
12. Robert Merton used the term goal displacement to refer to overzealous conformity to official regulations. (125)
13. True (125)
14. True (126)
15. True (126)

Multiple-Choice Questions
1. c (119)
2. a (119)
3. b (119)
4. d (121)
5. c (121)
6. d (122)
7. b (123)
8. a (123–124)
9. b (125)
10. c (125)
11. d (126)
12. d (128)
13. c (129)
14. b (130)
15. b (131)

Fill-In Questions
1. aggregate (119)
2. Charles (Horton) Cooley (119)
3. primary (119)
4. in-groups; out-groups (119)
5. reference (121)
6. dyad; triad; small (121–122)
7. divide-and-rule (122)
8. bureaucratic (123)
9. ideal type (123)
10. dysfunctions (124)
11. trained incapacity (124)
12. impersonality (125)
13. Robert Michels (126)
14. few (126)
15. Telecommuters (129)

Understanding Social Policy: The State of the Unions
1. Labor unions consist of organized workers who share either the same skill or the same employer. (130)

2. 1) Changes in the type of industry: manufacturing jobs, the traditional heart of the labor union, have declined, giving way to postindustrial service jobs that typically do not have union representation. 2) Growth in part-time jobs: Only in 2000 did laws governing collective bargaining allow temporary workers to join a union. 3) Changes in the legal system: Government measures have made it more difficult for labor unions to organize and bargain. 4) Globalization: The threat of jobs leaving the country has undercut the ability of union leaders to organize workers at home. 5) Employer offensive: Increasingly hostile employers have taken court action to block union efforts to represent their members. 6) Union rigidity and bureaucratization: Labor unions have been slow to embrace women, minorities and immigrants, and in some unions the election of leadership seems to dominate the organization's activity. (130–131)

3. Both Marxists and functionalists would view unions as a logical response to the emergence of impersonal, large-scale, formal, and often alienating organizations. Unions have become increasingly bureaucratized under a self-serving leadership. (131)

4. Right to work laws state that workers cannot be required to join or pay dues or fees to a union. This is evident in 21 states and displays an anti-union attitude. (131)

CHAPTER 7: THE MASS MEDIA

Sociological Perspectives on the Media
   Functionalist View
   Conflict View
   Feminist View
   Interactionist View

The Audience
   Who Is in the Audience?
   The Segmented Audience
   Audience Behavior

The Media Industry
   Media Concentration
   The Media's Global Reach

Social Policy and Mass Media: Media Violence
   The Issue
   The Setting
   Sociological Insights
   Policy Initiatives

BOXES
   SOCIAL INEQUALITY: *The Color of Network TV*
   SOCIOLOGY IN THE GLOBAL COMMUNITY: *Al Jazeera is on the Air*

KEY POINTS

Mass Media: By the term **mass media,** sociologists refer to the print and electronic instruments of communication that carry messages to often widespread audiences. The pervasiveness of the mass media in society is obvious. Few aspects of society are as central as the mass media. Through the media, we expand our understanding of people and events beyond what we experience in person. For sociologists, the key question is how the mass media affect our social institutions, and how they influence our social behavior. (136)

The Functionalist View: The most obvious function of the mass media is to entertain. We often think the purpose of media is to occupy our leisure time, but they also serve other important functions. The media also socialize us, enforce social norms, confer status, promote consumption, and keep us informed about our social environment. An important dysfunction is that they may act as a narcotic, desensitizing us to events. (137)

Socialization and Mass Media: The media act as agents of socialization. The media increase social cohesion by presenting a more or less standardized, common view of culture through mass communication. The mass media unquestionably play a significant role in providing a collective experience for members of a society. (137)

Enforcer of Social Norms: The mass media often reaffirm proper behavior by showing what happens to people who act in a way that violates societal expectations (138)

Conferral of Status, Promotion of Consumption, and Surveillance: The mass media confer status on people, organizations, and public issues by singling out one from thousands of other similarly placed issues or people to become significant. Media advertising contributes to a consumer culture that creates "needs" and raises unrealistic expectations of what is required to be happy or satisfied. Moreover, because the media depend heavily on advertising revenue, advertisers are able to influence media content. The decision-makers within the media organizations generally define the "facts," or determine how to portray a situation to the audience. The collection and distribution of information concerning events in the social environment is the **surveillance function** of the media. (138–139)

Dysfunctional Media—The Narcotizing Effect: Some refer to the media as having a narcotizing dysfunction. A **narcotizing dysfunction** refers to the phenomenon whereby the media provide such massive amounts of information that the audience becomes numb and generally fails to act on the information, regardless of how compelling the issue is. (140)

Conflict View: Conflict theorists emphasize that the media reflect and even exacerbate many of the divisions of our society and world, including those based on gender, race, ethnicity, and social class. Within the mass media, a relatively small number of people control what material eventually reaches the audience, a process known as **gatekeeping**. Conflict theorists argue that the mass media serve to maintain the privileges of certain groups. Moreover, while protecting their own interests, powerful groups may limit the representation of others in the media. (140)

Feminist View: Feminists continue the argument advanced by conflict theorists that the mass media stereotype and misrepresent social reality. They contend that their images of the sexes communicate unrealistic, stereotypical, and limiting perceptions. (143-144)

Interactionist View: Interactionists are especially interested in shared understandings of everyday behavior. They examine the media on the micro level to see how they shape day-to-day social behavior. The interactionist perspective also helps us to understand more about one important aspect of the entire mass media system—the *audience*. (144)

The Audience: We can look at the audience from both the level of microsociology and macrosociology. At the micro level, we would consider how the audience members interacting among themselves would respond to the media or, in the case of live performances, would perhaps influence the performers. At the macro level, we would examine broader societal consequences of the media, such as early childhood education through programming like *Sesame Street*. Despite the role of **opinion leaders** (someone who through day-to-day personal contact and communication, influences the opinions and decisions of others) members of an audience do not all interpret media in the same way. (146)

The Media Industry: The media industry is getting more and more concentrated, with just a handful of multinational corporations dominating the publishing, broadcasting, and film industries. The one significant exception to centralization and concentration is the Internet. (147)

KEY TERMS

Briefly define or identify the following terms in the spaces provided below. The definitions of these terms can be found later in this chapter of the study guide.

Mass media	Surveillance function
Narcotizing dysfunction	Stereotype

Gatekeeping	Opinion leader
Dominant ideology	

SELF-TEST

MODIFIED TRUE/FALSE QUESTIONS: If the statement below is true, write "true" in the space provided. If the statement is false, briefly correct the error.

1. Sociologists refer to the print and electronic means of communication that carry messages to often widespread audiences as television transmissions.

2. For sociologists, the key question is how the mass media affect our social institutions, and how they influence our social behavior.

3. While the media can serve to reinforce proper behavior, they don't endorse illicit activities, such as drag racing or drug use.

4. In 1997, a federal law required the television networks to provide one free minute for every minute the government bought for a public service announcement with an antidrug message. The networks have fully complied and continue support this law.

5. Viewer fatigue begins when the viewer experiences eyestrain and sore fingertips from overuse of the remote control.

6. The mass media constitute a form of big business in which profits are generally more important than the quality of the programming.

7. In many countries, the government plays a gatekeeping role. A study for the World Bank found that in 97 countries, only five percent of the top five TV stations and only three percent of the largest radio stations are government owned.

8. The Internet is a means of quick dissemination of information (or misinformation) without going through any significant gatekeeping process.

9. The Internet is totally without restrictions.

10. In 2003–2004 the 26 new prime-time television series more evenly portrayed minorities, which shows that the broadcasting industry is no longer supportive of biased programming.

11. Media observers believe that the networks will need to integrate the ranks of gatekeepers before they achieve true diversity in programming.

12. American movies make almost all of their profits from American audiences.

13. According to the feminist view, one of the three problems that arise from media coverage is the depiction of male-female relationships emphasizing traditional sex roles and discouraging violence against women.

14. Television literally serves as a babysitter, or a "playmate," for many children and even infants.

15. There are no exceptions to the centralization and concentration of the media.

MULTIPLE-CHOICE QUESTIONS: In each of the following, select the phrase that best completes the statement.

1. Sociologists consider mass media to include
   a. newspapers and magazines.
   b. television and radio.
   c. books and the Internet.
   d. all of the above

2. One obvious function of the mass media is
   a. to confer status.
   b. to enforce social norms.
   c. to inform us about our social environment.
   d. to entertain.

3. The socialization process of the mass media is not universally regarded. Many people worry about
   a. the effect of using the television as a "babysitter."
   b. the impact of violent programming on viewer behavior.
   c. the unequal ability of all individuals to purchase televisions.
   d. both a and b

4. In 1997, when networks made an agreement with the government to drop free minutes in exchange for embedding aggressive anti-drug messages in their programs, many thought it was a slippery slope that could
    a. allow an entertainer to quickly slide out of the limelight.
    b. open the way for government to plant messages in the media on topics such as abortion or gun control.
    c. cause the distribution of information related to the social environment.
    d. cause a crash in the stock market.

5. Regarding media advertising, sociologists are concerned that
    a. it creates unrealistic expectations of what is required to be happy.
    b. it creates new consumer needs.
    c. advertisers are able to influence media content.
    d. all of the above

6. In the United States the gatekeeping process is
    a. in the hands of private individuals who desire to maximize profits.
    b. in the hands of political leaders who desire to maintain control of the government.
    c. in the hands of church leaders who desire to maintain control of the government.
    d. none of the above

7. An example of television creating false images or stereotypes of subordinate groups that become accepted as accurate portrayals of reality are
    a. an all-White cast in an urban-based show situated in an ethnically diverse city.
    b. Blacks being repeatedly portrayed and featured in crime-based dramas.
    c. Latinos rarely being present in any television program.
    d. all of the above

8. Why should it matter that minority groups aren't visible on network television, if they are well represented on cable networks like BET, UPN, and Univision?
    a. Because everyone has the right to be a "star."
    b. An implication of the equal rights amendment is that all races and nationalities must be equally represented on television.
    c. A societal backlash may occur because minorities feel slighted by under representation.
    d. Whites as well as minorities see a distorted picture of their society every time they turn on network TV.

9. Which perspective contends that the mass media stereotype and misrepresent social reality influencing the way we view men and women?
    a. the functionalist perspective
    b. the conflict perspective
    c. the interactionist perspective
    d. the feminist perspective

10. Which perspective examines the media on the micro level to see how they shape day-to-day social behavior?
    a. the functionalist perspective
    b. the conflict perspective
    c. the interactionist perspective
    d. the feminist perspective

11. The one thing all media need in order to exist is
    a. cameras.
    b. fiber optic lines.
    c. laser dish transmission.
    d. an audience.

12. What statement about the televised news network Al Jazeera is true?
    a. Everyone agrees that Al Jazeera is far more biased than CNN or ABC.
    b. Since September 11, 2001, Al Jazeera has steadfastly refused to air videotaped messages from Osama bin Laden.
    c. Almost all of the Arab world would agree that Palestinian suicide bombings are wrong.
    d. Al Jazeera presents a diversity of viewpoints.

13. The key to creating a truly global network that reaches directly into workplaces, schools, and homes is
    a. cable networks.
    b. XFM radio broadcasting.
    c. distribution of major print media.
    d. the Internet.

14. The lack of one national home for the various forms of mass media points to a potential dilemma for users. One major concern is
   a. propaganda radio transmissions.
   b. cable theft.
   c. Internet crime.
   d. none of the above

15. Studies of media violence have found that
   a. witnessing violence in the home has no impact on one's own violent behavior.
   b. less media exposure is related to less observed physical aggression.
   c. on average, television shows contain about one violent act per episode.
   d. theatrical release movies contain less violence than broadcast and cable movies.

FILL-IN QUESTIONS: Fill in the blank spaces in the sentences below with the correct words. Where two or more words are required, there will be a corresponding number of blank spaces.

1. For sociologists, the key question is how the mass media affect our _____ _____ and how they influence our _____ _____.

2. In 1997, a federal law required television networks to provide one free minute for every minute the government bought for a public service announcement with a(n) _____ message.

3. The _____ generally define what are "facts" for the audience, using a definition that reflects the values and orientation of the decision makers within media organizations.

4. Paul Lazarsfeld and Robert Merton created the term _____ _____ to refer to the phenomenon whereby the media provide such massive amounts of information that the audience becomes numb, and generally fails to act on the information, regardless of how compelling the issue.

5. The content of media may create false images or _____ of subordinate groups.

6. The _____ perspective contends that television distorts the political process.

7. We risk being _____ if we overstress U.S. dominance and assume other nations do not play a role in media cultural exports.

8. Efforts by this organization to monitor media content that crosses the borders of developing nations, was one factor that prompted the United States to withdraw from _____ in the mid-1980s.

9. The fact that pornography presents women as sex objects is one reason why it is a continuing, troubling issue for _____.

10. _____ examine the media on the micro level to see how they shape day-to-day social behavior.

11. The _____ perspective helps us to understand more about one important aspect of the entire mass media system, the _____.

12. We can point to a handful of _____ _____ that dominate the publishing, broadcasting, and film industries.

13. Today, _____ _____ is no longer a barrier, and instant messaging is possible across the world.

14. A comparison of top-grossing movies in 2000 and 1998 shows a 6 percent increase in the number of episodes of _____ in 2000.

15. Both _____ and _____ theorists are troubled that the victims depicted in violent imagery are often those who are given less respect in real life: women, children, the poor, racial minorities, citizens of foreign countries and even the physically disabled.

UNDERSTANDING SOCIAL POLICY: All of the following questions are based on material that appears in the social policy section on Media Violence. Write a brief answer to each question in the space provided below.

1. How do conflict and feminist theorists interpret violence in the media?

2. How do interactionists interpret violence in the media?

3. How have policy makers responded to the issue of violence in the media?

DEFINITIONS OF KEY TERMS

Mass media: Print and electronic means of communication that carry messages to widespread audiences. (136)

Surveillance function: The collection and distribution of information concerning events in the social environment. (139)

Narcotizing dysfunction: The phenomenon in which the media provide such massive amounts of coverage that the audience becomes numb and fails to act on the information, regardless of how compelling the issue. (140)

Gatekeeping: The process by which a relatively small number of people in the media industry control what material eventually reaches the audience. (140)

Dominant ideology: A set of cultural beliefs and practices that helps to maintain powerful social, economic, and political interests. (141)

Stereotype: An unreliable generalization about all members of a group that does not recognize individual differences within the group. (141)

Opinion leader: Someone who influences the opinions and decisions of others through day-to-day personal contact and communication. (146)

ANSWERS TO SELF-TEST

Modified True/False Questions
1. Sociologists refer to the print and electronic means of communication that carry messages to often widespread audiences as mass media. (136)
2. True (137)
3. While the media can serve to reinforce proper behavior, they may also endorse illicit activity, such as physical violence or drug abuse. (138)
4. In 1997, a federal law required the television networks to provide one free minute for every minute the government bought for a public service announcement with an antidrug message. However, the networks subsequently made an agreement with the government to drop the free minutes in exchange for embedding aggressive antidrug messages in their programs, such as *ER* and *The Practice*. (138)

5. Viewer fatigue sets in sometime after a tragedy, such as a natural disaster or family crisis. (140)
6. True (140)
7. The study for the World Bank found that in 97 countries, 60 percent of the top five TV stations and 72 percent of the largest radio stations are government owned. (140)
8. True (140)
9. The Internet is not totally without restrictions. Laws in many nations try to regulate content on such issues as gambling, pornography, and even political views, and popular Internet service providers will terminate accounts for offensive behavior. (140)
10. During the 2003 – 2004 season, 74 percent of all characters shown in prime time were White non-Hispanic. (142)
11. True (142)
12. Many motion pictures, such as *The Titanic*, have brought in more revenues abroad than at home. (143)
13. According to the feminist view, one of the three problems that arise from media coverage is the depiction of male-female relationships, which emphasizes traditional sex roles and normalizes violence against women. (143–144)
14. True (144)
15. There is one exception to the centralization and concentration of the media—the Internet. (147)

Multiple-Choice Questions

1.	d (136)	6.	a (140)	11.	d (145)
2.	d (137)	7.	d (141)	12.	d (149)
3.	d (138)	8.	d (142)	13.	d (148)
4.	b (137)	9.	d (143)	14.	c (150)
5.	d (139)	10.	c (144)	15.	b (151)

Fill-In Questions

1. social institutions; social behavior (137)
2. antidrug (138)
3. media (139-140)
4. narcotizing dysfunction (140)
5. stereotypes (141)
6. conflict (141)
7. ethnocentric (143)
8. UNESCO (143)
9. feminists (144)
10. Interactionists (144)
11. interactionist; audience (144)
12. multinational corporations (147)
13. physical distance (148)
14. violence (151)
15. conflict; feminist (152)

Understanding Social Policy: Media Violence

1. Media violence raises basic questions about the function of media. If some of its functions are to entertain, socialize, and enforce social norms, how can violence be a part of its programming? Conflict and feminist theorists are troubled that the victims depicted in violent imagery are often those who are given less respect in real life: women, children, the poor, racial minorities, citizens of foreign countries, and even the physically disabled. (151–152)

2. Interactionists are especially interested in finding out if violence in media may then become a script for real-life behavior. Aggression is a product of socialization and people may model themselves after the violent behavior they see. (152)

3. Policy makers have responded to the links between violence depicted in the media and real-life aggression on two levels. In public statements politicians are quick to call for more family-oriented, less violent content. However, on the legislative level, policymakers are reluctant to engage in what could be regarded as censorship. (152)

CHAPTER 8
DEVIANCE AND SOCIAL CONTROL

Social Control
  Conformity and Obedience
  Informal and Formal Social Control
  Law and Society

Deviance
  What Is Deviance?
  Explaining Deviance

Crime
  Types of Crime
  Crime Statistics

Social Policy and Social Control: Gun Control
  The Issue
  The Setting
  Sociological Insights
  Policy Initiatives

BOXES
  SOCIOLOGY ON CAMPUS: Binge Drinking
  SOCIAL INEQUALITY: Discretionary Justice
  TAKING SOCIOLOGY TO WORK: Tiffany Zapata-Mancilla, Victim Witness Specialist, Cook County State Attorney's Office

KEY POINTS

Social Control: The term **social control** refers to the techniques and strategies for preventing deviant human behavior in any society. Social control occurs on all levels of society; in the family, in peer groups, and in bureaucratic organizations. Most of us respect and accept basic social norms and assume that others will do the same. If we fail to live up to a norm, we may face punishment through informal **sanctions,** such as fear and ridicule, or formal sanctions such as jail sentences or fines. (159)

Conformity and Obedience: Stanley Milgram made a useful distinction between two important levels of social control. He used the term **conformity** to mean going along with one's peers; individuals of a person's own status, who have no special right to direct our behavior. In contrast, **obedience** is compliance with higher authorities in a hierarchical structure. (158)

Informal and Formal Social Control: **Informal social control** is social control carried out by people casually through such means as smiles, laughter, and ridicule. **Formal social control** is carried out by authorized agents, such as police officers, school administrators, employers, military officers, and managers of movie theaters. It can serve as a last resort when socialization and informal sanctions do not bring about desired behavior. (159)

Law and Society: Some norms are so important to a society that they are formalized into laws controlling people's behavior. **Law** is governmental social control. Sociologists see the creation of laws as a social process. In their view, law is not merely a static body of rules handed down from generation to generation. Rather it reflects continually changing standards of what is right and wrong, of how violations are to be determined, and of what sanctions are to be applied. (160)

Deviance: For sociologists, **deviance** is behavior that violates the standards of conduct or expectations of a group or society. Deviance involves the violations of group norms, which may or may not be formalized into law. It is a comprehensive concept that includes not only criminal behavior but also many actions that are not subject to prosecution. Deviance can be understood only within its social context. (162)

Deviance and Social Stigma: While deviance can include relatively minor day-to-day decisions about our personal behavior, in some cases it can become part of a person's identity. This process is called stigmatization. The interactionist Erving Goffman coined the term **stigma** to describe the labels society uses to devalue members of certain social groups. Often people are stigmatized for deviant behaviors they may no longer engage in. Goffman draws a useful distinction between a prestige symbol that draws attention to a positive aspect of one's identity, such as a wedding band or a badge, and a stigma symbol that discredits or debases one's identity, such as a conviction for child molestation. (162–163)

The Functionalist View: According to functionalists, deviance is a common part of human existence, with positive (as well as negative) consequences for social stability. Deviance helps to define the limits of proper behavior. As Émile Durkheim observed, the punishments established within a culture (including both formal and informal mechanisms of social control) help to define acceptable behavior and thus contribute to stability. If improper acts were not sanctioned, people might stretch their standards as to what constitutes appropriate conduct. (166)

Merton's Theory of Deviance: Using a functionalist analysis, Robert Merton adapted Durkheim's notion of anomie to explain why people accept or reject the goals of a society, the socially approved means of fulfilling their aspirations, or both. Merton developed the **anomie theory of deviance**, which posits five basic forms of adaptation. (1) Conformity to social norms, the most common adaptation in Merton's typology, is the opposite of deviance. It involves acceptance of both the overall societal goal and the approved means. (2) The "innovator" accepts the goals of society but pursues them with means that are regarded as improper. (3) The "ritualist" has abandoned the goal of material success and becomes compulsively committed to the institutional means. (4) The "retreatist" has withdrawn from both the goals and the means of a society, and (5) the "rebel" feels alienated from the dominant means and goals, and may seek a dramatically different social order. (166–167)

Cultural Transmission and Differential Association: Sociologist Edwin Sutherland drew upon the **cultural transmission** school of criminology, which emphasizes that criminal behavior is learned through interactions with others. Sutherland maintained that through interactions with a primary group and significant others, people acquire definitions of proper and improper behavior. He used the term **differential association** to describe the process through which exposure to attitudes favorable to criminal acts leads to the violation of rules. People are more likely to engage in norm-defying behavior if they are part of a group or subculture that stresses deviant values. (167–168)

Labeling Theory: Reflecting the contribution of interactionist theorists, labeling theory attempts to explain why certain people are perceived as deviants, while others with similar behavior are not. Labeling theory is also called the **societal-reaction approach**, reminding us that it is the response to an act, not the behavior itself, which determines deviance. An important aspect of labeling theory is the recognition that some people or groups have the power to define labels and apply them to others. The popularity of labeling theory is reflected in the emergence of a related perspective called social constructionism. According to the **social constructionist perspective**, deviance is the product of the culture we live in. Social constructionists focus specifically on the decision-making process that creates the deviant identity. (169)

The Conflict View of Deviance: Sociologist Richard Quinney and other conflict theorists argue that lawmaking is often an attempt by the powerful to coerce others into their own brand of morality. On the whole, conflict theorists contend that the criminal justice system of the United States treats suspects and offenders differently based on racial, ethnic, and social class backgrounds. (169–170)

Feminist Perspective: When it comes to crime and to deviance in general, society tends to treat women in a stereotypical fashion. Cultural views and attitudes towards women influence how they are perceived and labeled. The feminist perspective also emphasizes that deviance, including crime, tends to flow from economic relationships. (170)

Crime Statistics: Crime statistics are not as accurate as social scientists would like. Reported crime is very high in the United States, and the public regards crime as a major social problem. However, there has been a significant decline in violent crime nationwide following many years of increases. Sociologists have several ways of measuring crime. Partly because of the deficiencies in official statistics, the National Crime Victimization Survey was initiated in 1972. The Bureau of Justice Statistics, in compiling this annual report, seeks information from law enforcement agencies, but also interviews members of over 42,000 households and asks if they have been victims of a specific set of crimes. In general, **victimization surveys** question ordinary people, not police officers, to learn how much crime occurs. (175)

International Crime Rates: During the 1980s and 1990s violent crimes were much more common in the United States than in Western Europe. Yet, the incidence of certain other types of crime appears to be higher elsewhere. For example, England, Italy, Australia, and New Zealand all have higher rates of car theft than in the United States. (176)

KEY TERMS

Briefly define or identify the following terms in the spaces provided below. The definitions of these terms can be found later in this chapter of the study guide.

Social control	Obedience
Sanction	Informal social control
Conformity	Formal social control

Law	Societal-reaction approach
Control theory	Social constructionist perspective
Deviance	Crime
Stigma	Victimless crime
Anomie	Professional criminal
Anomie theory of deviance	Organized crime
Cultural transmission	White-collar crime
Differential association	Victimless crime
Routine activities theory	Transnational crime
Labeling theory	Victimization survey

SELF-TEST

MODIFIED TRUE/FALSE QUESTIONS: If the statement below is true, write "true" in the space provided. If the statement is false, briefly correct the error.

1. A recruit entering military service will typically obey the habits and language of other recruits, and will conform to the orders of superior officers.

2. Viewed from an interactionist perspective, one important aspect of Milgram's findings concerning obedience to authority is that subjects in follow-up studies were more likely to inflict the supposed shocks as they were moved physically closer to their victims.

3. A 1998 policy statement by the American Academy of Pediatrics that corporal punishment is not effective, and can indeed be harmful, is supported by the majority of child development specialists and pediatricians in the United States.

4. In the view of sociologists, law is a static body of rules handed down from generation to generation.

5. Binge drinking is always regarded as deviant behavior.

6. Conflict theory suggests that our connection to members of society leads us to systematically conform to society's norms.

7. According to functionalists, deviance has only negative consequences for social stability.

8. Robert Merton made a key contribution to sociological understanding of deviance, by pointing out that deviants such as innovators and ritualists, share a great deal with conforming people.

9. Sociologist Edwin Sutherland popularized labeling theory.

10. Researchers have found that discretionary differences in the way social control is exercised puts deprived African Americans and Hispanics at a disadvantage in the justice system—both as juveniles and as adults.

11. Organized crime dominates the world of illegal business, just as large corporations dominate the conventional business world.

12. Conviction for a white-collar crime has serious implications for an individual's reputation and career aspirations.

13. The conflict perspective argues that the criminal justice system largely disregards the white-collar crimes of the affluent, while focusing on crimes committed by the poor.

14. Trafficking in human beings, sea piracy, and terrorism are among the most common types of transnational crime.

15. Sociologists agree that the high rates of violent crimes in the United States are the result of the emphasis our society places on individual economic achievement.

MULTIPLE-CHOICE QUESTIONS: In each of the following, select the phrase that best completes the statement.

1. If we fail to respect and obey social norms, we may face punishment through informal or formal
   a. techniques of neutralization.
   b. deviance.
   c. cultural transmission.
   d. sanctions.

2. Which sociological perspective emphasizes that societies literally could not function if massive numbers of people defied standards of appropriate conduct?
   a. the functionalist perspective
   b. the conflict perspective
   c. the interactionist perspective
   d. labeling theory

3. A useful distinction between conformity and obedience was made by social psychologist
   a. Richard Quinney.
   b. Émile Durkheim.
   c. Edwin Sutherland.
   d. Stanley Milgram.

4. Which of the following suggested that the punishments established within a culture help to define acceptable behavior, and thus contribute to stability?
   a. William Chambliss
   b. Émile Durkheim
   c. Richard Quinney
   d. Stanley Milgram

5. The most common adaptation in the anomie theory of deviance is
   a. conformity.
   b. innovation.
   c. ritualism.
   d. rebellion.

6. A burglar who wants to live in the suburbs along with lawyers and stockbrokers will pursue material success by violating the law. In Robert Merton's terms, the burglar is a(n)
   a. ritualist.
   b. retreatist.
   c. rebel.
   d. innovator.

7. In Merton's terms, a person who has abandoned the goal of material success and become compulsively committed to the institutional means is a(n)
   a. ritualist.
   b. retreatist.
   c. rebel.
   d. innovator.

8. Which of the following conducted observation research on two groups of high school males (the Saints and the Roughnecks), and concluded that social class played an important role in the varying fortunes of the two groups?
   a. Richard Quinney
   b. Edwin Sutherland
   c. Émile Durkheim
   d. William Chambliss

9. An important aspect of labeling theory is the recognition that some people or groups have the power to define labels and apply them to others. This view recalls the emphasis placed on the social significance of power by the
   a. functionalist perspective.
   b. conflict perspective.
   c. interactionist perspective.
   d. anomie theory of deviance.

10. Which of the following is a leading exponent of the view that the criminal justice system serves the interests of the powerful?
    a. Richard Quinney
    b. Edwin Sutherland
    c. Stanley Milgram
    d. William Chambliss

11. _____ view standards of deviant behavior as merely reflecting cultural norms; whereas _____ and _____ theorists point out that the most powerful groups in a society can shape laws and standards and determine who is (or is not) prosecuted as a criminal.
    a. Conflict theorists; functionalists; labeling
    b. Labeling theorists; conflict; functionalist
    c. Functionalists; conflict; labeling
    d. Conflict theorists; labeling; functionalist

12. Gambling, prostitution, and smoking marijuana are
    a. white-collar crimes.
    b. violent crimes against people.
    c. victimless crimes.
    d. organized crime.

13. Which of the following offered pioneering insights regarding professional criminals by publishing an annotated account written by a professional thief?
    a. Robert Merton
    b. Émile Durkheim
    c. Howard S. Becker
    d. Edwin Sutherland

14. Which of the following is considered a white-collar crime?
    a. consumer fraud
    b. bribery
    c. income tax evasion
    d. all of the above

15. Which one of the following crime rates was higher in the United States than in Europe during the 1980s and 1990s?
    a. murder
    b. rape
    c. robbery
    d. all of the above

FILL-IN QUESTIONS: Fill in the blank spaces in the sentences below with the correct words. Where two or more words are required, there will be a corresponding number of blank spaces.

1. _____ theorists are concerned that "successful functioning" of a society will consistently benefit the powerful and work to the disadvantage of other groups.

2. In the United States, one common and controversial example of _____ social control is parental use of corporal punishment.

3. _____ social control is carried out by authorized agents, such as police officers, judges, administrators, employers, military officers, and managers of movie theaters.

4. Some norms are considered so important by a society that they are formalized into _____ controlling people's behavior.

5. It is important to underscore the fact that _____ is the primary source of conformity and obedience, including obedience to law.

6. _____ involves the violation of group norms that may or may not be formalized into law.

7. In general, sociologists reject any emphasis on _____ roots of crime and deviance.

8. _____ is a state of normlessness that typically occurs during a period of profound social change and disorder, such as a time of economic collapse.

9. Sociologist _____ _____ advanced the argument than an individual undergoes the same basic socialization process whether learning conforming or deviant acts.

10. _____ _____ _____, a recent interactionist explanation of deviance, considers that for the requisite conditions for a crime or deviant act to occur, there must be at the same time and in the same place, a perpetrator, a victim, and/or an object of property.

11. _____ theorists argue that lawmaking is often an attempt by the powerful to coerce others into their own brand of morality.

12. _____ represents some type of deviation from formal social norms administered by the state.

13. Organizations such as Mothers Against Drunk Driving (MADD) and Students Against Drunk Driving (SADD) have had success in recent years in shifting public attitudes toward drunkenness, so that it is no longer being viewed as a "_____ crime."

14. Daniel Bell used the term _____ _____ to describe the process during which leadership of organized crime was transferred from Irish Americans to Jewish Americans and later to Italian Americans and others.

15. The most serious limitation of official crime statistics is that they include only those crimes actually _____ to law enforcement agencies.

UNDERSTANDING SOCIAL POLICY: All of the following questions are based on material that appears in the social policy section on Gun Control. Write a brief answer to each question in the space provided below.

1. What role do guns play in crimes in the United States?

2. It is estimated that about half of all adult Americans support stricter laws covering the sale of firearms. Discuss some of the reasons why this support has not resulted in stricter gun control laws.

3. What changes are recommended by advocates of stricter gun control laws?

DEFINITIONS OF KEY TERMS

Social control: The techniques and strategies for preventing deviant human behavior in any society. (157)

Sanction: A penalty or reward for conduct concerning a social norm. (157)

Conformity: Going along with one's peers—individuals of our own status, who have no special right to direct our behavior. (158)

Obedience: Compliance with higher authorities in a hierarchical structure. (158)

Informal social control: Social control that is carried out casually by ordinary people through such means as laughter, smiles, and ridicule. (159)

Formal social control: Social control that is carried out by authorized agents, such as police officers, judges, school administrators, and employers. (159)

Law: Governmental social control. (160)

Control theory: A view of conformity and deviance that suggests that our connection to members of society leads us to systematically conform to society's norms. (162)

Deviance: Behavior that violates the standards of conduct or expectations of a group or society. (162)

Stigma: A label used to devalue members of certain social groups. (162)

Anomie: Durkheim's term for the loss of direction felt in a society when social control of individual behavior has become ineffective. (166)

Anomie theory of deviance: Robert Merton's theory of deviance as an adaptation of socially prescribed goals or of the means governing their attainment, or both. (166)

Cultural transmission: A school of criminology that argues that criminal behavior is learned through social interactions. (167–168)

Differential association: A theory of deviance proposed by Edwin Sutherland that holds that violation of rules results from exposure to attitudes favorable to criminal acts. (168)

Routine activities theory: The notion that criminal victimization increases when motivated offenders and suitable targets converge. (168)

Labeling theory: An approach to deviance that attempts to explain why certain people are viewed as deviants while others engaged in the same behavior are not. (169)

Societal-reaction approach: Another name for *labeling theory*. (169)

Social constructionist perspective: An approach to deviance that emphasizes the role of culture in the creation of the deviant identity. (169)

Crime: A violation of criminal law for which some governmental authority applies formal penalties. (172)

Victimless crime: A term used by sociologists to describe the willing exchange among adults of widely desired, but illegal, goods and services. (172)

Professional criminal: A person who pursues crime as a day-to-day occupation, developing skilled techniques and enjoying a certain degree of status among other criminals. (172)

Organized crime: The work of a group that regulates relations among criminal enterprises involved in illegal activities, including prostitution, gambling, and the smuggling and sale of drugs. (173)

White-collar crime: Illegal acts committed by affluent, "respectable" individuals in the course of business activities. (174)

Transnational crime: Crime that occurs across multiple national borders. (174)

120 | Sociology

Victimization survey: A questionnaire or interview given to a sample of the population to determine whether people have been victims of crime. (175)

ANSWERS TO SELF-TEST

Modified True/False Questions

1. A recruit entering military service will typically *conform* to the habits and language of other recruits, and will obey the orders of superior officers. (158)
2. Viewed from an interactionist perspective, one important aspect of Milgram's findings is that subjects in follow-up studies were less likely to inflict the supposed shocks as they were moved physically closer to their victims. (159)
3. Despite a 1998 policy statement by the American Academy of Pediatrics that corporal punishment is not effective and can be harmful, 59 percent of pediatricians support the use of corporal punishment. (159)
4. In the view of sociologists, law is not merely a static body of rules handed down from generation to generation. Rather, it reflects continually changing standards of what is right and wrong, of how violations are to be determined, and of what sanctions are to be applied. (160)
5. On the one hand, binge drinking can be regarded as deviant, violating the standards of conduct expected of those in an academic setting. The other side of this potentially self-destructive behavior is that binge drinking represents conformity to the peer culture. (161)
6. Control theory suggests that our connection to members of society leads us to systematically conform to society's norms. (162)
7. According to functionalists, deviance is a normal part of human existence with positive (as well as negative) consequences for social stability. (166)
8. True (166)
9. Sociologist Howard S. Becker popularized labeling theory. (169)
10. True (171)
11. True (173)
12. Conviction for white-collar crimes does not generally harm a person's reputation and career aspirations nearly as much as conviction for an index crime would. (174)
13. True (174)
14. True (175)
15. Sociologists suggest that the United States places a greater emphasis on individual economic achievement than do other societies; tolerates, if not condones, many forms of violence; has sharp disparities between poor and affluent citizens; has significant unemployment; and has substantial alcohol and drug abuse. These factors combine to produce a climate conducive to crime. (176)

Multiple-Choice Questions

1.	d (157)	5.	a (167)	9.	b (169)	13.	d (173)
2.	a (157)	6.	d (167)	10.	a (169)	14.	d (174)
3.	d (158)	7.	a (167)	11.	c (170)	15.	d (176)
4.	b (166)	8.	d (169)	12.	c (172)		

Fill-In Questions

1. Conflict (158)
2. informal (159)
3. Formal (159)
4. laws (160)
5. socialization (162)
6. Deviance (162)
7. genetic (166)
8. Anomie (166)
9. Edwin Sutherland (167)
10. Routine activities theory (168)
11. Conflict (169)
12. Crime (172)
13. victimless (172)
14. ethnic succession (173)
15. reported (175)

Understanding Social Policy: Gun Control

1. While reported crime has declined in recent years, the role of firearms in crime has remained fairly consistent. Over the last five years, two-thirds of all murders were committed with firearms. Guns have been used in high-profile assassinations of public figures such as John F. Kennedy, Senator Robert Kennedy, Dr. Martin Luther King, Jr., and Beatle John Lennon. (176)

2. The nation's major anti-gun control lobby, the National Rifle Association (NRA), has been able to use its impressive power to block or dilute measures to enact stricter gun control policies. The NRA has been particularly successful in defeating political candidates who favor stricter laws, and in backing those who seek to weaken such restrictions. Except in a handful of states, office seekers rarely risk taking an antigun position. (177)

3. Advocates for stricter gun control laws would like to see: a total ban on assault weapons; tight restrictions on permits to carry concealed weapons; regulation of gun shows; and increased penalties for leaving firearms where they are easily accessible to children and others who could misuse them. (177)

CHAPTER 9: STRATIFICATION AND SOCIAL MOBILITY IN THE UNITED STATES

Understanding Stratification
   Systems of Stratification
   Perspectives on Stratification
   Is Stratification Universal?

Stratification by Social Class
   Measuring Social Class
   Wealth and Income
   Poverty
   Life Chances

Social Mobility
   Open versus Closed Stratification Systems
   Types of Social Mobility
   Social Mobility in the United States

Social Policy and Stratification: Rethinking Welfare in North America and Europe
   The Issue
   The Setting
   Sociological Insights
   Policy Initiatives

BOXES
   SOCIOLOGY IN THE GLOBAL COMMUNITY: *Under Pressure: The Caste System in India*
   SOCIOLOGY ON CAMPUS: *Social Class and Financial Aid*

KEY POINTS

Stratification and Social Inequality: The term **social inequality** describes a condition in which members of society have different amounts of wealth, prestige, or power. Some degree of social inequality characterizes every society. When a system of social inequality is based on a hierarchy of groups, sociologists refer to it as **stratification**: a structured ranking of entire groups of people that perpetuates unequal economic rewards and power in a society. **Ascribed status** is a social position "assigned" to a person without regard for that person's unique characteristics or talents. By contrast, **achieved status** is a social position attained by a person largely through his or her own efforts. (182–183)

The Class System of the United States: Sociologist Daniel Rossides has conceptualized the class system of the United States using a five-class model. Rossides categorizes about 1 to 2 percent of the people in the United States as upper class. In contrast, the lower class, which is approximately 20 to 25 percent of the population, disproportionately consists of Blacks, Hispanics, single mothers with dependent children, and people who cannot find regular work or must make do with low-paying jobs. Sandwiched between the upper and lower classes in Rossides's model are the upper middle class, the lower middle class, and the working class. (185)

Karl Marx's View of Class Differentiation: Karl Marx viewed class differentiation as the crucial determinant of social, economic, and political inequality. Marx focused on the two classes that began to emerge as the estate system declined; the bourgeoisie and the proletariat. The **bourgeoisie**, or capitalist class, owns the means of production, such as factories and machinery, while the **proletariat** is the working class. According to Marx, exploitation of the proletariat will inevitably lead to the destruction of the capitalist system. Ultimately, the proletariat will overthrow the rule of the bourgeoisie and the government (which Marx saw as representing the interests of capitalists). (186)

Max Weber's View of Stratification: Unlike Karl Marx, Max Weber insisted that no single characteristic (such as class) totally defines a person's position within the stratification system. He identified three distinct components of stratification: class, status, and power. A person's position in a stratification system reflects some combination of his or her class, status, and power. (186–187)

The Functionalist View of Stratification: In the view of Kingsley Davis and Wilbert Moore, society must distribute its members among a variety of social positions. Davis and Moore argue that stratification is universal and that social inequality is necessary so that people will be motivated to fill functionally important positions. However, critics note that even if stratification is inevitable, the functionalist explanation for differential rewards does not explain the wide disparity between the rich and the poor. (188–189)

The Conflict View of Stratification: Contemporary conflict theorists believe that human beings are prone to conflict over scarce resources such as wealth, status, and power. However, Marx focused primarily on class conflict. More recent theorists have extended the analysis to include conflicts based on gender, race, age, and other dimensions. Conflict theorists see stratification as a major source of societal tension and conflict. They do not agree that stratification is functional for a society or that it serves as a source of stability. Rather, conflict sociologists argue that stratification will inevitably lead to instability and to social change. (189-190)

Lenski's View of Stratification: Gerhard Lenski described how economic systems change as their level of technology becomes more complex, beginning with hunting and gathering and culminating eventually with industrial society. As a society advances in technology, it becomes capable of producing a considerable surplus of goods. The emergence of surplus resources greatly expands the possibilities for inequality in status, influence, and power and allows a well-defined, rigid class system to develop. (190)

Wealth and Income in the United States: By all measures, income in the United States is unevenly distributed. In 2003, members of the richest fifth (or top 20 percent) of the nation's population earned $86,867 or more. Wealth in the United States is much less evenly distributed than income is. In 2001, the richest fifth of the population held 84.5 percent of the nation's wealth. (191–192)

Poverty in the United States: Approximately one out of every nine people in this country lives below the poverty line established by the federal government. In 2003, 51 percent of poor people in the United States were living in central cities. According to many observers, the plight of the urban poor is growing worse because of the devastating interplay of inadequate education and limited employment prospects. William Julius Wilson and other social scientists have used the term **underclass** to describe long-term poor people who lack training and skills. (192–195)

Social Mobility in the United States: The belief in upward social mobility is an important value in our society. Occupational mobility (which can be intergenerational or intragenerational) has been common among males. The impact of education on mobility has diminished somewhat in the last decade. However, occupational mobility among African Americans remains sharply limited by racial discrimination. Gender, like race, is an important factor in one's mobility. In contrast to men, women have a rather large range of clerical occupations open to them. But the modest salary ranges and few prospects for advancement in many of these positions mean that there is not much possibility of upward mobility. (198–199)

Rethinking Welfare in North America and Europe: In 1996, the Personal Responsibility and Work Opportunity Reconciliation Act ended the long-standing federal guarantee of assistance to every poor family that meets eligibility requirements. The law set a lifetime limit of five years of welfare benefits, and required all able-bodied adults to work after receiving two years of benefits (although hardship exceptions were allowed). From a conflict perspective, this backlash against welfare recipients reflects deep fears and hostility toward the nation's urban, predominantly African American and Hispanic underclass. Those who take a conflict perspective also urge policy makers and the general public to look closely at **corporate welfare**, the tax breaks, direct payments, and grants that the government makes to corporations—rather than focus on the relatively small allowances being given to welfare mothers and their children. (199–200)

KEY TERMS

Briefly define or identify the following terms in the spaces provided below. The definitions of these terms can be found later in this chapter of the study guide.

Social inequality	Estate system
Stratification	Class system
Income	Capitalism
Wealth	Bourgeoisie
Ascribed status	Proletariat
Achieved status	Class consciousness
Slavery	False consciousness
Caste	Class

Status group	Life chances
Power	Social mobility
Dominant ideology	Open system
Objective method	Closed system
Prestige	Horizontal mobility
Esteem	Vertical mobility
Absolute poverty	Intergenerational mobility
Relative poverty	Intragenerational mobility
Underclass	Corporate welfare

SELF-TEST

MODIFIED TRUE/FALSE QUESTIONS: If the statement below is true, write "true" in the space provided. If the statement is false, briefly correct the error.

1. In ancient Greece, slave status was permanent.

2. Although the UN Declaration of Human Rights prohibits slavery in all its forms, millions of people around the world still live as slaves.

3. In recent decades, urbanization and technological changes have led to the end of India's famous caste system.

4. According to Daniel Rossides, the largest social class in the United States is the upper-middle class.

5. Unlike Karl Marx, Max Weber insisted that no single characteristic (such as class) totally defines a person's position within the stratification system.

6. Max Weber suggested that a person's status cannot diverge from his or her economic class standing.

7. Social science research has found that inequality exists in all societies—even the simplest.

8. Conflict sociologists argue that stratification will inevitably lead to instability and to social change.

9. The objective method of measuring social class views class largely as a social rather than a statistical category.

10. Sociologists have become increasingly aware that studies of social class tend to neglect the occupations and incomes of women as determinants of social rank.

11. Because federal tax policies of the past three decades have favored low-income Americans, the gap in income between rich Americans and others is now smaller than before.

12. A key factor in the feminization of poverty has been the increase in families with women as single heads of households.

13. Herbert Gans notes that the presence of poor people means that society's dirty work—physically dirty or dangerous, dead-end and underpaid, undignified and menial jobs—will be performed at low cost.

14. One trend in student financial aid is that colleges and universities are increasing the proportion of funds allocated as grants.

15. Gender has little influence in shaping social mobility within the United States.

MULTIPLE-CHOICE QUESTIONS: In each of the following, select the phrase that best completes the statement.

1. The most extreme form of legalized social inequality for individuals or groups is
   a. slavery.
   b. open class systems.
   c. closed caste systems.
   d. caste systems.

2. The caste system is generally associated with
   a. Hinduism.
   b. Islam.
   c. Judaism.
   d. Buddhism.

3. In sociologist Daniel Rossides's model of the class system of the United States, the class with the smallest proportion of the population is the
   a. upper class.
   b. upper middle class.
   c. lower middle class.
   d. lower class.

4. In Karl Marx's view, the destruction of the capitalist system will occur only if the working class first develops
   a. bourgeois consciousness.
   b. false consciousness.
   c. class consciousness.
   d. caste consciousness.

5. Which of the following were viewed by Weber as analytically distinct components of stratification?
   a. conformity, deviance, and social control
   b. class, status, and power
   c. class, caste, and age
   d. class, prestige, and esteem

6. Which sociological perspective argues that stratification is universal and that social inequality is necessary so that people will be motivated to fill socially important positions?
   a. functionalist perspective
   b. conflict perspective
   c. interactionist perspective
   d. labeling perspective

7. The intellectual tradition at the heart of conflict theory begins principally with the work of
   a. Max Weber.
   b. Émile Durkheim.
   c. Erving Goffman.
   d. Karl Marx.

8. _____ refers to the reputation that a specific person has earned within an occupation.

a. Prestige
   b. Esteem
   c. Status
   d. Power

9. In 2001, about what percentage of the wealth of the United States was held by the richest fifth (or top 20 percent) of the population?
   a. 23 percent
   b. 38 percent
   c. 85 percent
   d. 75 percent

10. In 2003, 51 percent of poor people in the United States were living in
    a. central cities.
    b. the suburbs.
    c. rural areas.
    d. Appalachia.

11. In central cities, about 49 percent of the underclass are
    a. Whites.
    b. Asians.
    c. Hispanics.
    d. African Americans.

12. Which sociologist has applied functionalist analysis to the existence of poverty and argues that various segments of society actually benefit from the existence of the poor?
    a. Émile Durkheim
    b. Max Weber
    c. Karl Marx
    d. Herbert Gans

13. The term Max Weber used to refer to people's opportunities to provide themselves with material goods, positive living conditions, and favorable life experiences is
    a. power.
    b. wealth.
    c. life chances.
    d. the Titanic effect.

14. The poor, minorities, and those who live in rural communities and inner cities are not as likely to have access to the Internet as other members of the United States. This situation is called
    e. cybervoid.
    f. electronic redlining.
    g. the digital divide.
    h. none of the above

15. A plumber whose father was a physician is an example of
    a. downward intergenerational mobility.
    b. upward intergenerational mobility.
    c. downward intragenerational mobility.
    d. upward intragenerational mobility.

FILL-IN QUESTIONS: Fill in the blank spaces in the sentences below with the correct words. Where two or more words are required, there will be a corresponding number of blank spaces.

1. _____ involves the ways in which one generation passes on social inequalities to the next, thereby producing groups of people arranged in rank order from low to high.

2. In the _____ system of stratification, peasants were required to work land in exchange for military protection and other services.

3. Karl Marx viewed _____ differentiation as the crucial determinant of social, economic, and political inequality.

4. In Karl Marx's view, a worker who feels that he or she is being treated fairly by the bourgeoisie is guilty of _____ consciousness.

5. _____ _____ is the term Thorstein Veblen used to describe the extravagant spending patterns of those at the top of the class hierarchy.

6. _____ theorists believe that a differential system of rewards and punishments is necessary for the efficient operation of society.

7. In Karl Marx's view, a capitalist society has a _____ ideology that serves the interests of the ruling class.

8. The key to the _____ method of measuring social class is that the researcher makes a determination about an individual's class position.

9. From 1929 through 1970, the United States government's economic and tax policies seemed to shift income shares slightly to the _____. However, in the last three decades federal tax policies favored the _____.

10. One commonly used measure of absolute poverty is the federal government's _____ _____, which serves as an official definition of which people are poor.

11. Since World War II, an increasing proportion of the poor people of the United States are women, many of whom are divorced or never-married mothers. This alarming trend is known as the _____ _____ _____.

12. Sociologist William Julius Wilson and other social scientists have used the term _____ to describe the long-term poor who lack training and skills.

13. _____ notes that it is functional for society to have poor people because the identification and punishment of the poor as deviants upholds the legitimacy of the conventional social norms and "mainstream" values regarding hard work, thrift, and honesty.

14. An open class system implies that the position of each individual is influenced by the person's _____ status.

15. A woman who enters the paid labor force as a teacher's aide and eventually becomes superintendent of the school district experiences upward _____ mobility.

UNDERSTANDING SOCIAL POLICY: All of the following questions are based on material that appears in the social policy section on Rethinking Welfare in North America and Europe. Write a brief answer to each question in the space provided below.

1. What is the Personal Responsibility and Work Opportunity Reconciliation Act?

2. Compare the commitment to social service programs in the United States with programs that exist in European nations.

3. Why do sociologists tend to view the debate over welfare throughout industrialized nations from a conflict perspective?

DEFINITIONS OF KEY TERMS

Social inequality: A condition in which members of society have different amounts of wealth, prestige, or power. (182)

Stratification: A structured ranking of entire groups of people that perpetuates unequal economic rewards and power in a society. (183)

Income: Salaries and wages. (183)

Wealth: An inclusive term encompassing all a person's material assets, including land, stocks, and other types of property. (183)

Ascribed status: A social position that is assigned to a person by society without regard for the person's unique talents or characteristics. (183)

Achieved status: A social position that a person attains largely through his or her own efforts. (183)

Slavery: A system of enforced servitude in which some people are owned by other people. (183)

Caste: A hereditary rank, usually religiously dictated, that tends to be fixed and immobile. (183)

Estate system: A system of stratification under which peasants were required to work land leased to them by nobles in exchange for military protection and other services. Also known as *feudalism*. (184)

Class system: A social ranking based primarily on economic position in which achieved characteristics can influence social mobility. (184)

Capitalism: An economic system in which the means of production are held largely in private hands and the main incentive for economic activity is the accumulation of profits. (186)

Bourgeoisie: Karl Marx's term for the capitalist class, comprising the owners of the means of production. (186)

Proletariat: Karl Marx's term for the working class in a capitalist society. (186)

Class consciousness: In Karl Marx's view, a subjective awareness held by members of a class regarding their common vested interests and need for collective political action to bring about social change. (186)

False consciousness: A term used by Karl Marx to describe an attitude held by members of a class that does not accurately reflect their objective position. (186)

Class: A group of people who have a similar level of wealth and income. (186)

Status group: People who have the same prestige or lifestyle, independent of their class positions. (187)

Power: The ability to exercise one's will over others. (187)

Dominant ideology: A set of cultural beliefs and practices that help to maintain powerful social, economic, and political interests. (189)

Objective method: A technique for measuring social class that assigns individuals to classes based on criteria such as occupation, education, income, and place of residence. (190)

Prestige: The respect and admiration that an occupation holds in a society. (190)

Esteem: The reputation that a specific person has earned within an occupation. (190)

Absolute poverty: A minimum level of subsistence that no family should be expected to live below. (193)

Relative poverty: A floating standard of deprivation by which people at the bottom of a society, whatever their lifestyles, are judged to be disadvantaged *in comparison with the nation as a whole*. (193)

Underclass: The long-term poor who lack training and skills. (195)

Life chances: The opportunities people have to provide themselves with material goods, positive living conditions, and favorable life experiences. (195)

Social mobility: Movement of individuals or groups from one position of a society's stratification system to another. (196)

Open system: A social system in which the position of each individual is influenced by his or her achieved status. (197)

Closed system: A social system in which there is little or no possibility of individual social mobility. (197)

Horizontal mobility: The movement of an individual from one social position to another of the same rank. (197)

Vertical mobility: The movement of a person from one social position to another of a different rank. (197)

Intergenerational mobility: Changes in the social position of children relative to their parents. (197)

Intragenerational mobility: Changes in social position within a person's adult life. (198)

Corporate welfare: Tax breaks, direct payments, and grants that the government makes to corporations. (200)

ANSWERS TO SELF-TEST

Modified True/False Questions
1. Although slave status in ancient Greece could be inherited by succeeding generations, it was not necessarily permanent. (183)
2. True (183)
3. Although urbanization and technological changes have weakened the caste system, they have not ended it. (184)
4. According to Daniel Rossides, the largest social class in the United States is the working class. (185)
5. True (185)
6. Max Weber suggested that status can diverge from economic class standing. For example, a successful pickpocket may be in the same income class as a college professor, yet the thief is widely regarded as a member of a lower status group than that of the professor. (186)
7. True (188)
8. True (190)
9. The objective method of measuring social class views class largely as a statistical category. (190)
10. True (190–191)
11. Tax policies during the past three decades have favored the affluent. As a result, the income gap has become larger. (192)
12. True (194)
13. True (195)

14. In recent years, colleges and universities have been allocating a higher proportion of financial aid in the form of low-interest students loans. (197)
15. Gender remains an important factor in shaping social mobility within the United States. (199)

Multiple-Choice Questions

1.	a (183)	6.	a (188)	11.	d (195)
2.	a (183)	7.	d (189)	12.	d (195)
3.	a (185)	8.	b (190)	13.	c (195)
4.	c (186)	9.	c (192)	14.	c (196)
5.	b (186)	10.	a (195)	15.	a (197)

Fill-In Questions

1. Stratification (183)
2. estate (184)
3. class (185)
4. false (186)
5. conspicuous consumption (188)
6. Functionalist (188)
7. dominant (189)
8. objective (190)
9. poor; affluent (192)
10. poverty line (193)
11. feminization of poverty (194)
12. underclass (195)
13. (Herbert) Gans (195)
14. achieved (197)
15. intragenerational (198)

Understanding Social Policy: Rethinking Welfare in North America and Europe

1. In late 1996, in a historic shift in federal policy, Congress passed the Personal Responsibility and Work Opportunity Reconciliation Act. This law ended the long-standing federal guarantee of assistance to every poor family that meets eligibility requirements. The law set a lifetime limit of five years of welfare and required all able-bodied adults to work after receiving two years of benefits. The federal government would give block grants to the states to use as they wished in assisting poor and needy residents, and it would permit states to experiment with ways to move people off welfare. (199)

2. Most industrialized nations devote higher proportions of their expenditures to housing, social security, welfare, health care, and unemployment compensation than the United States does. (199)

3. Sociologists tend to view the debate over welfare reform throughout industrialized nations from a conflict perspective: the "haves" in positions of policy making, listen to discussion of the interests of other "haves," while the cries of the "have-nots" are drowned out. From a conflict perspective, the backlash against welfare recipients reflects deep fears and hostility toward the nation's urban, predominantly African American, and Hispanic underclass. (199–200)

CHAPTER 10
GLOBAL INEQUALITY

The Global Divide
Open versus Closed Stratification Systems
Types of Social Mobility
Social Mobility in the United States

Stratification in the World System
The Legacy of Colonialism
Multinational Corporations
Modernization

Stratification within Nations: A Comparative Perspective
Distribution of Wealth and Income
Social Mobility

Case Study: Stratification in Mexico
Mexico's Economy
Race Relations in Mexico: The Color Hierarchy
The Status of Women in Mexico
The Borderlands

Social Policy and Global Inequality: HumanRights
The Issue
The Setting
Sociological Insights
Policy Initiatives

BOXES
SOCIOLOGY IN THE GLOBAL COMMUNITY: *The Global Disconnect*
RESEARCH IN ACTION: *Social Inequality: Stratification in Japan*

KEY POINTS

The Global Divide: Around the world, inequality is a significant determinant of human behavior. Disparities in life chances across the globe are extreme. However, a few centuries ago, such vast divides in global wealth did not exist. This was true until the Industrial Revolution and rising agricultural productivity produced explosive economic growth. The resulting rise in living standards was not evenly distributed across the world. (207)

Colonialism and Neocolonialism: **Colonialism** is the maintenance of political, social, economic, and cultural domination over a people by a foreign power for an extended period. In simple terms, it is rule by outsiders. By the 1980s, colonialism had largely disappeared. Most of the nations that were colonies before World War I had achieved political independence and established their own governments. However, their dependence on more industrialized nations, including their former colonial masters, for managerial and technical expertise, investment capital, and manufactured goods, kept former colonies in a subservient position. Such continuing dependence and foreign domination constitute **neocolonialism**. (208)

World Systems Theory and Dependency Theory: Drawing on the conflict perspective, sociologist Immanuel Wallerstein views the global economic system as being divided between nations who control wealth and those from which resources are taken. Wallerstein has advanced a **world systems analysis** to describe the unequal economic and political relationships in which certain industrialized nations (among them, the United States, Japan, and Germany) and their corporations dominate the core of the system. Wallerstein suggests that the poor developing countries of Asia, Africa, and Latin America are on the periphery of the world economic system. Core nations and their corporations control and exploit non-core nations' economies. (208–210)

Globalization: **Globalization** is the worldwide integration of government policies, cultures, social movements, and financial markets through trade and the exchange of ideas. Some observers see globalization and its effects as the natural result of advances in communications technology. Others view it more critically, as a process that allows multinational corporations to expand unchecked. (210–211)

Multinational Corporations: The term **multinational corporation** refers to commercial organizations that are headquartered in one country but do business throughout the world. Conflict theorists conclude that on the whole, multinational corporations have a negative social impact on workers in both industrialized and developing nations. Workers in the United States and other core countries are beginning to recognize that their own interests are served by helping to organize workers in developing nations. As long as multinationals can exploit cheap labor abroad, they will be in a strong position to reduce wages and benefits in industrialized countries. (211–212)

Modernization and Modernization Theory: Contemporary social scientists use the term **modernization** to describe the far-reaching process by which peripheral nations move from traditional or less developed institutions to those characteristic of more developed societies. Many sociologists are quick to note that terms such as modernization, and even development, contain an ethnocentric bias. A similar criticism has been made of **modernization theory**, a functionalist approach proposing that modernization and development will gradually improve the lives of people in developing nations. According to this theory, while countries develop at uneven rates, the development of peripheral countries will be assisted by innovations transferred from the industrialized world. (212–213)

Stratification within Nations—A Comparative Perspective: At the same time that the gap between rich and poor nations is widening, so too is the gap between rich and poor citizens within developing nations. In at least 24 nations around the world, the most affluent 10 percent of the population receives at least 40 percent of all income. Women in developing countries find life especially difficult. (214)

Comparative Social Mobility: It would be incorrect to assume that the degree of social mobility and the means for obtaining mobility are the same in all class systems. Studies of intergenerational mobility in industrial nations have found the following patterns: substantial similarities exist in the ways that parents' positions in stratification systems are transmitted to their children; mobility opportunities in other nations have been influenced by structural factors, such as labor market changes; and immigration continues to be a significant factor in shaping a society's level of intergenerational mobility. Within developing nations, micro-level movement from one occupation to another is often overshadowed by macro-level social and economic changes. (215)

Stratification in Mexico—A Case Study: Mexico lobbied strongly for acceptance of the North American Free Trade Agreement (NAFTA), ultimately signed in 1993, which provided for the dismantling of almost all trade barriers among the United States, Canada, and Mexico. Although U.S. investment in Mexico has increased since the signing of NAFTA, the implementation of the agreement has meant little in the day-to-day economic struggles of the average Mexican. Although Mexico is unquestionably a poor country, the gap between its richest and poorest citizens is one of the widest in the world. The subordinate status of Mexico's Indians is but one reflection of the nation's color hierarchy, which links social class to the appearance of racial purity. There is widespread denial of prejudice and discrimination against people of color in Mexico. Feminist sociologists emphasize that even when Mexican women work outside the home, they often are not recognized as active and productive household members, while men are typically viewed as heads of households. Water pollution is but one of the many ways in which the problems of Mexico and the United States intertwine. Growing recognition of the borderlands reflects the increasingly close and complex relationship between these two countries. (217–219)

Universal Human Rights: Poised on the third millennium, the world seemed capable of mighty feats, yet at the same time came constant reminders of how quickly people and their fundamental human rights could be trampled. **Human rights** refers to universal moral rights possessed by all people because they are human. The most important elaboration of human rights appears in the Universal Declaration of Human Rights, adopted by the United Nations in 1948. This declaration prohibits slavery, torture, and degrading punishment; grants everyone the right to a nationality and its culture; affirms freedom of religion and the right to vote; proclaims the right to seek asylum in other countries to escape persecution; and prohibits arbitrary interference with one's privacy and arbitrary taking of a person's property. Cultural relativism encourages understanding and respecting the distinctive norms, values, and customs of each culture. In some situations, conflicts arise between human rights standards and local social practices that rest on alternative views of human dignity. Functionalists would point out how much more quickly we become embroiled in "human rights" concerns when oil is at stake, or when military alliances come into play. In addition to the United Nations, non-governmental organizations (NGOs) such as Médecins sans Frontières and Amnesty International have become human rights watchdogs. (221–222)

KEY TERMS

Briefly define or identify the following terms in the spaces provided below. The definitions of these terms can be found later in this chapter of the study guide.

Colonialism	Modernization
Neocolonialism	Modernization theory
World systems analysis	Borderlands
Dependency theory	Remittances
Multinational corporation	Human rights

SELF-TEST

MODIFIED TRUE/FALSE QUESTIONS: If the statement below is true, write "true" in the space provided. If the statement is false, briefly correct the error.

1. The lifestyles portrayed in the media in countries like India are out of reach economically for all but a small percentage of the population.

2. In 2002, the average value of goods and services produced per citizen in the industrialized nations was equivalent to that of poorer countries.

3. The global debt crisis has lessened the Third World dependency begun under colonialism, neocolonialism, and multinational investment.

4. In the developing world, it is easy to build strong trade unions in factories run by multinational corporations.

5. Several sociologists who have surveyed the effects of foreign investment by multinationals conclude that, although it may initially contribute to a host nation's wealth, it eventually increases economic inequality within developing nations.

6. Many contemporary researchers view modernization as movement along a series of social indicators—among them, degree of urbanization, energy use, literacy, mass transit systems, political democracy, and use of birth control.

7. The main implication of the global disconnect is that people in "disconnected" countries are unable to play Internet games and surf the Net.

8. Karuna Chanana Ahmed, an anthropologist from India who has studied developing nations, calls Blacks the most exploited among oppressed people.

9. Japan's level of income inequality is among the highest of major industrial societies.

10. More than 25 percent of Japanese women in the work force hold management positions.

11. Cross-cultural studies suggest that intragenerational mobility has been increasing in recent decades, at least among men.

12. Mexico strongly opposed acceptance of the North American Free Trade Agreement (NAFTA).

13. The gross domestic product—the value of all money that is spent on groceries and other household goods—is a commonly used measure of an average resident's economic well-being.

14. As far back as 1973, women in Monterrey—Mexico's third largest city—began protesting the continuing disruptions of the city's water supply. Their efforts brought improvement in water service, but the issue of reliable and safe water remains a concern.

15. Maquiladoras are foreign factories established just across the border in Mexico that do not have to pay taxes, and are not required to provide insurance or benefits for their workers.

MULTIPLE-CHOICE QUESTIONS: In each of the following, select the phrase that best completes the statement.

1. Relations between the colonial nation and the colonized people are similar to those between the dominant capitalist class and the proletariat as described by
    a. Émile Durkheim.
    b. Max Weber.
    c. Karl Marx.
    d. Benito Juarez.

2. In viewing the global economic system as divided between nations who control wealth and those from whom capital is taken, sociologist Immanuel Wallerstein draws on the
    a. functionalist perspective.
    b. conflict perspective.
    c. interactionist perspective.
    d. dramaturgical approach.

3. Which of the following nations would Wallerstein classify as a core country within the world economic system?
    a. Germany
    b. South Korea
    c. Ireland
    d. Mexico

4. Which of the following nations would Wallerstein classify as on the periphery of the world economic system?
    a. Germany
    b. South Korea
    c. Ireland
    d. Mexico

5. Which sociological perspective emphasizes that multinational corporations exploit local workers to maximize profits?
   a. functionalist perspective
   b. conflict perspective
   c. interactionist perspective
   d. labeling theory

6. According to a ranking by revenues, the largest industrial company in the world is
   a. Wal-Mart.
   b. International Business Machines (IBM).
   c. General Motors.
   d. Mitsubishi.

7. Modernization theory is associated with
   a. the functionalist perspective.
   b. the conflict perspective.
   c. the interactionist perspective.
   d. labeling theory.

8. Current modernization studies generally take a _____ perspective: using various indicators, researchers show how societies are moving closer together despite traditional differences.
   a. dependency
   b. convergence
   c. labeling
   d. world systems

9. Which of the following nations has the greatest gap in income between its most affluent and least affluent residents?
   a. Brazil
   b. Jamaica
   c. Sweden
   d. United States

10. The gap between rich and poor in developing nations is
    a. increasing.
    b. decreasing.
    c. unchanged in the past half century.
    d. unchanged in the past century.

11. The Japanese minority group known as the Burakamin constitutes a low-status
    a. subculture.
    b. counterculture.
    c. neocolonialism.
    d. in-group.

12. Mobility patterns in industrialized countries are usually associated with
    a. intergenerational mobility.
    b. positive mobility.
    c. intragenerational mobility.
    d. both a and c

13. Since the early 20th century, the United States and Mexico have had a close _____ relationship.
    a. cultural
    b. economic
    c. political
    d. all of the above

14. Which term is used to refer to Mexico's large, impoverished majority, most of whom have brown skin and a mixed racial lineage due to intermarriage?
    a. criollo
    b. indio
    c. mestizo
    d. zapatista

15. Which perspective would view immigration into the United States from Mexico as a labor market issue, and emphasize that this is another example of a core industrialized nation exploiting a peripheral developing country?
    a. modernization theory
    b. labeling theory
    c. world systems theory
    d. anomie theory

FILL-IN QUESTIONS: Fill in the blank spaces in the sentences below with the correct words. Where two or more words are required, there will be a corresponding number of blank spaces.

1. The long reign of the British Empire over much of North America, parts of Africa, and India is an example of _____ domination.

2. When two countries have a _____ relationship, the dependence of a former colony on more industrialized nations for managerial and technical expertise, investment capital, and manufactured goods keeps it in a subservient position.

3. In a sense, dependency theory can be regarded as an application of the _____ perspective on a global scale.

4. As _____ industries become a more important part of the international marketplace, many companies have concluded that the low costs of overseas operations more than offset the expense of transmitting information around the world.

5. Viewed from a _____ perspective, the combination of skilled technology and management provided by multinationals and the relatively cheap labor available in developing nations is ideal for a global enterprise.

6. Members of societies that have undergone modernization shift allegiance from _____ sources of authority such as parents and priests to newer authorities such as government officials.

7. Many sociologists are quick to note that terms such as modernization and development contain an _____ bias.

8. The technological disconnect between developing and industrial nations is known as the _____ _____.

9. In 1985, Japan's parliament passed an equal employment bill that encourages employers to end _____ discrimination in hiring, assignment, and promotion policies.

10. Cross-cultural studies of industrial nations suggest that intergenerational mobility has been increasing in recent decades, at least among _____.

11. According to _____'s analysis, the United States is at the core while neighboring Mexico is still on the periphery of the world economic system.

12. The NAFTA trade agreement was signed in the year _____.

13. The _____ _____ _____—the value of all final goods and services produced within a country—is a commonly used measure of an average resident's economic well-being.

14. About _____ percent of adults in the United States have a high school education, compared to only _____ percent of those in Mexico.

15. Many Mexicans who have come to the United States send some part of their earnings back across the border to family members still in Mexico; this substantial flow of money is sometimes called "_____."

UNDERSTANDING SOCIAL POLICY: All of the following questions are based on material that appears in the social policy section on Rethinking Welfare in North America and Europe. Write a brief answer to each question in the space provided below.

1. What is the Universal Declaration of Human Rights?

2. In what way(s) is the sociological concept of cultural relativism relevant to the human rights issue?

3. How would functionalists approach the issue of universal human rights?

DEFINITIONS OF KEY TERMS

Colonialism: The maintenance of political, social, economic, and cultural dominance over a people by a foreign power for an extended period. (208)

Neocolonialism: Continuing dependence of former colonies on foreign countries. (208)

World systems analysis: A view of the global economic system as one divided between certain industrialized nations that control wealth and developing countries that are controlled and exploited. (208)

Dependency theory: An approach that contends that industrialized nations continue to exploit developing countries for their own gain. (210)

Multinational corporation: A commercial organization that is headquartered in one country but does business throughout the world. (211)

Modernization The far-reaching process by which periphery nations move from traditional or less developed institutions to those characteristic of more developed societies. (212)

150 | Sociology

Modernization theory A functionalist approach that proposes that modernization and development will gradually improve the lives of people in developing nations. (213)

Borderlands: The area of common culture along the border between Mexico and the United States. (219)

Remittances: The monies that immigrants return to their families of origin. Also called *migradollars*. (220)

Human Rights Universal moral rights possessed by all people because they are human. (221)

ANSWERS TO SELF-TEST

Modified True/False Questions

1. True (206)
2. In 2002, the average value of goods and services produced per citizen in the United States, Japan, Switzerland, Belgium, and Norway was more than $25,000. In at least thirteen poorer countries the value was $800 or less. (208)
3. The global debt crisis has intensified the Third World dependency begun under colonialism, neocolonialism, and multinational investment. (210)
4. In the developing world, it is difficult to build strong trade unions in factories run by multinational corporations. (212)
5. True (212)
6. Mass transit is not one of the social indicators that determines modernity. (212–213)
7. Becoming integrated into the global economy is not possible without access to the Internet. (213)
8. Karuna Chanana Ahmed calls women the most exploited among oppressed people. (214)
9. Japan's level of income inequality is among the lowest of major industrial societies. (215)
10. Only about 9 percent of Japan's managers are female. (215)
11. Cross-cultural studies suggest that intergenerational mobility has been increasing in recent decades, at least among men. (215)
12. Mexico strongly lobbied for acceptance of the North American Free Trade Agreement (NAFTA). (217)
13. The gross domestic product—the value of all final goods and services produced within a country—is a commonly used measure of an average resident's economic well-being. (217)
14. True (219)
15. True (219)

Multiple-Choice Questions

1.	c (208)	6.	a (212)	11.	a (215)
2.	b (210)	7.	a (213)	12.	d (215)
3.	a (210)	8.	b (214)	13.	d (217)
4.	d (210)	9.	a (214)	14.	c (218)
5.	b (211)	10.	a (214)	15.	c (220)

Fill-In Questions

1. colonial (208)
2. neocolonial (208)
3. conflict (210)
4. service (211)
5. functionalist (211)
6. traditional (212–213)
7. ethnocentric (213)
8. global disconnect (213)
9. sex (215)
10. men (210)
11. Wallerstein (217)
12. 1993 (217)
13. gross domestic product (217)
14. 88; 22 (217)
15. migradollars (219)

Understanding Social Policy: Universal Human Rights

1. The Universal Declaration of Human Rights, adopted by the United Nations in 1948, prohibits slavery, torture, and degrading punishment; grants everyone the right to a nationality and its culture; affirms freedom of religion and the right to vote; proclaims the right to seek asylum in other countries to escape persecution; and prohibits arbitrary interference with one's privacy and arbitrary taking of a person's property. It also emphasizes that mothers and children are entitled to special care and assistance. (221)

2. Cultural relativism encourages the understanding and respect for the distinctive norms, values, and customs of each culture. In some situations, conflicts arise between human rights standards and local social practices that rest on alternative views of human dignity. (221)

3. Functionalists would point out how much more quickly we become embroiled in "human rights" concerns when oil is at stake, as in the Middle East, or when military alliances come into play, as in Europe. The United States is less likely to want to interfere in an area where its economic concerns are modest (as in Africa) or where it is seeking to advance an economic agenda (as in China). (222)

CHAPTER 11: RACIAL AND ETHNIC INEQUALITY

Minority, Racial, and Ethnic Groups
    Minority Groups
    Race
    Ethnicity

Prejudice and Discrimination
    Prejudice
    Discriminatory Behavior
    The Privileges of the Dominant
    Institutional Discrimination

Studying Race and Ethnicity
    Functionalist Perspective
    Conflict Perspective
    Interactionist Perspective

Patterns of Intergroup Relations
    Amalgamation
    Assimilation
    Segregation
    Pluralism

Impact of Global Immigration

Race and Ethnicity in the United States
    Racial Groups
    Ethnic Groups

Social Policy and Race and Ethnicity: Racial Profiling
    The Issue
    The Setting
    Sociological Insights
    Policy Initiatives

BOXES
    RESEARCH IN ACTION: *Interracial and Interethnic Friendships*
    TAKING SOCIOLOGY TO WORK: *Prudence Hannis: Liason Officer, National Institute of Science Research, University of Québec*
    SOCIAL INEQUALITY: *Native Americans Gamble on Gaming*

KEY POINTS

Racial and Ethnic Groups: Sociologists frequently distinguish between racial groups and ethnic groups. The term **racial group** is used to describe a group that is set apart from others because of obvious physical differences. Whites, African Americans, and Asian Americans are all considered racial groups in the United States. Unlike racial groups, an **ethnic group** is set apart from others primarily because of its national origin or distinctive cultural patterns. In the United States, Puerto Ricans, Jews, and Polish Americans are all categorized as ethnic groups. (229)

Minority Groups: A **minority group** is a subordinate group whose members have significantly less control or power over their own lives than members of a dominant or majority group have over theirs. Sociologists have identified five basic properties of a minority group: (1) members experience treatment that is unequal to the treatment of those in the majority; (2) members share physical or cultural characteristics that distinguish them from the dominant group; (3) membership in the group is not voluntary; people are born into the group; (4) minority group members have a strong sense of group solidarity; and (5) members generally marry others from the same group. (229)

Prejudice: **Prejudice** is a negative attitude toward an entire category of people, often an ethnic or racial minority. One important and widespread form of prejudice is **racism**, the belief that one race is supreme and all others are innately inferior. When racism prevails in a society, members of subordinate groups generally experience prejudice, discrimination, and exploitation. (232)

Studying Race and Ethnicity: Viewing race from the macro level, functionalists observe that racial prejudice and discrimination serve positive functions for dominant groups, whereas conflict theorists see the economic structure as a central factor in the exploitation of minorities. The micro-level analysis of interactionist researchers stresses the manner in which everyday contact between people from different racial and ethnic backgrounds contributes to tolerance or leads to hostility. (236)

Patterns of Intergroup Relations: There are four identifiable patterns that describe typical intergroup relations. **Amalgamation** describes the result when a majority group and a minority group combine to form a new group. Through intermarriage over several generations, various groups in society combine to form a new group. **Assimilation** is the process through which a person forsakes his or her own cultural tradition to become part of a different culture. Generally, it is practiced by a minority group member who wants to conform to the standards of the dominant group. **Segregation** refers to the physical separation of two groups of people in terms of residence, workplace, and social events. Generally, a dominant group imposes this pattern on a minority group. **Pluralism** is based on mutual respect between various groups in a society for one another's cultures. This pattern allows a minority group to express its own culture, and still participate without prejudice in the larger society. (237–239)

African Americans: Despite their large numbers, African Americans have long been treated as second-class citizens. Currently, by the standards of the federal government, nearly 1 out of every 4 Blacks—as opposed to 1 out of every 12 Whites—is poor. Contemporary institutional discrimination and individual prejudice against African Americans are rooted in the history of slavery in the United States. During the 1960s, a vast civil rights movement emerged with many competing factions and strategies for change. Some African Americans—especially middle-class men and women—have made economic gains over the last 50 years. (241–242)

Native Americans: There are approximately 2.5 million Native Americans. They represent a diverse array of cultures, distinguishable by language, family organization, religion, and livelihood. Today, life remains difficult for members of the 554 tribal groups in the United States, whether they live in cities or on reservations. By the 1990s, an increasing number of people in the United States were openly claiming a Native American identity. Since 1960, the federal government's count of Native Americans has tripled, to an estimated 2.5 million. (243)

Asian Americans: Asian Americans are held up as a **model** or **ideal minority** group, supposedly because despite past suffering from prejudice and discrimination, they have succeeded economically, socially, and educationally without resorting to confrontations with Whites. This concept of a model minority ignores the diversity among Asian Americans: there are rich and poor Japanese Americans, rich and poor Filipino Americans, and so forth. The existence of a model minority seems to reaffirm the notion that anyone can get ahead in the United States with talent and hard work, and implies that those minorities that don't succeed are somehow responsible for their failures. Viewed from a conflict perspective, this attitude is yet another instance of "blaming the victims." (243)

Arab Americans: Arab Americans are immigrants and their descendents who hail from the 22 nations of the Arab world, located in North Africa and the Middle East. By some estimates, up to 3 million people of Arab ancestry reside in the United States. Despite the stereotype, most Arab Americans are not Muslim, and not all practice religion. Despite their great diversity, profiling of potential terrorists at airports has put Arab and Muslim Americans under special surveillance. (246)

Latinos—An Overview: The various groups included under the general category Latinos represent the largest minority in the United States. The various Latino groups share a heritage of Spanish language and culture, which can cause serious problems in their assimilation. The educational difficulties of Latino students contribute to the generally low economic status of Hispanics. (246–247)

Jewish Americans: Jews have not achieved equality in the United States. Despite high levels of education and professional training, they are still conspicuously absent from the top management of large corporations (except for the few firms founded by Jews). A

1994 tabulation by the Anti-Defamation League (ADL), indicated that in that year, anti-Semitic acts had reached their highest level of the previous 19 years in which the ADL has been recording such incidents. As is true for other minorities, Jewish Americans face choosing between maintaining ties to their long religious and cultural heritage, or becoming as indistinguishable as possible from gentiles. (248–249)

Racial Profiling: Racial profiling is any police-initiated action based on race, ethnicity, or national origin rather than on a person's behavior. Generally, profiling occurs when law enforcement officers, including customs officials, airport security personnel, and police, assume that people who fit certain descriptions are likely to engage in illegal activities. The evidence that racial profiling is misleading is overwhelming. Interactionists point out that when law enforcement officers or employers see people of a certain race or ethnicity as less trustworthy than others, intergroup relations suffer. Conflict theorists see racial profiling as one more way in which those in power seek to further social inequality. (250)

KEY TERMS

Briefly define or identify the following terms in the spaces provided below. The definitions of these terms can be found later in this chapter of the study guide.

Racial group	Racism
Ethnic group	Discrimination
Minority group	Hate crime
Stereotype	Glass ceiling
Prejudice	Institutional discrimination
Ethnocentrism	Affirmative action

Exploitation theory	Pluralism
Contact hypothesis	Black power
Genocide	Model or ideal minority
Amalgamation	Anti-Semitism
Assimilation	Symbolic ethnicity
Segregation	Racial profiling
Apartheid	

SELF-TEST

MODIFIED TRUE/FALSE QUESTIONS: If the statement below is true, write "true" in the space provided. If the statement is false, briefly correct the error.

1. When sociologists define a minority group, they are primarily concerned with the economic and political power, or powerlessness, of that group.

2. The one-drop rule was a vivid example of the biological construction of race.

3. When allowed to check off multiple racial categories on the 2000 census, nearly 7 million people reported that they were of two or more races.

4. Stratification along racial lines is more subject to change than stratification along ethnic lines.

5. A White corporate president with a completely respectful view of Vietnamese Americans refuses to hire such people for executive posts out of fear that biased clients will take their business elsewhere. The president's action constitutes prejudice without discrimination.

6. In early 1995, the federal Glass Ceiling Commission found that affirmative action has completely eliminated glass ceilings and allowed women and minority group men to win a significant proportion of top management positions in the nation's industries.

7. A rule requiring that only English be spoken at a place of work—even when it is not a business necessity—is an example of institutional discrimination.

8. Affirmative action refers to hiring women and minorities for job openings and admitting members of these groups to college regardless of their competency.

9. Both the enslavement of Blacks and the extermination and removal westward of Native Americans were, to a significant extent, economically motivated.

10. The term genocide has been used in reference to the killing of 1 million Armenians by Turkey beginning in 1915.

11. Great Britain is an example of a nation that has been notably successful in achieving cultural pluralism in a multiracial society.

12. During World War II, the federal government decreed that all German Americans on the East Coast leave their homes and report to "evacuation camps."

13. Politically, Puerto Ricans in the United States have been more successful than Mexican Americans in organizing for their rights.

14. Arab Americans and Muslims are two different names for the same social group.

15. Despite high levels of education and professional training, Jewish Americans are still conspicuously absent from the top management of large corporations (except for the few firms founded by Jews).

MULTIPLE-CHOICE QUESTIONS: In each of the following, select the phrase that best completes the statement.

1. Which sociologist, writing in 1906, noted that individuals make distinctions between members of their own group (the in-group) and everyone else (the out-group)?
    a. Charles Horton Cooley
    b. Émile Durkheim
    c. William I. Thomas
    d. William Graham Sumner

2. The largest racial minority group in the United States is
    a. Asians Americans.
    b. African Americans.
    c. Native Americans.
    d. Jewish Americans.

3. Which of the following is considered a racial group?
    a. Irish Americans
    b. Jewish Americans
    c. African Americans
    d. all of the above

4. Which of the following is considered an ethnic group?
    a. Puerto Ricans
    b. Jews
    c. Polish Americans
    d. all of the above

5. Suppose that a work place requires that only English be spoken, even when it is not a business necessity to restrict the use of other languages. This would be an example of:
    a. prejudice.
    b. scapegoating.
    c. a self-fulfilling prophecy.
    d. institutional discrimination.

6. Which sociological perspective sees the economic structure as a central factor in the exploitation of minority groups?
   a. functionalist perspective
   b. conflict perspective
   c. interactionist perspective
   d. labeling theory

7. A Hispanic woman and a Jewish man, working together as computer programmers for an electronics firm, overcome their initial prejudices and come to appreciate each other's strengths and talents. This is an example of
   a. the contact hypothesis.
   b. a self-fulfilling prophecy.
   c. amalgamation.
   d. reverse discrimination.

8. Which equation can be used to represent amalgamation?
   a. $A + B + C = A$
   b. $A + B + C = A + B + C$
   c. $A + B + C = D$
   d. $A + B + C = A + B + D$

9. Which equation can be used to represent pluralism?
   a. $A + B + C = A$
   b. $A + B + C = A + B + C$
   c. $A + B + C = D$
   d. $A + B + C = A + B + D$

10. Which person wrote the acclaimed novel *Invisible Man*?
    a. Malcolm X
    b. James Baldwin
    c. Alice Walker
    d. Ralph Ellison

11. The approximately 2.5 million Native Americans represent a diverse array of cultures distinguishable by
    a. language.
    b. family organization.
    c. religion.
    d. all of the above

12. The "model minority" stereotype of Asian Americans contains an implicit critique of Blacks, Hispanics, and others for failing to succeed as well as the model minority has. Which sociological perspective would view this as yet another instance of "blaming the victim?"
    a. functionalist perspective
    b. conflict perspective
    c. interactionist perspective
    d. dramaturgical approach

13. The largest Hispanic population of the United States is
    a. Mexican Americans.
    b. Puerto Ricans.
    c. Cuban Americans.
    d. refugees from Central America.

14. Which country has the world's largest concentration of Jews?
    a. Israel
    b. Russia
    c. United States
    d. Poland

15. The largest population of White ethnics in the United States consists of
    a. Italian Americans.
    b. Irish Americans.
    c. Polish Americans.
    d. German Americans.

FILL-IN QUESTIONS: Fill in the blank spaces in the sentences below with the correct words. Where two or more words are required, there will be a corresponding number of blank spaces.

1. Writing from the _____ perspective, sociologist William I. Thomas observed that people respond not only to the objective features of a situation or person, but also to the meaning that situation or person has for them.

2. A(n) _____ person judges other cultures by the standards of his or her own group, which leads quite easily into prejudice against cultures viewed as inferior.

3. When White Americans can use credit cards without suspicion and browse through stores without being shadowed by security guards, they are enjoying _____ _____.

4. Sociologists such as Oliver Cox and Robert Blauner have used the _____ theory to explain the basis of racial subordination in the United States.

5. The micro-level analysis of the _____ perspective stresses the manner in which everyday contact between people from different racial and ethnic backgrounds contributes to tolerance or leads to hostility.

6. In surveys of interracial and interethnic friendships, only _____ percent of Whites list a close friend who is of a different race or ethnicity.

7. In the United States, there are Italian Americans, Polish Americans, Hispanics, and Jews who have changed their names to those typically found among White, Protestant families. This is an example of _____.

8. In 1994, a prominent Black activist, _____ _____, was elected as South Africa's president in the nation's first election in which Blacks were allowed to vote.

9. Over the past 40 years, new immigrants to the United States have come primarily from _____ and _____ _____ countries.

10. The "_____ _____" laws of the southern United States, designed to enforce official segregation, were upheld as constitutional by the Supreme Court in 1896.

11. In the 1960s, proponents of _____ _____ rejected the goal of assimilation into White, middle-class society. They defended the beauty and dignity of Black and African cultures and supported the creation of Black-controlled political and economic institutions.

12. One _____ American teenager in six has attempted suicide—a rate four times higher than the rate for other teenagers.

13. During the 1992 Los Angeles riots, small businesses owned by _____ Americans were a particular target.

14. Despite the stereotype, most Arab Americans are not _____.

15. White ethnic and racial minorities have often been antagonistic to one another because of economic competition; an interpretation in line with the _____ approach to sociology.

UNDERSTANDING SOCIAL POLICY: All of the following questions are based on material that appears in the social policy section on Racial Profiling. Write a brief answer to each question in the space provided below.

1. What is racial profiling?

2. Is racial profiling justified by patterns of crime?

3. What was the impact of the 2001 terrorist attacks on efforts to end racial profiling?

DEFINITIONS OF KEY TERMS

Racial group: A group that is set apart from others because of physical differences that have taken on a social significance. (229)

Ethnic group: A group that is set apart from others primarily because of its national origin or distinctive cultural patterns. (229)

Minority group: A subordinate group whose members have significantly less control or power over their lives than the members of a dominant or majority group have over theirs. (229)

Stereotype: An unreliable generalization about all members of a group that does not recognize individual differences within the group. (231)

Prejudice: A negative attitude toward an entire category of people, often an ethnic or racial minority. (232)

Ethnocentrism: The tendency to assume that one's culture and way of life represent the norm or are superior to all others. (232)

Racism: The belief that one race is supreme and all others are innately inferior. (232)

Discrimination: The denial of opportunities and equal rights to individuals and groups because of prejudice or other arbitrary reasons. (232)

Hate crime: A criminal offense committed because of the offender's bias against a race, religion, ethnic group, national origin, or sexual orientation. (232)

Glass ceiling: An invisible barrier that blocks the promotion of a qualified individual in a work environment because of the individual's gender, race, or ethnicity. (232)

Institutional discrimination: The denial of opportunities and equal rights to individuals or groups that results from the normal operations of a society. (235)

Affirmative action: Positive efforts to recruit minority group members or women for jobs, promotions, and educational opportunities. (236)

Exploitation theory: A Marxist theory that views racial subordination in the United States as a manifestation of the class system inherent in capitalism. (237)

Contact hypothesis: An interactionist perspective which states that in cooperative circumstances, interracial contact between people of equal status will reduce prejudice. (237)

Genocide: The deliberate, systematic killing of an entire people or nation. (237)

Amalgamation: The process through which a majority group and a minority group combine to form a new group. (238)

Assimilation: The process through which a person forsakes his or her own cultural tradition to become part of a different culture. (239)

Segregation: The physical separation of two groups of people in terms of residence, workplace, and social events; often imposed on a minority group by a dominant group. (239)

Apartheid: A former policy of the South African government, designed to maintain the separation of Blacks and other non-Whites from the dominant Whites. (239)

Pluralism: Mutual respect for one another's cultures among the various groups in a society, which allows minorities to express their own cultures without experiencing prejudice. (239)

Black power: A political philosophy promoted by many younger Blacks in the 1960s that supported the creation of Black-controlled political and economic institutions. (241)

Model or **ideal minority**: A minority group that despite past prejudice and discrimination, succeeds economically, socially, and educationally without resorting to confrontations with Whites. (259)

Anti-Semitism: Anti-Jewish prejudice. (243)

Symbolic ethnicity: An ethnic identity that emphasizes concerns such as ethnic food or political issues rather than deeper ties to one's heritage. (249)

Racial profiling: Any police-initiated action initiated by an authority based on race, ethnicity, or national origin rather than on a person's behavior. (250)

ANSWERS TO SELF-TEST

Modified True/False Questions
1. True (229)
2. The one-drop rule was a vivid example of the social construction of race. (230)
3. True (230)
4. Stratification along racial lines is less subject to change than stratification along ethnic lines. (231)
5. The president's action constitutes discrimination without prejudice. (232)
6. In early 1995, the federal Glass Ceiling Commission found that glass ceilings continue to block women and minority group men from top management positions in the nation's industries. (232)
7. True (235)
8. Affirmative action refers to positive efforts to recruit minority members or women for jobs, promotions, and educational opportunities. (236)
9. True (237)
10. True (237)
11. Great Britain is an example of a nation that has had difficulty achieving cultural pluralism in a multiracial society. (240)
12. During World War II, the federal government decreed that all Japanese Americans on the West Coast leave their homes and report to "evacuation camps." (245)
13. Politically, Puerto Ricans in the United States have not been as successful as Mexican Americans in organizing for their rights. (248)
14. While these groups overlap, many Arab Americans are Christians, and many Muslims are non-Arabs. (246)
15. True (248)

Multiple-Choice Questions

1.	d (229)	6.	b (237)	11.	d (243)
2.	b (230)	7.	a (237)	12.	b (243)
3.	c (230)	8.	c (238)	13.	a (247)
4.	d (231)	9.	b (239)	14.	c (248)
5.	d (235)	10.	d (241)	15.	d (249)

Fill-In Questions
1. interactionist (231)
2. ethnocentric (232)
3. White privilege (234)
4. exploitation (237)
5. interactionist (237)
6. 6 (238)

Chapter 11 *Racial and Ethnic Inequality* | 167

7. assimilation (239)
8. Nelson Mandela (239)
9. Asian; Latin American (240)
10. Jim Crow (241)
11. Black power (241)
12. Native (243)
13. Korean (246)
14. Muslim (246)
15. conflict (249)

Understanding Social Policy: Racial Profiling

1. Racial profiling is any police-initiated action based on race, ethnicity, or national origin rather than on a person's behavior. Generally, profiling occurs when law enforcement officers, including customs officials, airport security personnel, and police, assume that people who fit certain descriptions are likely to engage in illegal activities. (250)

2. The evidence that racial profiling is misleading is overwhelming. In areas where minority group members are targeted disproportionately, Whites are more likely than Blacks to be found carrying drugs. Nationwide, 80 percent of cocaine users are White. Nevertheless, law enforcement officials prefer to concentrate on the inner-city drug trade, creating a kind of self-fulfilling prophecy. (250)

3. Efforts to end racial profiling came to an abrupt end after the terrorist attacks of September 11, 2001. As suspicions about Muslims and Arabs in the United States increased, foreign students from Arab countries were summoned by police for special questioning. Arabs or Muslims who were legal immigrants were scrutinized for an illegal activity and prosecuted for routine violations of immigration law—ones that immigration officials customarily overlooked among people of other ethnic and religious backgrounds. In 2003, President George W. Bush issued guidelines that barred federal agents from using race and ethnicity in routine investigations, but specifically exempted cases involving terrorism and national security. (251)

CHAPTER 12
STRATIFICATION BY GENDER

Social Construction of Gender
    Gender Roles in the United States
    Cross-Cultural Perspective

Explaining Stratification by Gender
    The Functionalist View
    The Conflict Response
    The Feminist Perspective
    The Interactionist Approach

Women: The Oppressed Majority
    Sexism and Sex Discrimination
    Sexual Harassment
    The Status of Women Worldwide
    Women in the Workforce of the United States
    Women: Emergence of a Collective Consciousness

Intersection of Gender, Race, and Class

Social Policy and Gender Stratification: The Battle over Abortion from a Global Perspective
    The Issue
    The Setting
    Sociological Insights
    Policy Initiatives

BOXES
    RESEARCH IN ACTION: *Communication Differences between Female and Male Physicians*
    SOCIOLOGY IN THE GLOBAL COMMUNITY: *The Head Scarf and the Veil: Complex Symbols*

KEY POINTS

Social Construction of Gender: In studying gender, sociologists are interested in the gender-role socialization that leads females and males to behave differently. The application of dominant gender roles leads to many forms of differentiation between women and men. Gender roles are evident not only in our work and behavior but in how we react to others. We are constantly "doing gender" without realizing it. We construct our behavior socially to create or exaggerate male-female differences. (257)

Gender Role Socialization in the United States: According to traditional gender-role patterns that have been influential in the socialization of children in the United States, boys must be masculine—active, aggressive, tough, daring, and dominant—but girls must be feminine—soft, emotional, sweet, and submissive. It is adults, of course, who play a critical role in guiding children into those gender roles deemed appropriate in a society. Parents are normally the first and most crucial agents of socialization. But other adults, older siblings, the mass media, and religious and educational institutions also exert an important influence on gender role socialization, in the United States and elsewhere. (258)

The Functionalist View of Gender Stratification: Functionalists maintain that gender differentiation has contributed to overall social stability. Sociologists Talcott Parsons and Robert Bales argued that in order to function most effectively, the family requires adults who specialize in particular roles. They contended that women take the expressive, emotionally supportive role, and men take the instrumental, practical role, with the two roles complementing each other. Parsons and Bales did not explicitly endorse traditional gender roles, but they imply that a division of tasks between spouses is functional for the family as a unit. (261)

The Conflict View of Gender Stratification: Conflict theorists see gender differences as a reflection of the subjugation of one group (women) by another group (men). If we use an analogy to Marx's analysis of class conflict, we can say that males are like the bourgeoisie, or capitalists; they control most of the society's wealth, prestige, and power. Females are like the proletariat, or workers; they can acquire valuable resources only by following the dictates of their "bosses." (261)

The Feminist Perspective: A significant component of the conflict approach to gender stratification draws on feminist theory. Feminist sociologists would find little to disagree with in the conflict theorists' perspective. But the feminist perspective would also argue that until recently, the very discussion of women and society, however well meant, was distorted by the exclusion of women from academic thought, including sociology. (261–262)

The Interactionist View of Gender Stratification: While functionalists and conflict theorists who study gender stratification typically focus on macro-level social forces and institutions, interactionist researchers tend to examine gender stratification on the micro level of everyday behavior. For example, in conversations men are more likely than women to change the topic, to ignore topics chosen by members of the opposite sex, to minimize the contributions and ideas of members of the opposite sex, and to validate their own contributions. These patterns reflect the conversational (and in a sense, political) dominance of males. From an interactionist perspective, these simple, day-to-day exchanges are one more battleground in the struggle for sexual equality—as women try to get a word in edgewise in the midst of men's interruptions and verbal dominance. (262)

Women—The Oppressed Majority: When one looks at the political structure of the United States, women remain noticeably underrepresented. This lack of women in decision-making positions is evidence of women's powerlessness in the United States. Women can be said to suffer both from individual acts of sexism and from institutional sexism. All the major institutions of our society are controlled by men. These institutions, in their "normal" day-to-day operations, often discriminate against women and perpetuate sexism. (262–263)

The Status of Women Worldwide: Women experience second-class treatment throughout the world. They constitute one-third of the world's paid labor force, but are generally found in the lowest-paying jobs. Single parent households headed by women, which appear to be on the increase in many nations, are typically found in the poorest sections of the population. The feminization of poverty has become a global phenomenon. (264)

Women in the Workforce of the United States: Women's participation in the paid labor force increased steadily throughout the twentieth century. A majority of women are now members of the paid labor force. Unfortunately, women entering the job market find their options restricted in important ways. Particularly damaging is occupational segregation, or confinement to sex-typed "women's jobs" that pay less than "men's" jobs. Women from all groups and men from minority groups sometimes encounter attitudinal or organizational bias that prevents them from reaching their full potential. The **glass ceiling** refers to an invisible barrier that blocks the promotion of a qualified individual in a work environment. (266)

Social Consequences of Women's Employment: Studies indicate that there is still a clear gender gap in the performance of housework, although it is narrowing. Women do more housework and spend more time on childcare than men do, whether on a workday or a non-workday. Sociologist Arlie Hochschild has used the phrase **second shift** to describe the double burden that many women face—work outside the home followed by child care and housework—and few men share equitably. (267)

Women—The Emergence of a Collective Consciousness: The feminist movement of the United States was born in Seneca Falls, New York in the summer of 1848.

Ultimately, the early feminists won many victories, among them the passage and ratification of the Nineteenth Amendment to the Constitution, which granted women the right to vote in national elections beginning in 1920. The second wave of feminism in the United States emerged in the 1960s and came into full force in the 1970s. A sense of sisterhood, much like the class consciousness that Marx hoped would emerge in the proletariat, became evident. Individual women identified their interests with those of the collectivity women. No longer were women happy in submissive, subordinate roles ("false consciousness" in Marxist terms). (267–268)

The Battle over Abortion from a Global Perspective: A critical victory for the struggle for legalized abortion in the United States came in 1973, when the Supreme Court granted women the right to terminate pregnancies in the Roe v. Wade ruling. The debate that has followed Roe v. Wade revolves around prohibiting abortion altogether or, at the very least, putting limits on it. In 1979, for example, Missouri required parental consent for minors wishing to obtain an abortion, and the Supreme Court upheld the law. Sociologists see gender and social class as the defining issues surrounding abortion. In terms of social class, the first major restriction on the legal right to terminate a pregnancy affected poor people. In 1976, Congress passed the Hyde Amendment, which banned the use of Medicaid and other federal funds for abortions. Viewed from a conflict perspective, this is one more financial burden that falls especially heavily on low-income women. (269–270)

KEY TERMS

Briefly define or identify the following terms in the spaces provided below. The definitions of these terms can be found later in this chapter of the study guide.

Gender role	Sexism
Homophobia	Institutional discrimination
Instrumentality	Sexual harassment
Expressiveness	Glass ceiling

Second shift	

SELF-TEST

MODIFIED TRUE/FALSE QUESTIONS: If the statement below is true, write "true" in the space provided. If the statement is false, briefly correct the error.

1. Azadeh Moaveni's research in Iran suggests that gender roles are fairly consistent from one society to another.

2. Gender roles are biologically determined.

3. Homophobia significantly reduces rigid gender-role socialization.

4. Studies of children's books suggest that females are now shown in the same kinds of social roles as males are.

5. The research of anthropologist Margaret Mead points to the importance of biological factors in defining the social roles of males and females.

6. Conflict theorists see gender differences as a reflection of the subjugation of one group (women) by another group (men).

7. Feminist sociologists would find little to disagree with in the functionalist perspective.

8. Sociologists associated with the interactionist approach generally agree with the conflict perspective that men hold a dominant position over women.

9. By the year 2003 female representation in our political arenas was equal to that of men.

10. Among Muslims, both men and women are expected to cover themselves and avoid wearing revealing clothes in public.

11. Sociologist Michelle Budig found that men in predominantly female professions benefited from hidden advantages gained from their status as men.

12. As married women have taken on more and more hours of paid employment, they have been extremely successful in getting their husbands to assume a greater role in needed homemaking duties.

13. In the U.S., women and men in the same occupations typically have very similar incomes.

14. The first wave of feminism in the United States emerged in the 1960s and came into full force in the 1970s.

15. A sense of sisterhood, much like the false consciousness that Marx hoped would emerge in the proletariat, became evident in the feminist movement of the 1960s and 1970s.

MULTIPLE-CHOICE QUESTIONS: In each of the following, select the phrase that best completes the statement.

1. The most crucial agent of socialization in teaching gender roles in the United States is
   a. peers.
   b. teachers.
   c. media personalities.
   d. parents.

2. Which of these statements is true?
   a. More boys than girls take AP exams.
   b. Women in the United States are more likely to attend college than men.
   c. Women in the U.S. are less likely to obtain doctoral degrees than men.
   d. all of the above

3. In which culture of New Guinea were expectations of each sex almost the reverse of those found in the United States?
   a. Arapesh
   b. Mundugumor
   c. Tchambuli
   d. Klingons

4. Which sociological perspective makes the distinction between instrumental and expressive roles?
   a. functionalist perspective
   b. conflict perspective
   c. interactionist perspective
   d. labeling theory

5. Which sociological perspective emphasizes that the relationship between females and males has been one of unequal power, with men in a dominant position over women?
   a. functionalist perspective
   b. conflict perspective
   c. interactionist perspective
   d. dramaturgical perspective

6. Which sociological perspective acknowledges that it is not possible to change gender roles drastically without dramatic revisions in a culture's social structure?
   a. functionalist perspective
   b. conflict perspective
   c. interactionist perspective
   d. both a and b

7. In studying gender stratification, which sociological perspective typically focuses on the micro level of everyday behavior, such as cross-sex conversation?
   a. functionalist perspective
   b. conflict perspective
   c. interactionist perspective
   d. all of the above

8. In 1981, Sandra Day O'Connor was sworn in as the nation's first female
   a. senator.
   b. governor.
   c. Supreme Court justice.
   d. attorney general.

9. In what way do female physicians interact differently with patients than do male physicians?
   a. They take on an aggressive interactional style to compensate for their lack of authority.
   b. They have poor bedside manner.
   c. They spend 10 percent more time with patients.
   d. both a and c

10. The courts recognize two kinds of sexual harassment,
   a. quid pro quo and a hostile environment.
   b. squid con so and a hostile environment.
   c. quid pro con and a hostile environment.
   d. none of the above

11. Which of the following statements about the status of women around the world is correct?
   a. They rarely own land.
   b. They generally work in the lowest-paid jobs.
   c. Households headed by single women are typically found in relatively poor areas.
   d. all of the above

12. In 2001, what percentage of adult women in the United States held jobs outside the home?
   a. 24 percent
   b. 38 percent
   c. 60 percent
   d. 87 percent

13. Which sociologist has used the phrase second shift to describe the double burden—work outside the home followed by child care and housework—that many women face and few men share equitably?
   a. Heidi Hartmann
   b. Arlie Hochschild
   c. Talcott Parsons
   d. Kristin Luker

14. Which early feminist leader was arrested for attempting to vote in the presidential election of 1872?
   a. Elizabeth Cady Stanton
   b. Abigail Adams
   c. Sojourner Truth
   d. Susan B. Anthony

15. The sense of sisterhood that became evident during the rise of the contemporary feminist movement resembled the Marxist concept of
    a. alienation.
    b. dialectics.
    c. class consciousness.
    d. false consciousness.

FILL-IN QUESTIONS: Fill in the blank spaces in the sentences below with the correct words. Where two or more words are required, there will be a corresponding number of blank spaces.

1. _____ contributes significantly to rigid gender-role socialization, since many people stereotypically associate male homosexuality with femininity and lesbianism with masculinity.

2. In Margaret Mead's analysis of New Guinea tribes, she indicates that among the _____, gender roles for both men and women are similar to female gender roles in the United States.

3. Within the general framework of their theory, _____ sociologists maintain that gender differentiation has contributed to overall social stability.

4. Talcott Parsons and Robert Bales contend that women take the _____, emotionally supportive role in the family and men take the _____, practical role.

5. _____ theorists would say males are like the bourgeoisie, or capitalists (they control most of the society's wealth, prestige, and power), and females are like the proletarians, or workers.

6. Studies show that up to 96 percent of all interruptions in cross-sex (male-female) conversations are initiated by _____.

7. It is not simply that particular men in the United States are biased in their treatment of women. All the major institutions of our society—including the government, armed forces, large corporations, the media, the universities, and the medical establishment—are controlled by men. This situation is symptomatic of institutional _____.

8. In the country of _____, the banning of head scarves in public schools has been a source of controversy.

9. Women from all groups and men from minority groups sometimes encounter attitudinal or organizational bias that prevents them from reaching their full potential. This is known as the _____ _____.

10. Sociologist Arlie Hochschild has used the phrase _____ _____ to describe the double burden that many women face and few men share equitably: working outside the home followed by child care and housework.

11. The _____ Amendment to the Constitution granted women the right to vote in national elections beginning in 1920.

12. The author of the pioneering argument for women's rights, *The Feminine Mystique*, is _____ _____.

13. Through the rise of contemporary _____, women are developing a greater sense of group solidarity.

14. A critical victory in the struggle for legalized abortion in the United States came in 1973 when the Supreme Court granted women the right to terminate pregnancies in the _____ v. _____ decision.

15. The Supreme Court currently supports the general right to terminate a pregnancy by a narrow _____.

UNDERSTANDING SOCIAL POLICY: All of the following questions are based on material that appears in the social policy section on The Battle Over Abortion from a Global Perspective. Write a brief answer to each question in the space provided below.

1. What is at the heart of the abortion controversy in the United States today?

2. In what way has changing technology had an impact on the abortion controversy?

3. What is the sociological interest in abortion rights?

4. In the battle between pro-choice and pro-life activists, what are the most recent policy initiatives that have been made with respect to abortion rights in the United States?

DEFINITIONS OF KEY TERMS

Gender role: Expectations regarding the proper behavior, attitudes, and activities of males and females. (257)

Homophobia: Fear of and prejudice against homosexuality. (258)

Instrumentality: An emphasis on tasks, a focus on more distant goals, and a concern for the external relationship between one's family and other social institutions. (261)

Expressiveness: Concern for the maintenance of harmony and the internal emotional affairs of the family. (261)

Sexism: The ideology that one sex is superior to the other. (263)

Institutional discrimination: The denial of opportunities and equal rights to individuals and groups that results from the normal operations of a society. (263)

Sexual harassment: Behavior that occurs when work benefits are made contingent on sexual favors (as a quid pro quo), or when touching, lewd comments, or the exhibition of pornographic material creates a "hostile environment" in the workplace. (264)

Glass ceiling: An invisible barrier that blocks the promotion of a qualified individual in a work environment because of the individual's gender, race, or ethnicity. (266)

Second shift: The double burden—work outside the home followed by child care and housework—that many women face and few men share equitably. (267)

ANSWERS TO SELF-TEST

Modified True/False Questions
1. Moaveni found not only that gender roles are very different in Iran than they are in the United States, but also that they changed dramatically with the Iranian Revolution. (256–257)
2. We socially construct our behavior so that male-female differences are either created or exaggerated. (257)
3. Homophobia contributes significantly to rigid gender-role socialization. (258)

4. Studies of children's books suggest that while males are portrayed as a variety of characters, females tend to be shown mostly in traditional roles, such as mother, grandmother, or volunteer. (259)
5. The research of anthropologist Margaret Mead points to the importance of cultural conditioning—as opposed to biological factors—in defining the social roles of males and females. (260)
6. True (261)
7. Feminist sociologists would find little to disagree with in the conflict perspective. (262)
8. True (262)
9. Women remain noticeably underrepresented. In 2003, only 6 of the nation's 50 states had a female governor. (262)
10. True (265)
11. True (267)
12. As married women have taken on more and more hours of paid employment, they have been only partially successful in getting their husbands to assume a greater role in needed homemaking duties. (267)
13. Data from the Census Bureau show that, even when women and men are in the same occupation, men typically earn more than women. (266)
14. The first wave of feminism in the United States emerged in the mid-1800s; the second wave emerged in the 1960s and came into full force in the 1970s. (267–268)
15. A sense of "sisterhood," much like the class consciousness that Marx hoped would emerge in the proletariat, became evident in the feminist movement of the 1960s and 1970s. (268)

Multiple-Choice Questions

1. d (258)
2. b (259)
3. c (260)
4. a (261)
5. b (261)
6. d (262)
7. c (262)
8. c (263)
9. c (263)
10. a (264)
11. d (264)
12. c (266)
13. b (267)
14. d (268)
15. c (268)

Fill-In Questions

1. Homophobia (258)
2. Arapesh (260)
3. functionalist (261)
4. expressive; instrumental (261)
5. Conflict (261)
6. men (262)
7. discrimination (263)
8. France (265)
9. glass ceiling (266)
10. second shift (267)
11. Nineteenth (268)
12. Betty Friedan (268)
13. feminism (268)
14. Roe, Wade (269)

15. majority (270)

Understanding Social Policy: The Battle over Abortion from a Global Perspective

1. A critical victory in the struggle for legalized abortion in the United States came in 1973 in the Supreme Court case of Roe v. Wade, which was based on a woman's right to privacy. The Court's decision was generally applauded by pro-choice groups, which believe women should have the right to make their own decisions about their bodies and should have access to safe and legal abortions. However, for pro-life groups, abortion is a moral and often religious issue. In their view, human life begins at the moment of conception rather than at the moment of a baby's delivery, so that its termination through abortion is essentially an act of murder. (269)

2. "Day-after" pills are now prescribed in the United States. These pills can abort a fertilized egg the day after conception. Doctors, guided by ultrasound, can now end a pregnancy as early as eight days after conception. Pro-life activists are concerned that the use of ultrasound technology will allow people to abort unwanted females in nations where a premium is placed on male offspring. (270)

3. Sociologists see gender and social class as the defining issues surrounding abortion. The intense conflict over abortion reflects broader differences over women's position in society. Feminists involved in defending abortion rights typically believe that men and women are essentially similar; they support women's full participation in work outside the home and oppose all forms of sex discrimination. In contrast, most anti-abortion activists believe that men and women are fundamentally different. In their view, men are best suited to the public world of work, while women are best suited to the demanding and crucial task of rearing children. These activists are troubled by women's growing participation in work outside the home, which they view as destructive to the family, and ultimately to society. (270)

4. The Supreme Court currently supports the general right to terminate a pregnancy by a narrow 5-4 majority. While pro-life activists continue to hope for an overruling of Roe v. Wade, they have focused in the interim on weakening the decision through tactics such as limiting the use of fetal tissue in medical experiments and prohibiting late-term abortions. In 1998 the Court gave the states authority to prohibit abortions at the point where the fetus is viable outside the mother's womb. (270–271)

CHAPTER 13
STRATIFICATION BY AGE

Aging and Society

Explaining the Aging Process
    Functionalist Approach:
        Disengagement Theory
    Interactionist Approach: Activity
        Theory
    The Conflict Approach

Role Transitions throughout the Life Course
    The Sandwich Generation
    Adjusting to Retirement
    Death and Dying

Age Stratification in the United States
    The "Graying of America"
    Wealth and Income
    Ageism
    Competition in the Labor Force
    The Elderly: Emergence of a
        Collective Consciousness

Social Policy and Age Stratification: The Right to Die Worldwide
    The Issue
    The Setting
    Sociological Insights
    Policy Initiatives

BOXES
    RESEARCH IN ACTION: *Naturally Occurring Retirement Communities (NORCs)*
    SOCIOLOGY IN THE GLOBAL COMMUNITY: *Aging Worldwide—Issues and Consequences*

KEY POINTS

Aging and Society: "Being old" is a master status that commonly overshadows all others in the United States. Once people have been labeled "old," the designation has a major impact on how others perceive them, and even on how they view themselves. Negative stereotypes of the elderly contribute to their position as a minority group subject to discrimination. The elderly experience unequal treatment in employment, and may face prejudice and discrimination; they share physical characteristics that distinguish them from younger people; their membership in a disadvantaged minority is involuntary; they have a strong sense of group solidarity; and they are generally married to others of a comparable age. (277)

Disengagement Theory: Elaine Cumming and William Henry introduced an explanation of the impact of aging during one's life course known as **disengagement theory**. This theory contends that society and the aging individual mutually sever many of their relationships. In keeping with the functionalist perspective, disengagement theory emphasizes that passing social roles on from one generation to another ensures social stability. Implicit in disengagement theory is the view that society should help older people to withdraw from their accustomed social roles. Although functionalist in its approach, disengagement theory ignores the fact that postretirement employment has been increasing in recent decades. (277–278)

Activity Theory: Often seen as an opposing approach to disengagement theory, **activity theory** argues that the elderly person who remains active will be best adjusted. Proponents of activity theory view older people's withdrawal from society as harmful for both the elderly and society. Activity theorists focus on the potential contributions of older people to the maintenance of society. In their opinion, aging citizens will feel satisfied only when they can be useful and productive in society's terms; primarily by working for wages. (279)

The Conflict Approach: Conflict theorists have criticized both disengagement theorists and activity theorists for failing to consider the impact of social structure on aging patterns. According to the conflict approach, the treatment of older people in the United States reflects the many divisions in our society. The low status of older people is seen in prejudice and discrimination against them, in age segregation, and in unfair job practices, none of which are directly addressed by either disengagement theory or activity theory. (279–280)

Role Transitions throughout the Life Course: How we move through the life course varies dramatically, depending on the individual. Still, it is possible to identify a series of developmental periods, with critical transitions between the various stages, as shown in the model devised by psychologist Daniel Levinson. The first transitional period identified by Levinson begins at about age 17 and extends to age 22. It marks the time at which an individual gradually enters the adult world. At about age 40, men and women often experience a stressful period of self-evaluation, commonly known as the **midlife crisis**. During the late 1990s social scientists focused on the **sandwich generation**—adults who simultaneously try to meet the competing needs of their parents and their children. (281)

Adjusting to Retirement: Retirement is a rite of passage that marks a critical transition from one phase of a person's life to another. Retirement is not a single transition, but rather a series of adjustments that varies from one person to another. Like other aspects of life in the United States, the experience of retirement varies according to gender, race, and ethnicity. (281–283)

The "Graying of America": An increasing proportion of the population of the United States is composed of older people. Men and women aged 65 years and over constituted only 4.1 percent of the national population in the year 1900, but by 2005 this figure is expected to grow to 12.6 percent. In 2005, a higher percentage of non-Hispanic whites are projected to be older than 65, compared to African Americans and Asian Americans. These differences reflect the shorter life spans of the latter groups, as well as immigration patterns among Asians and Hispanics. Politicians court the votes of older people, since they are the age group most likely to register and vote. (285)

The Elderly—Emergence of a Collective Consciousness: In the 1970s, many older people became aware that they were being treated as second-class citizens and turned to collective action. The largest organization representing the nation's elderly is the American Association of Retired Persons (AARP). The potential power of the AARP is enormous. It is the third largest voluntary association in the United States (behind only the Roman Catholic church and the American Automobile Association), representing one out of every four registered voters in the United States. (287)

The Right to Die Worldwide: The issue of physician-assisted suicide is but one aspect of the larger debate in the United States and other countries over the ethics of suicide and euthanasia. Many societies are known to have practiced senilicide, the killing of the aged because of extreme difficulties in providing basic necessities such as food and shelter. Conflict theorists question whether by endorsing physician-assisted suicide we are devaluing the disabled through an acceptance of their premature death. Conflict theorists are also concerned that economically and politically disadvantaged groups might be pushed into consenting to euthanasia. (288)

KEY TERMS

Briefly define or identify the following terms in the spaces provided below. The definitions of these terms can be found later in this chapter of the study guide.

Gerontology	Sandwich generation
Disengagement theory	Hospice care
Activity theory	Ageism
Midlife crisis	Euthanasia

SELF-TEST

MODIFIED TRUE/FALSE QUESTIONS: If the statement below is true, write "true" in the space provided. If the statement is false, briefly correct the error.

1. Unlike gender, age is an achieved status that forms the basis for social differentiation.

2. Gerontologists rely heavily on sociological principles to explain the impact of aging on the individual and society.

3. According to activity theory, the approach of death forces people to drop most of their social roles, including those of worker, volunteer, spouse, hobby enthusiast, and even reader.

Chapter 13 *Stratification by Age* | 187

4. During the tragic 1995 heat wave that resulted in 733 deaths in Chicago, older Hispanics and Asian Americans had higher death rates from the heat wave than did other racial and ethnic groups.

5. Conflict theorists have criticized both disengagement theory and activity theory for failing to consider the impact of social structure on patterns of aging.

6. Conflict theorists have noted that as societies make the transition from agricultural economies to industrialization and capitalism, the importance of older people within the economy tends to increase.

7. The sandwich generation refers to older people who are providing support for their children and grandchildren simultaneously.

8. According to gerontologist Robert Atchley, the fourth stage of dying is depression.

9. NORCs are retirement communities established through a federal initiative, whose purpose is to create more communities for older people as the population ages.

10. In 2002, the Senate Special Committee on Aging sharply criticized media and marketing executives for bombarding audiences with negative images of the aged.

11. Many people continue to view older workers as "job stealers," a biased judgment similar to that directed against illegal immigrants.

12. The AARP is the largest organization representing the nation's elderly, and it is the third-largest voluntary association in the United States.

13. The debate over euthanasia and assisted suicide is an issue that is exclusively the concern of older people and those who care for them.

14. Euthanasia is widely accepted in Europe and in most other industrial societies other than the United States.

15. In the United States, the only state to pass a law permitting assisted suicide is Oregon, with its Death with Dignity Act in 1997.

MULTIPLE-CHOICE QUESTIONS: In each of the following, select the phrase that best completes the statement.

1. Which one of the following statements about the elderly is correct?
   a. Being old is a master status.
   b. Once people are labeled as old, it has a major impact on how others perceive them.
   c. Once people are labeled as old, it has a major impact on how they view themselves.
   d. all of the above

2. What is the one crucial difference between older people and other subordinate groups, such as racial and ethnic minorities or women?
   a. Older people do not experience unequal treatment in employment.
   b. Older people have a strong sense of group solidarity and other groups do not.
   c. All of us who live long enough will eventually assume the ascribed status of being an older person.
   d. Older people are generally married to others of comparable age and other minorities do not marry within their group.

3. Which field of study was originally developed in the 1930s as an increasing number of social scientists became aware of the plight of the elderly?
   a. sociology
   b. gerontology
   c. gerontocracy
   d. senilicide

4. Elaine Cumming and William Henry introduced an explanation of the impact of aging known as
   a. disengagement theory.
   b. activity theory.
   c. labeling theory.
   d. the contact hypothesis.

5. Activity theory is associated with the
   a. functionalist perspective.
   b. conflict perspective.
   c. interactionist perspective.
   d. labeling perspective.

6. Which sociological perspective is most likely to emphasize the important role of social networks in providing life satisfaction for the elderly?
   a. functionalist perspective
   b. conflict perspective
   c. interactionist perspective
   d. labeling theory

7. Which sociological perspective views the treatment of older people as reflective of the many divisions in our society?
   a. functionalist perspective
   b. conflict perspective
   c. interactionist perspective
   d. labeling theory

8. _____ theorists regard older people as victimized by social structure with their social roles relatively unchanged but devalued.
   a. Functionalist
   b. Conflict
   c. Interactionist
   d. Dramaturgical

9. Men and women often experience a stressful period of self-evaluation, commonly known as
   a. passage confusion.
   b. old "old" dementia.
   c. altimetry division.
   d. midlife crisis.

10. Retirement is an example of a
    a. rite of passage.
    b. gerontocracy.
    c. functional prerequisite.
    d. trained incapacity.

11. According to psychologist Elisabeth Kübler-Ross, the first stage of the experience of dying that a person may undergo is
    a. denial.
    b. anger.
    c. depression.
    d. bargaining.

12. Which sociological perspective would be most likely to emphasize the tasks of those who are dying, such as settling insurance and legacy matters, restoring harmony to social relationships, and making funeral plans?
    a. functionalist perspective
    b. conflict perspective
    c. interactionist perspective
    d. labeling theory

13. As of 2000, which state had the highest percentage of elderly?
    a. Iowa
    b. New Jersey
    c. Florida
    d. California

14. The largest organization representing the nation's older people is the
    a. Gray Panthers.
    b. Older Women's League (OWL).
    c. American Association of Retired Persons (AARP).
    d. Americans for Generational Equality (AGE).

15. In 1996, the American Association of Retired Persons (AARP) chose Margaret Dixon as its president. Dixon became the first president of the AARP who was
    a. African American.
    b. 85 years old or over.
    c. born outside the United States.
    d. active in the Republican party.

FILL-IN QUESTIONS: Fill in the blank spaces in the sentences below with the correct words. Where two or more words are required, there will be a corresponding number of blank spaces.

1. The elderly are _____ regarded in the traditional Sherpa (Tibet) culture.

2. In keeping with the _____ perspective of sociology, disengagement theory emphasizes that a society's stability is ensured when social roles are passed on from one generation to another.

3. Implicit in _____ theory is the view that society should help older people withdraw from their accustomed social roles.

4. The improved health of older people, which is sometimes overlooked by social scientists, has strengthened the arguments of _____ theorists regarding how society should deal with the elderly.

5. _____ theorists argue that both the disengagement and the activity perspectives often ignore the impact of social class in the lives of the elderly.

6. During the late 1990s, growing attention in the United States focused on the _____ generation: adults who simultaneously try to meet the competing needs of their parents and their children.

7. For both men and women in the United States, the average age of retirement _____ between 1950 and the mid-1990s.

8. The final phase of retirement, according to Robert Atchley, is the _____, which begins when the person can no longer engage in basic, day-to-day activities such as self-care and housework.

9. According to psychologist Elisabeth Kübler-Ross, the final stage of the experience of dying, _____, is not always reached by the dying person.

10. Recent studies in the United States suggest that in many ways people have broken through the historic taboos about death and are attempting to arrange certain aspects of the idealized "_____ death."

11. Hospice programs currently serve more than _____ people each year.

12. The fastest-growing age group in the United States is people over _____ years old.

13. The "old old" segment of the population of the United States—people _____ years old and over—is growing rapidly.

14. In a study of 41 non-industrialized societies, Anthony Glascock found some form of _____ in 21 of them.

15. Currently, public policy in the United States does not permit _____ euthanasia (such as deliberate injection of lethal drugs to a terminally ill patient) or physician-assisted suicide.

UNDERSTANDING SOCIAL POLICY: All of the following questions are based on material that appears in the social policy section on The Right to Die Worldwide. Write a brief answer to each question in the space provided below.

1. What is euthanasia and what are the different kinds of euthanasia?

2. What is the conflict approach to the right to die?

3. Is euthanasia legal anywhere in the world?

DEFINITIONS OF KEY TERMS

Gerontology: The scientific study of the sociological and psychological aspects of aging and the problems of the aged. (277)

Disengagement theory: A functionalist theory of aging that suggests that society and the aging individual mutually sever many of their relationships. (277)

Activity theory: An interactionist theory of aging that suggests that those elderly people who remain active and socially involved will be best adjusted. (279)

Midlife crisis: A stressful period of self-evaluation that begins at about age 40. (281)

Sandwich generation: The generation of adults who simultaneously try to meet the competing needs of their parents and their children. (281)

Hospice care: Treatment of the terminally ill in their own homes, or in special hospital units or other facilities, with the goal of helping them to die easily, without pain. (284)

Ageism: Prejudice and discrimination based on a person's age. (286)

Euthanasia: The act of bringing about the death of a hopelessly ill and suffering person in a relatively quick and painless way for reasons of mercy. (288)

ANSWERS TO SELF-TEST

Modified True/False Questions
1. Like gender, age is an ascribed status that forms the basis for social differentiation. (276)
2. True (277)
3. According to disengagement theory, the approach of death forces people to drop most of their social roles. (277)
4. During the tragic 1995 heat wave that resulted in 733 deaths in Chicago, older Hispanics and Asian Americans had lower death rates from the heat wave than did other racial and ethnic groups. (279)
5. True (279)
6. Conflict theorists have noted that as societies make the transition from agricultural economies to industrial societies and capitalism, the importance of older people within the economy tends to erode. (280)
7. The sandwich generation refers to adults who simultaneously try to meet the competing needs of their parents and their children. (281)
8. According to Elizabeth Kübler-Ross, the fourth stage of dying is depression. (284)
9. NORCs are areas that have gradually become informal centers for senior citizens, not through any government initiative. (283)
10. True (286)
11. True (286)
12. True (287)
13. The debate over euthanasia and assisted suicide often focuses on cases involving older people, although it can involve younger adults with terminal and degenerative diseases. (288)
14. In the industrialized world, euthanasia is widely accepted only in the Netherlands. (289)
15. True (289)

Multiple-Choice Questions
1. d (277)
2. c (277)
3. b (277)
4. a (277)
5. c (279)
6. c (279)
7. b (280)
8. b (280)
9. d (281)
10. a (281)
11. a (284)
12. a (284)
13. c (285)
14. c (287)
15. a (287)

Fill-In Questions
1. highly (277)
2. functionalist (277)

3. disengagement (278)
4. activity (279)
5. Conflict (279)
6. sandwich (281)
7. declined (281)
8. termination (282)
9. acceptance (284)
10. good (284)
11. 880,000 (284)
12. 100 (285)
13. 85 (285)
14. senilicide (288)
15. active (288)

Understanding Social Policy: The Right to Die Worldwide

1. Euthanasia has been defined by the American Medical Association as the "act of bringing about the death of a hopelessly ill and suffering person in a relatively quick and painless way for reasons of mercy." Active euthanasia may involve the deliberate injection of lethal drugs to a terminally ill patient, whereas passive euthanasia might involve disconnecting life support equipment from a comatose patient. (288)

2. Conflict theorists question whether we are devaluing the disabled through an acceptance of their premature death. Critics of euthanasia charge that many of its supporters are guilty of ageism and other forms of bias. In a society that commonly discriminates against the elderly and people with disabilities, medical authorities and even family members may decide too quickly that such people should die "for their own good" or (in a view somewhat reminiscent of the disengagement theory) "for the good of society." (288–289)

3. In the industrialized world, euthanasia is widely accepted only in the Netherlands. Dutch law provides for euthanasia after a patient has voluntarily requested assistance in committing suicide and has received a second medical opinion. In the United States, the only state to allow assisted suicide is Oregon. (289)

CHAPTER 14: THE FAMILY AND INTIMATE RELATIONSHIPS

Global View of the Family
- *Composition: What Is the Family?*
- *Kinship Patterns: To Whom Are We Related?*
- *Authority Patterns: Who Rules?*

Studying the Family
- *Functionalist View*
- *Conflict View*
- *Interactionist View*
- *Feminist View*

Marriage and Family
- *Courtship and Mate Selection*
- *Variations in Family Life and Intimate Relationships*
- *Child-Rearing Patterns in Family Life*

Divorce
- *Statistical Trends in Divorce*
- *Factors Associated with Divorce*
- *Impact of Divorce on Children*

Diverse Lifestyles
- *Cohabitation*
- *Remaining Single*
- *Marriage without Children*
- *Lesbian and Gay Relationships*

Social Policy and the Family: Gay Marriage
- *The Issue*
- *The Setting*
- *Sociological Insights*
- *Policy Initiatives*

BOXES
- **SOCIOLOGY IN THE GLOBAL COMMUNITY**: Domestic Violence
- **RESEARCH IN ACTION**: The Lingering Impact of Divorce

KEY POINTS

Composition—What Is the Family? A **family** can be defined as a set of people related by blood, marriage, some other agreed-upon relationship, or adoption, who share the primary responsibility for reproduction and caring for members of society. In the United States, many people still think of the family in very narrow terms; as a married couple and their unmarried children living together. However, this is but one type of family; what sociologists refer to as a **nuclear family**. By contrast, an **extended family** is a family in which relatives, in addition to parents and children, live in the same home. (295)

Kinship Patterns—To Whom Are We Related? The state of being related to others is called **kinship**. The United States follows the system of **bilateral descent**, which means that both sides of a person's family are regarded as equally important. In **patrilineal descent,** only the father's relatives are important in terms of property, inheritance, and emotional ties. Conversely, in societies that favor **matrilineal descent**, only the mother's relatives are significant. New forms of reproductive technology will necessitate a new way of looking at kinship. Today, a combination of biological and social processes can "create" a family member, requiring that more distinctions be made about who is related to whom. (298)

Authority Patterns—Who Rules? Societies vary in the way that power is distributed within the family. A society that expects males to dominate in all family decision making is termed a **patriarchy**. In contrast, in a **matriarchy**, women have greater authority than men. In a third type of authority pattern, the **egalitarian family**, spouses are regarded as equals. This does not mean, however, that all decisions are shared in such families. Wives may hold authority in some spheres, husbands in others. (298–299)

Functionalist View of the Family: The family performs six paramount functions, first outlined more than 65 years ago by sociologist William F. Ogburn. These are (1) reproduction, (2) protection, (3) socialization, (4) regulation of sexual behavior, (5) affection and companionship, and (6) provision of social status. (299)

Conflict View of the Family: Conflict theorists view the family not as a contributor to social stability, but as a reflection of the inequality in wealth and power that is found within the larger society. Feminist and conflict theorists note that the family has traditionally legitimized and perpetuated male dominance. While the egalitarian family has become a more common pattern in the United States in recent decades, male dominance within the family has hardly disappeared. Conflict theorists also view the family as an economic unit that contributes to societal injustice. Children inherit the privileged or less-than-privileged social and economic status of their parents. (299)

Interactionist View: Interactionists focus on the micro level of family and other intimate relationships. They are interested in how individuals interact with one another, whether they are cohabiting partners or long-time married couples. Interactionists might, for example, study the relationship between parents and children in stepfamilies. (300)

Feminist View: Feminist sociologists have taken a strong interest in the family as a social institution. Sociologists have looked particularly closely at how women's work outside the home impacts their childcare and housework duties. Feminist theorists have urged social scientists and social agencies to rethink the notion that families in which no adult male is present are automatically cause for concern. (300)

Parenthood: The socialization of children is essential to the maintenance of any culture. Consequently, parenthood is one of the most important (and most demanding) social roles in the United States. Sociologist Alice Rossi has identified four factors that complicate the transition to parenthood and the role of socializer. First, there is little anticipatory socialization for the social role of caregiver. Second, only limited learning occurs during the period of pregnancy itself. Third, the transition to parenthood is quite abrupt. Finally, in Rossi's view, our society lacks clear and helpful guidelines for successful parenthood. (305)

Dual-Income Families: The idea of a family consisting of a wage-earning husband with a wife who stays at home has largely given way to the dual-income household. Among married people between the ages of 25 and 34, 92 percent of the men and 75 percent of the women were in the labor force in 2002. A major factor in the rise of dual-income couples is economic need. Other factors include the nation's declining birthrate, the increase in the proportion of women with a college education, the shift in the economy of the United States from manufacturing to service industries, and the impact of the feminist movement in changing women's consciousness. (306)

Single-Parent Families: In 2000, a single parent headed about 21 percent of white families with children under 18, 35 percent of Hispanic families with children, and 55 percent of African American families with children. A family headed by a single mother faces especially difficult problems when the mother is a teenager. While 82 percent of single parents in the United States are mothers, the number of households headed by single fathers more than quadrupled over the period from 1980 to 2000. (306–307)

Factors Associated with Divorce: Perhaps the most important factor in the increase in divorce in the last hundred years has been the greater social acceptance of divorce. More important, various religious denominations have relaxed their negative attitudes toward divorce, and most religious leaders no longer treat it as a sin. In addition, many states have adopted more liberal divorce laws, families have fewer children, more couples can afford divorces, and increasing numbers of women are becoming less economically and emotionally dependent on their husbands. (308)

Cohabitation: One of the most dramatic trends of recent years has been the tremendous increase in male-female couples who choose to live together without marrying, thereby engaging in what is commonly called **cohabitation**. The number of such households in the United States rose sixfold in the 1960s and increased another 72 percent between 1990 and 2000. Working couples are almost twice as likely to cohabit as college students, and half of all people involved in cohabitation in the United States have been previously married. In much of Europe, cohabitation is also very common. Government policies in these countries make few legal distinctions between married and unmarried couples or households. (308–309)

Remaining Single: More and more people are postponing entry into first marriages. As of 2000, one out of every three households with children in the United States (accounting for 28 million people) was a single-member household. The trend toward maintaining a single lifestyle is related to the growing economic independence of young people. This trend is especially significant for women. Freed from financial needs, women don't necessarily need to marry to enjoy a satisfying life. (310)

Gay Marriage: The idea of same-sex marriage strikes some people as only the latest of many attacks on traditional marriage. To others, it seems an overdue acknowledgement of the formal relationships that faithful, monogamous gay couples have long maintained. Functionalists have traditionally seen marriage as a social institution that is closely tied to human reproduction. But many same-sex couples are entrusted with the socialization of young children. Conflict theorists have charged that denial of the right to marry reinforces the second-class status of gays and lesbians. Interactionists generally avoid the policy question and focus instead on the nature of same-sex households. (311)

KEY TERMS

Briefly define or identify the following terms in the spaces provided below. The definitions of these terms can be found later in this chapter of the study guide.

Family	Monogamy
Nuclear family	Serial monogamy
Extended family	Polygamy

Polygyny	Exogamy
Polyandry	Homogamy
Kinship	Incest taboo
Bilateral descent	Machismo
Patrilineal descent	Familism
Matrilineal descent	Adoption
Patriarchy	Single-parent family
Matriarchy	Cohabitation
Egalitarian family	Domestic partnership
Endogamy	

SELF-TEST

MODIFIED TRUE/FALSE QUESTIONS: If the statement below is true, write "true" in the space provided. If the statement is false, briefly correct the error.

1. By 2000, more than one-half of all households in the United States fit the nuclear family model.

2. 2. In polygynous societies, most men have multiple spouses.

3. Kinship is totally determined by biological or marital ties.

4. Many sociologists believe that the matriarchal family has begun to replace the patriarchal family as the social norm in the United States, as more women become self-sufficient.

5. The functionalist perspective encourages us to examine the ways in which the family gratifies the needs of its members and contributes to the stability of society.

6. Currently, over 95 percent of all men and women in the United States marry at least once.

7. Endogamy is intended to reinforce the cohesiveness of the group by suggesting to the young that they should marry someone "of our own kind."

8. The number of interracial marriages between African Americans and whites in the United States has increased more than seven times, jumping from 51,000 in 1960 to 416,000 in 2003.

9. Among the poor, adult women often play a significant role in the economic support of the family.

10. 10. Adopters must be married.

11. Approximately 10 percent of all people in the United States will marry, divorce, and then remarry.

12. Men are less likely to remarry than women are, because men cannot afford to make child support payments and establish a new family simultaneously.

13. Cohabitation only involves male-female couples.

14. The number of households in the United States engaged in cohabitation increased 72 percent between 1990 and 2000.

15. Current data indicate that more people in the United States are entering marriage at an earlier age than was true in the past.

MULTIPLE-CHOICE QUESTIONS: In each of the following, select the phrase that best completes the statement.

1. Alice, age 7, lives in a private home with her parents, her grandmother, and her aunt. Alice's family is an example of a(n)
    a. nuclear family.
    b. dysfunctional family.
    c. extended family.
    d. polygynous family.

2. Some observers, noting the high rate of divorce in the United States, have suggested that the most accurate description for the form that monogamy takes in this country is
    a. functional monogamy.
    b. communal monogamy.
    c. serial monogamy.
    d. regressive monogamy.

3. According to anthropologist George Murdock, the most common type of polygamy is
    a. polygyny.
    b. polyandry.
    c. serial polygamy.
    d. matriarchy.

4. Which system of descent is followed in the United States?
    a. matrilineal
    b. patrilineal
    c. unilateral
    d. bilateral

5. Which of the following is not a function of the family discussed by William Ogburn?
    a. provision of social status
    b. reproduction
    c. economic support
    d. protection

6. Which statement about domestic violence is not true?
    a. Family violence is at least as dangerous as assault committed by strangers.
    b. Violence within intimate relationships tends to lessen over time.
    c. Emotional and psychological abuse can be as debilitating as physical abuse.
    d. Women are most at risk of abuse from the men they know.

7. 7. In the United States in 2000, domestic abuse resulted in
    a. more than 3 million reports of child abuse or neglect.
    b. 2 million violent crimes committed by current or former spouses, boyfriends, or girlfriends.
    c. injuries to more than 25 percent of wives.
    d. all of the above

8. Pride in the extended family among Mexican Americans is referred to as
    a. familism.
    b. machismo.
    c. bilateralism.
    d. extended family.

9. One recent development in family life in the United States has been the extension of parenthood as adult children continue to (or return to) live at home. The reason for this is
    a. the rising divorce rate.
    b. skyrocketing rent and real estate prices.
    c. financial difficulties.
    d. all of the above

10. Which term has been used in the popular press to refer to adult children who continue to (or return to) live at home?
    a. "boomerang generation"
    b. counterculture
    c. "Brady Bunch" cohort
    d. Generation X

11. Which sociological perspective emphasizes that government has a strong interest in encouraging adoption?
    a. functionalist perspective
    b. conflict perspective
    c. interactionist perspective
    d. labeling theory

12. Which of the following is a factor that has contributed to the rise of the dual-income model of the family?
    a. increasing number of men with a college education
    b. increasing birthrate
    c. shift in the economy of the United States from manufacturing to service industries
    d. all of the above

13. Since 1980, the rate of African-American teenage pregnancy in the United States
    a. increased dramatically.
    b. decreased.
    c. increased slightly.
    d. remained steady.

14. Of those in the United States who obtain a divorce, about what percent later remarry?
    a. 10 percent
    b. 45 percent
    c. 63 percent
    d. 80 percent

15. Which of the following factors is associated with the high divorce rate in the United States?
    a. the liberalization of divorce laws
    b. contemporary families have fewer children than earlier families
    c. the increase in family incomes
    d. all of the above

FILL-IN QUESTIONS: Fill in the blank spaces in the sentences below with the correct words. Where two or more words are required, there will be a corresponding number of blank spaces.

1. People in the United States see the _____ family as the preferred form of family arrangement.

2. Anthropologist George Murdock sampled 565 societies and found that over 80 percent had some type of _____ as their preferred form of marriage.

3. The principle of _____ assigns people to kinship groups according to their relationship to an individual's mother or father.

4. In patriarchal societies, the _____ male often wields the greatest power.

5. _____ emerged among Native American tribal societies, and in nations in which men were absent for long periods for warfare or food gathering.

6. In the view of many sociologists, the _____ family has begun to replace the patriarchal family as the social norm in the United States.

7. As _____ theorists point out, the social class of couples and their children significantly influences the socialization experiences to which they are exposed, and the protection they receive.

8. Mate selection based on love is not a cultural universal. In many societies, marriages are instead _____ by parents or religious authorities.

9. Although social class differences in family life are less striking than they once were, _____ class families were found to be more authoritarian in rearing children and more inclined to use physical punishment.

10. Caring for children is a _____ function of the family, yet the ways in which different societies assign this function to family members can vary significantly.

11. Sociologist Alice Rossi points out that there is little _____ socialization in the United States for the social roles of caregiver.

12. Viewed from a(n) _____ perspective, having a child may provide a sense of motivation and purpose for a low-income teenager whose economic worth in our society is limited at best.

13. Although _____ percent of single parents in the United States are mothers, the number of households headed by single fathers has more than _____ over the period from 1980 to 2000.

14. The rising rates of divorce and remarriage in the United States have led to a noticeable increase in _____ relationships.

15. Certain municipalities have passed legislation allowing for the registration of _____ _____, couples who live in close and committed personal relationships, but have not married.

UNDERSTANDING SOCIAL POLICY: All of the following questions are based on material that appears in the social policy section on Gay Marriage. Write a brief answer to each question in the space provided below.

1. How do functionalists, conflict theorists, and interactionists view gay marriage?

2. Describe public opinion toward gay marriage and civil unions.

3. Describe recent policy changes toward gay marriage and civil unions.

DEFINITIONS OF KEY TERMS

Family: A set of people related by blood, marriage or some other agreed-upon relationship, or adoption, who share the primary responsibility for reproducing and caring for members of society. (294–295)

Nuclear family: A married couple and their unmarried children living together. (295)

Extended family: A family in which relatives—such as grandparents, aunts, or uncles—live in the same home as parents and their children (295)

Monogamy: A form of marriage in which one woman and one man are married only to each other. (295)

Serial monogamy: A form of marriage in which a person may have several spouses in his or her lifetime, but only one spouse at a time. (295)

Polygamy: A form of marriage in which an individual may have several husbands or wives simultaneously. (295)

Polygyny: A form of polygamy in which a man may have more than one wife at the same time. (295)

Polyandry: A form of polygamy in which a woman may have more than one husband at the same time. (295)

Kinship: The state of being related to others. (298)

Bilateral descent: A kinship system in which both sides of a person's family are regarded as equally important. (298)

Patrilineal descent: A kinship system in which only the father's relatives are significant. (298)

Matrilineal descent: A kinship system in which only the mother's relatives are significant. (298)

Patriarchy: A society in which men dominate in family decision making. (298)

Matriarchy: A society in which women dominate in family decision making. (299)

Egalitarian family: An authority pattern in which spouses are regarded as equals. (299

Endogamy: The restriction of mate selection to people within the same group. (302)

Exogamy: The requirement that people select a mate outside certain groups. (302)

Homogamy: The conscious or unconscious tendency to select a mate with personal characteristics similar to one's own. (302)

Incest taboo: The prohibition of sexual relationships between certain culturally specified relatives. (302)

Machismo: A sense of virility, personal worth, and pride in one's maleness. (304)

Familism: Pride in the extended family, expressed through the maintenance of close ties and strong obligations to kinfolk outside the immediate family. (304)

Adoption: In a legal sense, a process that allows for the transfer of the legal rights, responsibilities, and privileges of parenthood to a new legal parent or parents. (305)

Single-parent family: A family in which only one parent is present to care for the children. (306)

Cohabitation: The practice of living together as a male-female couple without marrying. (308)

Domestic partnership: Two unrelated adults who share a mutually caring relationship, reside together, and agree to be jointly responsible for their dependents, basic living expenses, and other common necessities. (312)

ANSWERS TO SELF-TEST

Modified True/False Questions

1. By 2000 only about one-third of the nation's families fit the nuclear family model. (295)
2. In polygynous societies, relatively few men actually have multiple spouses. (295)
3. Kinship is culturally learned and is not totally determined by biological or marital ties. (298)
4. Many sociologists believe the egalitarian family has begun to replace the patriarchal family as the social norm in the United States. (299)
5. True (299)
6. True (301)
7. True (302)
8. True (302)
9. True (303)
10. In some cases, adopters are not married and are not required to be married. (306)
11. Approximately 45 percent of all people in the United States will marry, divorce, and then remarry. (307)
12. Women are less likely to remarry than men are, because women most often retain custody of children after a divorce, which complicates establishing a new adult relationship. (307)
13. True (308)
14. True (308)
15. Current data indicate that more people in the United States are postponing entry into first marriages than was true in the past. (310)

Multiple-Choice Questions

1. c (295)
2. c (295)
3. a (295)
4. d (298)
5. c (299)
6. b (300)
7. a (300)
8. a (304)
9. d (305)
10. a (305)
11. a (305)
12. c (306)
13. b (307)
14. c (307)
15. d (308)

Fill-In Questions

1. nuclear (295)
2. polygamy (295)
3. descent (298)
4. eldest (298)
5. Matriarchies (299)
6. egalitarian (299)
7. conflict (299–300)
8. arranged (303)
9. lower (303)
10. universal (305)

11. anticipatory (305)
12. interactionist (306–307)
13. 82; quadrupled (307)
14. stepfamily (307)
15. domestic partners (322)

Understanding Social Policy: Gay Marriage

1. Functionalists have traditionally seen marriage as a social institution that is closely tied to human reproduction. Many same-sex couples are entrusted with the socialization of young children, whether or not their partnership is recognized by the state. Conflict theorists have charged that the denial of the right to marry reinforces the second-class status of gays and lesbians. Interactionists generally avoid the policy questions and focus instead on the nature of same-sex households. (311)

2. Recently, national surveys of attitudes toward gay marriage have been showing volatile shifts in public opinion. Typically, people are more opposed to gay marriage than to civil union: about one-fourth of respondents favor gay marriage, while as many as half favor civil union. Still, as of 2005, the majority of the population endorsed a constitutional amendment to ban gay marriage. (312)

3. In 1999, Vermont gave gay couples the legal benefits of marriage through civil union. Then, in 2003, the Massachusetts Supreme Court ruled 4-3 that under the state's constitution, gay couples have the right to marry—a ruling the Supreme Court has refused to review. Many local jurisdictions have also passed legislation allowing for the registration of domestic partnerships, and have extended employees benefits to those relationships. Recently, pressure has been mounting for national legislation. The Defense of Marriage Act, passed in 1996, provided that no state is obliged to recognize same-sex marriages performed in another state. In 2003, opponents of gay marriage proposed a constitutional amendment that would limit marriage to heterosexual couples. (312)

CHAPTER 15
RELIGION

Durkheim and the Sociological Approach to Religion

World Religions

The Role of Religion
The Integrative Function of Religion
Religion and Social Support
Religion and Social Change
Religion and Social Control: A Conflict View

Religious Behavior
Belief
Ritual
Experience

Religious Organization
Ecclesiae
Denominations
Sects
New Religious Movements or Cults
Comparing Forms of Religious Organization

Case Study: Religion in India
The Religious Tapestry in India
Religion and the State in India

Social Policy and Religion: Religion in the Schools
The Issue
The Setting
Sociological Insights
Policy Initiatives

BOXES
SOCIAL INEQUALITY: *The Stained Glass Ceiling*
RESEARCH IN ACTION: *Islam in the United States*

KEY POINTS

Émile Durkheim: Émile Durkheim was perhaps the first sociologist to recognize the critical importance of religion in human societies. He saw its appeal for the individual, but more importantly, he stressed the social impact of religion. In Durkheim's view, religion is a collective act that includes many forms of behavior in which people interact with others. Durkheim defined **religion** as a "unified system of beliefs and practices relative to sacred things." (319)

The Integrative Function of Religion: Émile Durkheim viewed religion as an integrative power in human society, a perspective that is reflected in functionalist thought today. Religion gives people certain ultimate values and ends to hold in common. In some instances, however, religious loyalties are dysfunctional; that is, they contribute to tension and even conflict between groups or nations. (324)

Religion and Social Support: Through its emphasis on the divine and supernatural, religion allows us to "do something" about the calamities we face. Religion encourages us to view our personal misfortunes as relatively unimportant in the broader perspective of human history, or even as part of an undisclosed divine purpose. This perspective may be much more comforting than the terrifying feeling that any of us can die senselessly at any moment, and that there is no divine answer as to why one person lives a long and full life, whereas another dies tragically at a relatively early age. (325)

Religion and Social Change—The Weberian Thesis: Max Weber carefully examined the connection between religious allegiance and capitalist development in his pioneering work, *The Protestant Ethic and the Spirit of Capitalism*. Weber pointed out that the followers of John Calvin, a leader of the Protestant Reformation, emphasized a disciplined work ethic, this-worldly concerns, and a rational orientation to life that has become known as the **Protestant ethic**. Like Durkheim, Weber demonstrated that religion is not solely a matter of intimate personal beliefs. He stressed that the collective nature of religion has social consequences for society as a whole. (325)

Religion and Social Control—A Conflict View: For Karl Marx, the relationship between religion and social change was clear: religion impeded social change by encouraging oppressed people to focus on otherworldly concerns rather than on their immediate poverty or exploitation. He felt that religion often drugged the masses into submission by offering a consolation for their harsh lives on earth: the hope of salvation in an ideal afterlife. Marxists suggest that by inducing a "false consciousness" among the disadvantaged, religion lessens the possibility of collective political action that can end capitalist oppression and transform society. (326)

Religious Behavior: Religious beliefs, religious rituals, and religious experience all help to define what is sacred, and to differentiate the sacred from the profane. **Religious beliefs** are statements to which members of a particular religion adhere. **Religious rituals** are practices required or expected of members of a faith. The term **religious experience** refers to the feeling or perception of being in direct contact with the ultimate reality, such as a divine being, or of being overcome with religious emotion. (326–328)

Religious Organization: Sociologists find it useful to distinguish among four basic forms of religious organization. An **ecclesia** is a religious organization that claims to include most or all members of a society, and is recognized as the national or official religion. A **denomination** is a large, organized religion that is not officially linked with the state or government. A **sect** can be defined as a relatively small religious group that has broken away from some other religious organization to renew what it considers the original vision of the faith. A **new religious movement** or **cult** is generally a small, secretive religious group that represents either a new religion or a major innovation of an existing faith. (329–332)

Religion in India—A Case Study: Hinduism and Islam are the two most important religions in India. Today, Muslims account for 11 percent of India's population; Hindus make up 83 percent. Another religion, the Sikh faith, originated in the fifteenth century A.D. Sikhism shows the influence of Islam in India, in that it is monotheistic. A fourth faith that has been influential beyond its numbers in India is Jainism. According to the Jain faith, there is no god; each person is responsible for his or her own spiritual well-being. Religion was influential in India's drive to overturn British colonialism. A proponent of nonviolent resistance, Gandhi persuaded Hindus and Muslims, ancient enemies, to join in defying British domination. (333)

Religion in the Schools: The government must protect the right to practice one's religion; on the other hand, it cannot take any measures that would seem to "establish" one religion over another (the separation of church and state). In the key case of *Engle v. Vitale*, the Supreme Court ruled in 1962 that the use of nondenominational prayer in New York schools was "wholly inconsistent" with the First Amendment's prohibition against government establishment of religion. In the "monkey trial" of 1925, a high school biology teacher, John T. Scopes, was convicted of violating a Tennessee law making it a crime to teach the scientific theory of evolution in schools. Drawing on the interactionist perspective and small group research, opponents of school prayer and creationism suggest that children will face enormous social pressure to conform to the beliefs and practices of a religious majority. (334–335)

KEY TERMS

Briefly define or identify the following terms in the spaces provided below. The definitions of these terms can be found later in this chapter of the study guide.

Cultural universal	Religious ritual
Secularization	Religious experience
Religion	Ecclesia
Sacred	Denomination
Profane	Sect
Protestant ethic	Established sect
Liberation theology	New religious movement (NRM) or cult
Religious belief	Creationism

SELF-TEST

MODIFIED TRUE/FALSE QUESTIONS: If the statement below is true, write "true" in the space provided. If the statement is false, briefly correct the error.

1. The same object can be either sacred or profane, depending on how it is viewed.

2. A church service is a meeting ground for unmarried members. This is a manifest function of religions.

3. The "cultural war" taking place in the United States is between Christian fundamentalists, conservative Catholics, and Orthodox Jews.

4. In Max Weber's *The Protestant Ethic and the Spirit of Capitalism,* he noted that in European nations with both Jewish and Protestant citizens, an overwhelming number of business leaders, owners of capital, and skilled workers were Jewish.

5. Karl Marx argued that religion impeded social change by encouraging oppressed people to focus on otherworldly concerns rather than on their immediate poverty or exploitation.

6. For Jews, a very important ritual is the hajj, a pilgrimage to the holy land that every Jew is expected to make at least once in their life.

7. In the modern world, ecclesiae tend to be increasing in power.

8. Denominations resemble sects in that generally few demands are made on members.

9. Because of its immigrant heritage, the United States is home to a large number of denominations.

10. Sects are often short-lived, but those that are able to survive may, over time, become less antagonistic and begin to resemble denominations.

11. Ecclesiae and denominations are much more likely to be at odds with the larger culture than are sects and cults.

12. Different Muslim sects are sometimes antagonistic toward each other.

13. According to one 2005 survey, about 1 million "blogs" have been established in the United States, primarily to address people's views about religion or their personal spiritual experiences.

14. Because of their distinctive dress, Sikhs who live in the United States are often mistaken for Muslims.

15. Although Hindus and Muslims joined to defy British colonization, immediately after independence India was divided into two separate states, Pakistan for the Muslims, and India for the Hindus.

MULTIPLE-CHOICE QUESTIONS: In each of the following, select the phrase that best completes the statement.

1. Which of the following sociologists stressed the social impact of religion, and was perhaps the first to recognize the critical importance of religion in human societies?
    a. Max Weber
    b. Émile Durkheim
    c. Karl Marx
    d. Talcott Parsons

2. Religion defines the spiritual world and gives meaning to the divine. These are _____ functions of religion.
    a. manifest
    b. latent
    c. positive
    d. negative

3. Which sociological perspective emphasizes the integrative power of religion in human society?
    a. functionalist perspective
    b. conflict perspective
    c. interactionist perspective
    d. all of the above

4. A Roman Catholic parish church offers services in the native language of an immigrant community. This is an example of
    a. the integrative function of religion.
    b. the social support function of religion.
    c. the social control function of religion.
    d. none of the above

5. John Calvin, a leader of the Protestant Reformation, emphasized
    a. disciplined work ethic.
    b. this-worldly concerns.
    c. a rational orientation to life.
    d. all of the above

6. In Max Weber's pioneering work, *The Protestant Ethic and the Spirit of Capitalism*, one by-product of Protestantism was
   a. a drive to accumulate savings.
   b. a commitment to serve God without pursuit of tangible items.
   c. a recognition that "God's will" will be understood another time.
   d. none of the above

7. Liberation theology is the use of the Roman Catholic church in a political effort to eliminate poverty, discrimination, and other forms of injustice, especially in
   a. Europe.
   b. East Africa.
   c. Latin America.
   d. Southeast Asia.

8. Which sociological perspective argues that to whatever extent religion actually does influence social behavior, it reinforces existing patterns of dominance and inequality?
   a. functionalist perspective
   b. conflict perspective
   c. interactionist perspective
   d. all of the above

9. The Adam and Eve account of creation found in Genesis, the first book of the Old Testament, is an example of a religious
   a. ritual.
   b. experience.
   c. custom.
   d. belief.

10. Which one of the following religious denominations is most likely to report the experience of being "born again"?
    a. Southern Baptists
    b. Roman Catholics
    c. Episcopalians
    d. Unitarians

11. Which of the following is not an example of an ecclesia?
    a. the Lutheran church in Sweden
    b. Islam in Saudi Arabia
    c. Buddhism in Thailand
    d. the Episcopal church in the United States

12. In a society with a(n) _____, the political and religious institutions often act in harmony and mutually reinforce each other's powers over their relative spheres of influence.
    a. denomination
    b. ecclesia
    c. cult
    d. sect

13. By far the largest single denomination in the United States is
    a. Lutheranism.
    b. Episcopalianism.
    c. Southern Baptists.
    d. Roman Catholicism.

14. Which of the following is an example of a cult?
    a. the Catholic church
    b. the Lutheran church in Sweden
    c. the Unitarian church
    d. Heaven's Gate

15. Which one of the following has a set of doctrines that are innovative and path breaking?
    a. cults
    b. ecclesiae
    c. denominations
    d. sects

FILL-IN QUESTIONS: Fill in the blank spaces in the sentences below with the correct words. Where two or more words are required, there will be a corresponding number of blank spaces.

1. The _____ encompasses elements beyond everyday life that inspire awe, respect, and even fear, as compared to the _____, which includes the ordinary and commonplace.

2. _____ _____ noted that in European nations with both Protestant and Catholic citizens, an overwhelming number of business leaders, owners of capital, and skilled workers were Protestant.

3. Weber pointed out that followers of John Calvin, a leader of the Protestant Reformation, emphasized a disciplined work ethic, this-worldly concerns, and a rational orientation to life that have become known as the _____ _____.

4. _____ theorists caution that Weber's theory of the Protestant ethic, even if it is accepted, should not be regarded as an analysis of mature capitalism as reflected in the rise of large corporations that transcend national boundaries.

5. A possible dysfunction of _____ _____ would be the belief that when Roman Catholics focus on political and governmental injustice, the clergy are no longer addressing their personal and spiritual needs.

6. Because they are _____, most religions tend to reinforce men's dominance in secular as well as spiritual matters.

7. In _____ _____ view, religion impeded social change by encouraging oppressed people to focus on other-worldly concerns rather than on their immediate poverty or exploitation.

8. _____ _____ are statements to which members of a particular religion adhere.

9. _____ are recognized as national churches; _____, although not officially approved by the state, are generally widely respected.

10. The single largest denomination in the United States is _____ _____.

11. Unlike ecclesiae and denominations, _____ require intensive commitments and demonstrations of belief by members.

12. _____ and _____ are much more likely to be at odds with the larger culture than ecclesiae or denominations.

13. Eighty-three percent of India's population practice _____.

14. The "big bang" theory is challenged by _____ who hold to the biblical account of the creation of humans and the universe.

15. The issue of religion in our schools goes to the heart of the _____ Amendment provisions on religious freedoms. The government is required to protect the right to practice one's religion, but it cannot take any measure that would seem to "establish" one religion over another: this is known as the separation of church and state.

UNDERSTANDING SOCIAL POLICY: All of the following questions are based on material that appears in the social policy section on Religion in the Schools. Write a brief answer to each question in the space provided below.

1. What is creationism and why is it a social issue in the United States?

2. What is the "monkey trial"?

3. What do opponents of school prayer and creationism argue?

DEFINITIONS OF KEY TERMS

Cultural universal: A common practice or belief found in every culture. (318)
Secularization: The process through which religion's influence on other social institutions diminishes. (319)
Religion: A unified system of beliefs and practices relative to sacred things. (319)

Sacred: Elements beyond everyday life that inspire awe, respect, and even fear. (319)

Profane: The ordinary and commonplace elements of life, as distinguished from the sacred. (319)

Protestant ethic: Max Weber's term for the disciplined work ethic, this-worldly concerns, and rational orientation to life emphasized by John Calvin and his followers. (325)

Liberation theology: Use of a church, primarily Roman Catholicism, in a political effort to eliminate poverty, discrimination, and other forms of injustice from a secular society. (325)

Religious belief: A statement to which members of a particular religion adhere. (327)

Religious ritual: A practice required or expected of members of a faith. (327)

Religious experience: The feeling or perception of being in direct contact with the ultimate reality, such as a divine being, or of being overcome with religious emotion. (328)

Ecclesia: A religious organization that claims to include most or all members of a society and is recognized as the national or official religion. (329)

Denomination: A large, organized religion that is not officially linked to the state or government. (329)

Sect: A relatively small religious group that has broken away from some other religious organization to renew what it considers the original vision of the faith. (330)

Established sect: A religious group that is the outgrowth of a sect, yet remains isolated from society. (332)

New Religious Movement (NRM) or **cult**: A small, secretive religious group that represents either a new religion or a major innovation of an existing faith. (332)

Creationism: A literal interpretation of the Bible regarding the creation of humanity and the universe, used to argue that evolution should not be presented as established scientific fact. (334)

ANSWERS TO SELF-TEST

Modified True/False Questions

1. True (319)
2. Church services are a meeting ground for unmarried members. This is a latent function of religions. (324)
3. The "cultural war" refers to Christian fundamentalists, conservative Catholics, and Orthodox Jews joining forces in many communities to battle against their liberal counterparts for control of the secular culture. (324)
4. In Max Weber's *The Protestant Ethic and the Spirit of Capitalism*, he noted that in European nations with both Catholic and Protestant citizens an overwhelming number of business leaders, owners of capital, and skilled workers were Protestants. (325)
5. True (326)

6. For Muslims, a very important ritual is the hajj, a pilgrimage to the Grand Mosque in Mecca, Saudi Arabia. Every Muslim who is physically and financially able is expected to make this trip at least once. (328)
7. In the modern world, ecclesiae tend to be declining in power. (329)
8. Denominations resemble ecclesiae in that generally few demands are made on members. (329)
9. True (329)
10. True (332)
11. Sects and cults are much more likely to be at odds with the larger culture than are ecclesiae and denominations. (332)
12. True (331)
13. True (333)
14. True (333)
15. True (333)

Multiple-Choice Questions
1. b (319)
2. a (324)
3. a (324)
4. a (324)
5. d (325)
6. a (325)
7. c (325)
8. b (326)
9. d (327)
10. a (328)
11. d (329)
12. b (329)
13. d (330)
14. d (332)
15. a (332)

Fill-In Questions
1. sacred; profane (319)
2. Max Weber (325)
3. Protestant ethic (325)
4. Conflict (325)
5. liberation theology (325)
6. patriarchal (326)
7. Karl Marx's (326)
8. Religious beliefs (327)
9. Ecclesiae; denominations (329)
10. Roman Catholicism (330)
11. sects (330)
12. Sects; NRMs (332)
13. Hinduism (333)
14. creationists (334)
15. First (334–335)

Understanding Social Policy: Religion in the Schools
1. Creationism is a viewpoint regarding the creation of humans and the universe, used to argue that evolution should not be presented as established scientific fact. Creationists want their theory taught in schools as the only one, or at the very least, as an alternative to the theory of evolution. (334)
2. The controversy over whether the biblical account of creation should be presented in school curricula recalls the famous "monkey trial" of 1925. In that trial, high school

biology teacher John T. Scopes was convicted of violating a Tennessee law making it a crime to teach the scientific theory of evolution in public schools. (335)

3. Opponents of school prayer and creationism argue that a religious majority in a community might impose religious viewpoints specific to its faith, at the expense of religious minorities. (335)

CHAPTER 16
EDUCATION

Sociological Perspectives on Education
    Functionalist View
    Conflict View
    Interactionist View

Schools as Formal Organizations
    Bureaucratization of Schools
    Teachers: Employees and Instructors
    Student Subcultures
    Homeschooling

Social Policy and Religion: No Child Left Behind Program
    The Issue
    The Setting
    Sociological Insights
    Policy Initiatives

BOXES
TAKING SOCIOLOGY TO WORK: Ray Zapata, Business Owner and Former Regent, Texas State University
SOCIOLOGY ON CAMPUS: The Debate over Title IX
RESEARCH IN ACTION: Violence in the Schools

KEY POINTS

Transmitting Culture: As a social institution, education performs a rather conservative function; transmitting the dominant culture. Schooling exposes each generation of young people to the existing beliefs, norms, and values of their culture. In our society, we learn respect for social control and reverence for established institutions such as religion, the family, and the presidency. (341)

Promoting Social and Political Integration: Education serves the latent function of promoting social and political integration by transforming a population composed of diverse racial, ethnic, and religious groups into a society whose members share—to some extent—a common identity. From a functionalist perspective, the common identity and social integration fostered by education contribute to societal stability and consensus. In the past, the integrative function of education was most obvious in its emphasis on promoting a common language. (342)

Maintaining Social Control: Through the exercise of social control, schools teach students various skills and values essential to their future positions in the labor force. Schools direct and even restrict students' aspirations in a manner that reflects societal values and prejudices. Socialization into traditional gender roles can be viewed as a form of social control. (342)

Conflict View of Schooling: The functionalist perspective portrays contemporary education as a basically benign institution. For example, it argues that schools rationally sort and select students for future high-status positions, thereby meeting society's need for talented and expert personnel. In contrast, the conflict perspective views education as an instrument of elite domination. Conflict theorists point out the sharp inequalities that exist in the educational opportunities available to different racial and ethnic groups. (343)

Bestowal of Status: Conflict sociologists stress that schools sort pupils according to social class background. Although the educational system helps certain poor children to move into middle-class professional positions, it denies most disadvantaged children the same educational opportunities afforded to children of the affluent. In this way, schools tend to preserve social class inequalities in each new generation. Even a single school can reinforce class differences by putting students in tracks. Thus, working-class children, whom many assume are destined for subordinate positions, are likely to be placed in high school vocational and general tracks, which emphasize close supervision and compliance with authority. (344–345)

Treatment of Women in Education: In the twentieth century, sexism in education showed up in many ways; in textbooks with negative stereotypes of women, counselors' pressure on female students to prepare for "women's work," and unequal funding for women's and men's athletic programs. But perhaps nowhere has educational discrimination been more evident than in the employment of teachers. Men generally fill the positions of university professor and college administrator, which hold relatively high status in the United States. (345)

Education—The Interactionist View: The labeling approach suggests that if we treat people in particular ways, they may fulfill our expectations. A dominant group's stereotyping of racial minorities may limit their opportunities to break away from expected roles. Studies in the United States have revealed that teachers wait longer for an answer from a student they believe to be a high achiever, and they are more likely to give such children a second chance. (346–347)

Schools as Formal Organizations: Max Weber noted five basic characteristics of bureaucracy, all of which are evident in the vast majority of schools. (1) A division of labor: Specialized experts teach particular age levels and specific subjects. (2) Hierarchy of authority: Each employee of a school system is responsible to a higher authority. (3) Written rules and regulations: Teachers and administrators must conform to numerous rules and regulations in the performance of their duties. (4) Impersonality: Large class sizes and bureaucratic norms encourage teachers to treat all students in the same way. (5) Employment based on technical qualifications: At least in theory, the hiring of instructors is based on professional competence and expertise. (347)

No Child Left Behind Program: In 2001, Congress voted to approve the No Child Left Behind Act, and initiative designed to improve the performance of public schools in the United States, proposed by President George W. Bush. The NCLB Act increased federal standards of accountability for states, school districts, and schools, and gave parents more flexibility in choosing which schools their children would attend. The NCLB Act has created a national debate about how best to offer high-quality schooling to all children. From a functionalist point of view, the development of common curricular objectives promotes social integration. Conflict theorists support the need to educate all students, regardless of their socioeconomic status, but they question the wisdom of pursuing that goal through testing programs like those involved in the NCLB Act. (351–352)

KEY TERMS

Briefly define or identify the following terms in the spaces provided below. The definitions of these terms can be found later in this chapter of the study guide.

Education	Hidden curriculum

Credentialism	Correspondence principle
Tracking	Teacher-expectancy effect

SELF-TEST

MODIFIED TRUE/FALSE QUESTIONS: If the statement below is true, write "true" in the space provided. If the statement is false, briefly correct the error.

1. Jonathan Kozol found that whereas White students in affluent suburban towns enjoyed state-of-the-art science labs, superb music and art programs and elaborate athletic facilities, inner-city children were crowded into antiquated, decrepit buildings, deprived of even the most basic requirements like textbooks, classrooms, computers and counselors.

2. Through the exercise of social control, schools teach students various skills and values essential to their future positions within the labor force. They learn punctuality, discipline, scheduling, and responsible work habits, as well as how to negotiate their way through the complexities of a bureaucratic organization.

3. Numerous sociological studies have revealed that increased years of formal schooling are associated with openness to new ideas and more liberal social and political viewpoints.

4. According to the "hidden curriculum" of schools, students are expected to concentrate on their own work rather than assist other students who learn more slowly.

5. The hidden curriculum is a unique characteristic of schools in the United States, which is fostered by the bureaucratic structure of that institution.

6. Upgrading credentials serves the self-interest of the two groups most responsible for this trend: the government and the upper class.

7. As early as 1916, Karl Marx had already anticipated the phenomenon of credentialism.

8. It has been estimated that about 2 percent of elementary schools in the United States, and 3 percent of secondary schools, use some form of tracking.

9. In the view of conflict theorists, the educational inequalities resulting from tracking are designed to meet the needs of modern capitalist society.

10. According to the correspondence principle, schools promote the values of the White middle class to further the process of cultural assimilation.

11. In 1833, Oberlin College became the first institution of higher learning in the United States to admit female students.

12. The labeling approach suggests that if we treat people in a particular way, they may fulfill our expectations.

13. Female participation in high school sports has doubled since Title IX was implemented.

14. Teachers are employees of formal organizations with bureaucratic structure.

15. Schools provide for students' social and recreational needs, thereby fulfilling a manifest function of education.

MULTIPLE-CHOICE QUESTIONS: In each of the following, select the phrase that best completes the statement.

1. The most basic manifest function of education is
    a. transmitting culture.
    b. transmitting knowledge.
    c. serving as an agent of change.
    d. maintaining social control.

2. Which one of the following is a manifest function of education?
    a. bestowing status
    b. transmitting culture
    c. promoting social and political change
    d. all of the above

3. In 1996, Great Britain's chief curriculum adviser proposed that British schools socialize students into a set of core values that included
    a. a sense of fair play.
    b. politeness.
    c. faithfulness.
    d. all of the above

4. Which sociological perspective emphasizes that the common identity and social integration fostered by education contribute to overall societal stability and consensus?
    a. the functionalist perspective
    b. the conflict perspective
    c. the interactionist perspective
    d. labeling theory

5. Which one of the following was introduced into school systems to promote social change?
    a. sex education classes
    b. affirmative action programs
    c. Project Head Start
    d. all of the above

6. Who developed the concept of the hidden curriculum?
    a. Max Weber
    b. Philip Jackson
    c. Christopher Hurn
    d. Émile Durkheim

7. The trend toward credentialism was anticipated as far back as 1916 by
    a. Émile Durkheim.
    b. Max Weber.
    c. Karl Marx.
    d. Charles Horton Cooley.

8. Which sociological perspective emphasizes that the widening bestowal of status granted by the educational system is beneficial not only to particular recipients but to the society as a whole?
    a. the functionalist perspective
    b. the conflict perspective
    c. the interactionist perspective
    d. labeling approach

9. Which perspective contends that schools tend to preserve social class inequalities in each new generation?
   a. the functionalist perspective
   b. the conflict perspective
   c. the interactionist perspective
   d. anomie theory

10. Most recent research on ability grouping raises questions about its
    a. effectiveness, especially for lower-achieving students.
    b. failure to improve the prospects of higher-achieving students.
    c. ability to improve the prospects of lower- and higher-achieving students.
    d. both a and b

11. The correspondence principle was developed by
    a. Max Weber.
    b. Karl Marx and Friedrich Engels.
    c. Samuel Bowles and Herbert Gintis.
    d. James Thurber.

12. The teacher-expectancy effect is most closely associated with
    a. the functionalist perspective.
    b. the conflict perspective.
    c. the interactionist perspective.
    d. anomie theory.

13. Which of the following is not required by Title IX legislation?
    a. Require all-male athletic teams to accept women.
    b. Eliminate sex-segregated classes.
    c. Provide more opportunities for women to play sports.
    d. End sex discrimination in admissions and financial aid.

14. Which of the following statements about school violence is true?
    a. A child has only a one in 1,000 chance of being killed at school.
    b. School-associated violent deaths increased every year from 1992 through 2000.
    c. Forty-seven percent of violent deaths of school-aged children in 1992–1999 occurred outside school grounds.
    d. Fewer students are now being found with guns in school.

15. The student subculture that is hostile to the college environment and seeks out ideas that may or may not relate to studies is called the
    a. collegiate subculture.
    b. academic subculture.
    c. vocational subculture.
    d. nonconformist subculture.

FILL-IN QUESTIONS: Fill in the blank spaces in the sentences below with the correct words. Where two or more words are required, there will be a corresponding number of blank spaces.

1. Schools provide a variety of _____ functions, such as transmitting culture, promoting social and political integration, and maintaining social control.

2. The _____ perspective stresses the importance of education in transmitting culture, maintaining social control, and promoting social change.

3. From a _____ perspective, the common identity and social integration fostered by education contributes to societal stability and consensus.

4. In the past, the integrative function of education was most obvious through its emphasis on promoting a common _____.

5. _____ _____ in admissions—giving priority to females or minorities—has been endorsed as a means of countering racial and sexual discrimination.

6. Numerous sociological studies have revealed that _____ years of formal schooling are associated with openness to new ideas and more _____ social and political viewpoints.

7. Sociologist _____ _____ points out that better-educated people tend to have greater access to information, more diverse opinions, and the ability to make subtle distinctions in analysis.

8. According to the _____ curriculum, children must not speak until the teacher calls on them, and must regulate their activities according to the clock or bell.

9. _____ theorists have observed that credentialism may reinforce social inequality and may be especially damaging for applicants from poor and minority backgrounds.

10. In the twentieth century, _____ in education has been manifested in many ways: in textbooks with negative stereotypes of women, counselors' pressure on female students to prepare for "women's work," and unequal funding for women's and men's athletic programs.

11. Women's education tends to suffer in those cultures with traditional _____ _____.

12. The _____ of schools in the United States has resulted not only from the growing number of students being served by individual schools and school systems, but also from the greater degree of specialization required within a technologically complex society.

13. The bureaucratic characteristic of written rules and regulations can become _____ in schools, since the time invested in completing required forms could instead be spent in preparing lessons or conferring with students.

14. The _____ subculture identifies with the intellectual concerns of the faculty and values knowledge for its own sake.

15. _____ and _____ are major issues in constructing any test, but rarely are they totally resolved.

UNDERSTANDING SOCIAL POLICY: All of the following questions are based on material that appears in the social policy section on the No Child Left Behind Program. Write a brief answer to each question in the space provided below.

1. What is the No Child Left Behind Act?

2. What are some of the common criticisms of the No Child Left Behind Act?

3. How are the concepts of validity and reliability relevant to school testing programs, such as those mandated by the No Child Left Behind program?

DEFINITIONS OF KEY TERMS

Education: A formal process of learning in which some people consciously teach while others adopt the social role of learner. (341)

Hidden curriculum: Standards of behavior that are deemed proper by society and are taught subtly in schools. (344)

Credentialism: An increase in the lowest level of education required to enter a field. (344)

Tracking: The practice of placing students in specific curriculum groups on the basis of their test scores and other criteria. (345)

Correspondence principle: The tendency of schools to promote the values expected of individuals in each social class and to prepare students for the types of jobs typically held by members of their class. (345)

Teacher-expectancy effect: The impact that a teacher's expectations about a student's performance may have on the student's actual achievements. (346)

ANSWERS TO SELF-TEST

Modified True/False Questions
1. True (340)
2. True (342)
3. True (343)
4. True (344)
5. A hidden curriculum is evident in schools around the world. (344)
6. Upgrading credentials serves the self-interest of the two groups most responsible for this trend: educational institutions and current jobholders. (344)
7. As early as 1916, Max Weber had already anticipated the phenomenon of credentialism. (344)
8. It has been estimated that about 60 percent of elementary schools in the United States, and 80 percent of secondary schools, use some form of tracking. (345)
9. True (345)
10. According to the correspondence principle, schools promote the values expected of individuals in each class, and perpetuate social class divisions from one generation to the next. (345)

238 | Sociology

11. True (345)
12. True (346)
13. In 1971—just before Title IX was implemented—only 300,000 girls participated in high school sports. In 2003, the figure was 2.7 million. (346)
14. True (348)
15. Schools provide for students' social and recreational needs, thereby fulfilling a latent function of education. (348)

Multiple-Choice Questions

1. b (341)
2. a (341)
3. d (341–342)
4. a (342)
5. d (343)
6. b (344)
7. b (344)
8. a (344)
9. b (345)
10. a (345)
11. c (345)
12. c (346)
13. a (346)
14. d (346)
15. d (350)

Fill-In Questions

1. latent (341)
2. functionalist (341)
3. functionalist (342)
4. language (342)
5. Affirmative action (343)
6. increased; liberal (343)
7. Robin Williams (343)
8. hidden (344)
9. Conflict (344)
10. sexism (345)
11. gender roles (345)
12. bureaucratization (347)
13. dysfunctional (347)
14. academic (350)
15. validity; reliability (352)

Understanding Social Policy: No Child Left Behind Program

1. No Child Left Behind Act, and initiative designed to improve the performance of public schools in the United States, proposed by President George W. Bush. The NCLB Act increased federal standards of accountability for states, school districts, and schools, and gave parents more flexibility in choosing which schools their children would attend. In addition, states are now required to conduct annual assessments of all public school students, with penalties for those that fail to meet them. (351)

2. Some critics charge that the program has no substance—that the required testing is just academic exercise. Others charge that it overemphasizes reading and math at the expense of other subjects, such as art, music, and social studies. Finally, state and local educators have complained bitterly about federal intrusion in local schools. (351)

3. Reliability and validity are major issues in constructing any test; rarely are these concerns totally resolved. Scholars who design standardized tests are constantly tweaking the questions to improve the tests' reliability and validity. From preschool

to graduate and professional programs, the reliability and validity of tests affects everything from the allocation of funds to admissions decisions in highly competitive programs. With high-stakes testing—testing that determines whether a public school closes or remains open, for instance—these issues become even more important. (352)

CHAPTER 17
GOVERNMENT AND POLITICS

Power and Authority
   Power
   Types of Authority

Types of Government
   Monarchy
   Oligarchy
   Dictatorship and Totalitarianism
   Democracy

Political Behavior in the United States
   Participation and Apathy
   Women in Politics

Models of Power Structure in the United States
   Power Elite Models
   Pluralist Model

War and Peace
   War
   Peace
   Terrorism

Political Activism

Social Policy and the Government: Campaign Financing
   The Issue
   The Setting
   Sociological Insights
   Policy Initiatives

BOXES
   RESEARCH IN ACTION: *Why Don't More Young People Vote?*
   SOCIAL INEQUALITY: *Gender Quotas at the Box*

KEY POINTS

The Political System: By **political system**, sociologists mean the social institution that is founded on a recognized set of procedures for implementing and achieving society's goals. Like religion and the family, the political system is a cultural universal: It is found in every society. (356)

Power: Power lies at the heart of a political system. Max Weber defined **power** as the ability to exercise one's will over others. Power relations can involve large organizations, small groups, or even people in an intimate association. There are three basic sources of power within any political system: force, influence, and authority. (357)

Types of Authority: Max Weber identified three ideal types of authority. In a political system based on **traditional authority**, legitimate power is conferred by custom and accepted practice. Authority does not rest in personal characteristics, technical competence, or even written law. Power made legitimate by law is known as **rational-legal authority**. Leaders derive their rational-legal authority from the written rules and regulations of political systems. The term **charismatic authority** refers to power made legitimate by a leader's exceptional personal or emotional appeal to his or her followers. Charisma lets a person lead or inspire without relying on set rules or traditions. (358)

Types of Government: There are five basic types of government. A **monarchy** is a form of government headed by a single member of a royal family, usually a king, queen, or some other hereditary ruler. An **oligarchy** is a form of government in which a few individuals rule. A **dictatorship** is a government in which one person has nearly total power to make and enforce laws. Frequently, dictators develop such overwhelming control over people's lives that their governments are called **totalitarian**. **Democracy** means government by the people. The United States is commonly classified as a **representative democracy**, since the elected members of Congress and state legislators make our laws. (358–359)

Women in Politics: Women continue to be dramatically underrepresented in the halls of government. As of mid-2005, there were only 80 women in Congress; they accounted for 66 of the 435 members of the House of Representatives and 14 of the 100 members of the Senate. Only 8 states had female governors. A new dimension of women and politics emerged beginning in the 1980s. Surveys detected a growing "gender gap" in the political preferences and activities of males and females. (360–361)

Elite and Pluralist Models of Power Relations: Who really holds power in the United States? Like others who hold an **elite model** of power relations, Karl Marx believed that society is ruled by a small group of individuals who share a common set of political and economic interests. Sociologist C. Wright Mills argued that power rested in the hands of a few, both inside and outside government—the **power elite**. Sociologist G. William Domhoff stresses the role played both by elites of the corporate community and by the leaders of policy-formation organizations, such as chambers of commerce and labor unions. Critics of the elite model of power relations insist that power is shared more widely than Marx, Mills, and Domhoff indicate. In their view, a **pluralist model** more accurately describes the nation's political system. In a pluralist model, many competing groups within the community have access to government so that no single group is dominant. (361–363)

War, Peace, and Terrorism: Conflict is a central aspect of social relations. Too often it becomes ongoing and violent, engulfing innocent bystanders as well as intentional participants. **War** is defined as conflict between organizations that possess trained combat forces equipped with deadly weapons. Sociologists have considered **peace** both as the absence of war and as a proactive effort to develop cooperative relations among nations. Sociologists and other social scientists who draw on sociological theory and research have tried to identify conditions that deter war. **Terrorism** is the use or threat of violence against random or symbolic targets in pursuit of political aims. (365–366)

Campaign Financing: The Federal Campaign Act of 1974 placed restrictions on so-called hard money, or donations made to specific candidates for national office. But soon after passage of the act, contributors and politicians found loopholes in the new law. In 2002, for the first time limitations were placed on contributions of soft money. Functionalists would say that political contributions keep the public involved in the democratic process and connected to the candidates. Conflict theorists would counter that since money brings influence, this use of material wealth allows donors to influence government policy makers in ways that tend to preserve their own wealth. Interactionists would point out the symbolic significance of the public perception that big money drives elections in the United States. Accurate or not, this impression encourages voter apathy, which is reflected in low turnout at the polls. (368–369)

KEY TERMS

Briefly define or identify the following terms in the spaces provided below. The definitions of these terms can be found later in this chapter of the study guide.

Political system	Power
Politics	Force

Influence	Democracy
Authority	Representative democracy
Traditional authority	Elite model
Rational-legal authority	Power elite
Charismatic authority	Pluralist model
Monarchy	War
Oligarchy	Peace
Dictatorship	Terrorism
Totalitarianism	Representative democracy

SELF-TEST

MODIFIED TRUE/FALSE QUESTIONS: If the statement below is true, write "true" in the space provided. If the statement is false, briefly correct the error.

1. There are four basic sources of power within any political system: force, influence, coercion, and authority.

2. Max Weber developed a classification system regarding authority in which he distinguished among rational, traditional-legal, and charismatic types of authority.

3. In societies based on rational-legal authority, legitimate power is conferred by custom and accepted practice.

4. Observing from an interactionist perspective, sociologist Carl Couch points out that the growth of the electronic media has facilitated the development of rational authority.

5. Political apathy and low voter turnout are unique to the political process in the United States.

6. In the United States, voter turnout has been particularly high among younger adults.

7. With respect to the "gender gap" in political preferences, women are more likely to register as Democrats than as Republicans.

8. Karl Marx believed that society is ruled by a small group of individuals who share a common set of political and economic interests.

9. The power elite model developed by C. Wright Mills is, in many respects, similar to the work of Max Weber.

10. Ratified in 1950, the 26th Amendment to the Constitution lowered the voting age from 21 to 18.

11. Sociologist G. William Domhoff argued that the United States is controlled by a powerful elite, that is largely White, male, and upper class.

12. Robert Dahl's study lends support to the power elite model of social power.

13. One critique of the pluralist model focuses on the possible power of elites to keep certain matters out of the realm of government debate.

14. While terrorists may wish to keep secret their individual identities, they want their political messages and goals to receive as much publicity as possible.

15. The Internet has led to the development of borderless political organizations that unite people of a like mind from around the world.

MULTIPLE-CHOICE QUESTIONS: In each of the following, select the phrase that best completes the statement.

1. Which one of the following is a cultural universal?
   a. religion
   b. the political system
   c. family
   d. all of the above

2. There are three basic sources of power within any political system:
   a. force, influence, and authority.
   b. force, influence, and democracy.
   c. force, legitimacy, and charisma.
   d. influence, charisma, and bureaucracy.

3. Which of the following is not part of the classification system of authority that was developed by Max Weber?
   a. traditional authority
   b. pluralist authority
   c. legal-rational authority
   d. charismatic authority

4. A king or queen is accepted as ruler of a nation simply by virtue of inheriting the crown. This is an example of
   a. totalitarianism.
   b. charismatic authority.
   c. traditional authority.
   d. rational-legal authority.

5. The authority of Congress and that of the president of the United States are legitimized by the Constitution. This is an example of
   a. political efficacy.
   b. charismatic authority.
   c. traditional authority.
   d. rational-legal authority.

6. Which of the following can be classified as a charismatic leader?
   a. Joan of Arc
   b. Malcolm X
   c. Adolf Hitler
   d. all of the above

7. Totalitarian states typically control which of the following institutions?
   a. family
   b. economy
   c. politics
   d. all of the above

8. The U.S. government can best be described as a(n):
   a. oligarchy.
   b. dictatorship.
   c. democracy.
   d. representative democracy.

9. Almost _____ percent of eligible voters in the United States went to the polls in the presidential election of 1896 as compared to less than _____ percent in the 2000 election.
   a. 75; 25
   b. 80; 51
   c. 15; 10
   d. 73; 70

10. Which nation has witnessed a significant decline in voter turnout in recent elections?
    a. Japan
    b. Great Britain
    c. the United States
    d. all of the above

11. In what way does media coverage of male and female politicians differ?
    a. Male reporters give more coverage of male candidates.
    b. Reporters pay special attention to the voting records of female candidates.
    c. Reporters write more about the personal life, appearance, or personality of a female candidate than about those of a male candidate's.
    d. Reporters are more reluctant to ask female candidates about financial issues.

12. A new dimension of women and politics emerged beginning in the 1980s. Surveys detected that women were more likely to register as Democrats than as Republicans and were also more critical of the Reagan and Bush administrations. This is known as a
    a. gender gap.
    b. glass ceiling.
    c. plastic floor.
    d. gender apathy quotient.

13. In C. Wright Mills's power elite framework, which one of the following is not at the top of the power structure in the United States?
    a. the corporate rich
    b. leaders of the executive branch of government
    c. heads of the military
    d. members of the Supreme Court and legislative leaders

14. G. William Domhoff's model is an example of
    a. an elite theory of power.
    b. a pluralist theory of power.
    c. a functionalist theory of power.
    d. an interactionist theory of power.

15. Which of the following social scientists is associated with the pluralist model of power relations?
    a. Robert Dahl
    b. C. Wright Mills
    c. G. William Domhoff
    d. Max Weber

FILL-IN QUESTIONS: Fill in the blank spaces in the sentences below with the correct words. Where two or more words are required, there will be a corresponding number of blank spaces.

1. _____ is the actual or threatened use of coercion to impose one's will on others.

2. Joan of Arc, Mahatma Gandhi, Malcolm X, and Martin Luther King are all examples of _____ leaders.

3. Observing from an interactionist perspective, sociologist Carl Couch points out that the growth of the electronic media has facilitated the development of _____ authority.

4. In most of today's _____, kings and queens have little practical power.

5. The elite model of political power implies that the U.S. has a(n) _____ as its form of government.

250 | Sociology

6. Studies reveal that only _____ percent of the people in the United States belong to a political club or organization.

7. _____ has been the most serious barrier to women interested in holding office.

8. A new dimension of women and politics emerged beginning in the 1980s. Surveys detected a growing "_____ _____" in the political preferences and activities of males and females. Women were more likely than men to register as Democrats than as Republicans.

9. G. William Domhoff noted that in the electoral arena two different coalitions have exercised influence. One of these coalitions, the _____-_____ coalition, is based in unions, local government organizations, some minority group communities, liberal churches, and the university and arts communities.

10. Robert Dahl argued for the _____ model of power.

11. Advocates of the _____ model suggest that conflicting groups within the community have access to government so that no single group is dominant.

12. _____ is the use or threat of violence against random or symbolic targets in pursuit of political aims.

13. _____ refers to the use of the Internet for political purposes.

14. The Bipartisan Campaign Reform Act, passed in 2002, placed limitations on contributions of _____ _____ in political campaigns.

15. _____ theorists are concerned that wealthy campaign donors can influence government policymakers in ways that tend to preserve that wealth.

UNDERSTANDING SOCIAL POLICY: All of the following questions are based on material that appears in the social policy section on Campaign Financing. Write a brief answer to each question in the space provided below.

1. What were the provisions of the Federal Campaign Act of 1974?

2. What is the functionalist view of campaign financing?

3. What is the conflict view of campaign financing?

4. What is the position of national reform groups about campaign financing?

DEFINITIONS OF KEY TERMS

Political system: The social institution that is founded on a recognized set of procedures for implementing and achieving society's goals. (356)

Politics: In Harold Lasswell's words, "who gets what, when, and how." (357)

Power: The ability to exercise one's will over others. (357)

Force: The actual or threatened use of coercion to impose one's will on others. (357)

Influence: The exercise of power through a process of persuasion. (357)

Authority: Institutionalized power that is recognized by the people over whom it is exercised. (357)

Traditional authority: Legitimate power conferred by custom and accepted practice. (358)

Rational-legal authority: Power made legitimate by law. (358)

Charismatic authority: Power made legitimate by a leader's exceptional personal or emotional appeal to his or her followers. (358)

Monarchy: A form of government headed by a single member of a royal family, usually a king, queen, or some other hereditary ruler. (358)

Oligarchy: A form of government in which a few individuals rule. (358)

Dictatorship: A government in which one person has nearly total power to make and enforce laws. (359)

Totalitarianism Virtually complete government control and surveillance over all aspects of a society's social and political life. (359)

Democracy: In a literal sense, government by the people. (359)

Representative democracy: A form of government in which certain individuals are selected to speak for the people. (359)

Elite model: A view of society as being ruled by a small group of individuals who share a common set of political and economic interests. (361)

Power elite: A small group of military, industrial, and government leaders who control the fate of the United States. (361)

Pluralist model: A view of society in which many competing groups within the community have access to government, so that no single group is dominant. (363)

War: Conflict between organizations that possess trained combat forces equipped with deadly weapons. (365)

Peace: The absence of war, or more broadly, a proactive effort to develop cooperative relations among nations. (365)

Terrorism: The use or threat of violence against random or symbolic targets in pursuit of political aims. (366)

ANSWERS TO SELF-TEST

Modified True/False Questions

1. There are three basic sources of power within any political system: force, influence, and authority. (357)
2. Max Weber developed a classification system regarding authority in which he distinguished among traditional, rational-legal, and charismatic types of authority. (358)
3. In societies based on traditional authority, legitimate power is conferred by custom and accepted practice. (358)
4. Observing from an interactionist perspective, sociologist Carl Couch points out that the growth of the electronic media has facilitated the development of charismatic authority. (358)
5. While a few nations still command high voter turnout, it is increasingly common to hear national leaders of other countries complain of voter apathy. (360)
6. In the United States, voter turnout has been particularly low among younger adults. (360)
7. True (361)
8. True (361)
9. The power elite model developed by C. Wright Mills is, in many respects, similar to the work of Karl Marx. (361)
10. Ratified in 1971, the 26th Amendment to the Constitution lowered the voting age from 21 to 18. (362)
11. True (363)
12. Robert Dahl's study lends support to the pluralist model of social power. (363)
13. True (363)
14. True (366–367)
15. True (368)

Multiple-Choice Questions

1. d (356)
2. a (357)
3. b (358)
4. c (358)
5. d (358)
6. d (358)
7. d (359)
8. d (359)
9. b (360)
10. d (360)
11. c (360)
12. a (361)
13. d (361)
14. a (363)
15. a (363)

Fill-In Questions

1. Force (357)
2. Charismatic (358)
3. charismatic (358)
4. monarchies (358)
5. oligarchy (359)
6. 8 (360)
7. Sexism (360)
8. gender gap (361)
9. liberal-labor (363)
10. pluralist (363)
11. pluralist (363)
12. Terrorism (366)
13. Cyberactivism (368)
14. soft money (368)
15. Conflict (369)

Understanding Social Policy: Campaign Financing

1. The Federal Campaign Act of 1974 placed restrictions on so-called hard money or donations made to specific candidates for national office. Hard money is now limited to $10,000 per organization or $2,000 per individual donor per election cycle. These limits were intended to keep national candidates or elected officials from being "bought" by the wealthy or by powerful special interest groups. (368)

2. Functionalists would say that political contributions keep the public involved in the democratic process and connected to the candidates. Issue advocacy money also offers voters a way to express their views on issues directly, rather than through the candidates. (369)

3. Conflict theorists note that since money brings influence, campaign contributions allow donors to influence government policymakers in ways that tend to preserve their own wealth. (369)

4. On the national level, traditional reform groups—Common Cause, the League of Women Voters, and Ralph Nader's organization, Public Citizen—continue to call for tighter limits on contributions by both individuals and organizations. But other interest groups, including the American Civil Liberties Union and the Cato Institute, claim that limiting anyone's involvement in the political process is unfair. (369)

CHAPTER 18: THE ECONOMY AND WORK

Economic Systems
- Capitalism
- Socialism
- The Informal Economy

Case Study: Capitalism in China
- The Road to Capitalism
- The Chinese Economy Today
- Chinese Workers in the New Economy

Work and Alienation
- Marx's View
- Worker Satisfaction

The Changing Economy
- The Changing Face of the Workforce
- Deindustrialization

Social Policy and the Economy: Global Offshoring
- The Issue
- The Setting
- Sociological Insights
- Policy Initiatives

BOXES
- **TAKING SOCIOLOGY TO WORK**: Richard J. Hawk, Vice President and Financial Consultant, Smith Barney
- **SOCIOLOGY IN THE GLOBAL COMMUNITY**: Working Women in Nepal
- **SOCIAL INEQUALITY**: Affirmative Action

KEY POINTS

The Economic System: The term **economic system** refers to the social institution through which goods and services are produced, distributed, and consumed. As with social institutions such as the family, religion, and government, the economic system shapes other aspects of the social order and is in turn influenced by them. (374)

Capitalism: **Capitalism** is an economic system in which the means of production are held largely in private hands, and the main incentive for economic activity is the accumulation of profit. In practice, capitalist systems vary in the degree to which the government regulates private ownership and economic activity. Contemporary capitalism features government regulation of economic relations and tolerance of monopolistic practices. (375–376)

Socialism: Socialist theory was refined in the writings of Karl Marx and Friedrich Engels. Under **socialism**, the means of production and distribution in a society are collectively, rather than privately owned. The basic objective of the economic system is to meet people's needs rather than to maximize profits. In theory, the wealth of the people as a collectivity is used to provide health care, housing, education, and other key services to each individual and family. Marx believed that each socialist state would eventually "wither away" and evolve into a communist state. As an ideal type, **communism** refers to an economic system under which all property is communally owned and no social distinctions are made based on people's ability to produce. (377)

Capitalism in China: When the communists assumed leadership of China in 1949, they cast themselves as the champions of workers and peasants, and the enemies of those who exploited them; namely landlords and capitalists. Profit making was outlawed, and by the 1960s, China was dominated by huge state-controlled enterprises. But the centralization of production did not work well economically. In the 1980s, the government eased restrictions against private enterprise somewhat, permitting the creation of small businesses. By the mid-1990s, party officials had begun to hand some ailing state-controlled businesses to over to private enterprises. The transition from an economy dominated by state-owned companies to one in which private firms can flourish has been surprisingly rapid. (378–380)

Work and Alienation: Émile Durkheim argued that as labor becomes more and more differentiated, individuals experience anomie, or loss of direction. Marx believed that as the process of industrialization advanced, workers were robbed of any meaningful relationship with their work. For Marx, the specialization of tasks contributed to a growing sense of alienation among industrial workers. The term **alienation** refers to the situation of being estranged or disassociated from the surrounding society. In his view, a deep cause of alienation was the powerlessness of workers in capitalist economic systems. Workers had no control over their occupational tasks, the products of their labor, or the distribution of profits. (381)

The Changing Face of the Workforce: The number of Black, Latino, and Asian American workers continues to increase at a rate faster than the number of White workers. Increasingly, the workforce reflects the diversity of the population. This is due to ethnic minorities entering the labor force, and immigrants and their children moving from marginal jobs or employment in the informal economy, to positions of greater visibility and responsibility. Interactionists note that people will find themselves supervising and being supervised by people very different from themselves. (383)

Deindustrialization and Downsizing: The term **deindustrialization** refers to the systematic, widespread withdrawal of investment in basic aspects of productivity such as factories and plants. Some companies relocate from northeastern and midwestern states to southern states, while others relocate outside the United States to countries with lower rates of prevailing wages. The term **downsizing** was introduced in 1987 to refer to reductions taken in a company's workforce as part of deindustrialization. Viewed from a conflict perspective, the unprecedented attention given to downsizing in the mid-1990s reflected the continuing importance of social class in the United States. Conflict theorists note that job loss among workers has long been a feature of deindustrialization. But when large numbers of middle-class managers and other white-collar employees with substantial incomes began to be laid off, suddenly there was great concern in the media over downsizing. (383–385)

Global Offshoring: U.S. firms have been outsourcing certain types of work for generations. The new trend toward offshoring carries this practice one step further, by transferring new types of work to foreign countries. Office and professional jobs are being exported, too, thanks to advanced telecommunications and the growth of skilled, English-speaking labor forces in developing nations with relatively low wage scales. Because offshoring, and outsourcing in general, tend to improve the efficiency of business operations, they can be viewed as functional to society. Conflict theorists question whether this aspect of globalization furthers global inequality. (385–386)

KEY TERMS

Briefly define or identify the following terms in the spaces provided below. The definitions of these terms can be found later in this chapter of the study guide.

Economic system	Industrial society
Capitalism	Alienation

Laissez-faire	Affirmative action
Monopoly	Deindustrialization
Socialism	Downsizing
Communism	Offshoring
Informal economy	

SELF-TEST

MODIFIED TRUE/FALSE QUESTIONS: If the statement below is true, write "true" in the space provided. If the statement is false, briefly correct the error.

1. In *The End of Work*, Jeremy Rifkin takes a positive view of technology and how it will impact work.

2. Monopolistic practices are a key component of laissez-faire capitalism as it was explained by British economist Adam Smith.

3. Government ownership of all major industries, including steel production, automobile manufacturing, and agriculture, is a major feature of socialism as an ideal type.

4. In Marx's view, communist societies will naturally evolve out of the stage of capitalism.

5. In reality, the economy of each industrial society—the United States, Great Britain, and Japan—includes elements of both capitalism and socialism.

6. In the informal economy, transfers of money, goods, and services are reported to the government, but in approximately numbers and without receipts.

7. A key reason why women's work is often underreported and underestimated in Nepal is that it is undervalued in the culture.

8. Following several decades of socialism, the Chinese government began to allow private businesses to emerge in the 1980s.

9. The shift to a market economy in China has resulted in great advances in economic status for women.

10. By the end of the 1990s Japanese companies had set aside the notion of lifetime employment, with the result that Japan now has the highest unemployment rate of any industrial society.

11. Some sociologists believe that by 2020 the female workforce may be only three percent smaller than the male workforce.

12. John F. Kennedy was the first president to enact and executive order for affirmative action.

13. Although there are significant racial and ethnic differences in people's views of affirmative action, gender differences are largely absent.

14. Viewed from a functionalist perspective, the unprecedented attention given to downsizing in the mid-1990s reflected the continuing importance of social class in the United States.

15. Outsourcing is a relatively new practice among U.S. firms.

MULTIPLE-CHOICE QUESTIONS: In each of the following, select the phrase that best completes the statement.

1. Which two basic types of economic system distinguish contemporary industrial societies?
    a. capitalism and communism.
    b. capitalism and socialism.
    c. socialism and communism.
    d. capitalism and dictatorships.

2. Which one of the following is an economic system that is typically found in contemporary societies?
    a. socialism
    b. feudalism
    c. slavery
    d. all of the above

3. The principle of laissez-faire was expounded and endorsed by the British economist
   a. John Maynard Keynes.
   b. Adam Smith.
   c. Paul Samuelson.
   d. Arthur Scargill.

4. Which sociological perspective points out that while pure monopolies are not a basic element of the economy of the United States, competition is much more restricted than one might expect in what is called a free enterprise system?
   a. the functionalist perspective
   b. the conflict perspective
   c. the interactionist perspective
   d. labeling theory

5. Socialist theory was refined in the writings of Karl Marx and
   a. Émile Durkheim.
   b. Adam Smith.
   c. Friedrich Engels.
   d. the Marx Brothers.

6. Karl Marx is associated with which of the following concepts?
   a. anomie
   b. assimilation
   c. apartheid
   d. alienation

7. Which is not an example of the informal economy?
   a. trading a haircut for a computer lesson
   b. selling illegal drugs
   c. working for a major corporation as a computer programmer
   d. offering child care out of a private home, without reporting the income to the IRS

8. Approximately what proportion of work in the Nepalese informal economy is performed by women?
    a. 5 percent
    b. 25 percent
    c. 50 percent
    d. 60 percent

9. By 2004, approximately what proportion of urban Chinese workers were still employed in state-owned companies?
    a. 5 percent
    b. 35 percent
    c. 75 percent
    d. 90 percent

10. Which sociologist, using the interactionist perspective, noted that "one key source of job satisfaction lies in the informal interaction shared by members of a work group"?
    a. Robert Blauner
    b. Donald Roy
    c. George Ritzer
    d. Karl Marx

11. Sociologists and labor specialists foresee a workforce increasingly composed of
    a. women.
    b. racial minorities.
    c. ethnic minorities.
    d. all of the above

12. In 1978, in the _____ case, the United States Supreme Court ruled that it was unconstitutional to have fixed quotas for minority students.
    a. Brown
    b. Bakke
    c. Roe
    d. Weber

13. In which of these states have residents voted to abolish affirmative action?
    a. Washington
    b. California
    c. Iowa
    d. both A and B

14. The systematic, widespread withdrawal of investment in basic aspects of productivity such as factories and plants is called
    a. deindustrialization.
    b. downsizing.
    c. postindustrialization.
    d. "banana time."

15. The most recent trend in offshoring is that _____ jobs are being transferred to foreign contractors.
    a. manufacturing
    b. office and professional
    c. post-modern
    d. agricultural

FILL-IN QUESTIONS: Fill in the blank spaces in the sentences below with the correct words. Where two or more words are required, there will be a corresponding number of blank spaces.

1. The industrial revolution took place largely in _____ during the period 1760 to 1830.

2. A(n) _____ society depends on mechanization to produce its goods and services.

3. Under _____ as an ideal type, government rarely takes over ownership of an entire industry.

4. Some capitalist nations, such as the United States, outlaw _____ through anti-trust legislation.

5. _____ theorists point out that while pure monopolies are not a basic element of the economy of the United States, competition is much more restricted than one might expect in what is called a free enterprise system.

6. _____ is an economic system under which all property is communally owned and no social distinctions are made based on people's ability to produce.

7. Capitalism and socialism serve as _____ _____ of economic systems; the economy of each industrial society includes certain elements of both these types of economic systems.

8. Émile Durkheim argued that as labor becomes more and more differentiated, individuals experience _____ or loss of direction.

9. Most studies of alienation have focused on how _____ changes in the economy serve to increase or decrease worker satisfaction.

10. By the 1980s the term _____ was increasingly being used to describe the stress experienced by a wide range of workers, including professionals, self-employed persons, and even unpaid volunteers.

11. Sociologist _____ _____ has suggested that the relatively positive impression many workers present is misleading. In his view, manual workers are so deeply alienated that they come to expect little from their jobs.

12. Regarding affirmative action, the "Q word" refers to _____.

13. While _____ often involves relocation, in some instances it takes the form of corporate restructuring, as companies seek to reduce costs in the face of growing worldwide competition.

14. The annual turnover rate in offshored, high-tech jobs is more than _____ percent.

15. By 2015, it is estimated that _____ million white collar jobs will have been offshored from the United States.

UNDERSTANDING SOCIAL POLICY: All of the following questions are based on material that appears in the social policy section on Global Offshoring. Write a brief answer to each question in the space provided below.

1. To what does the term offshoring refer?

2. How extensive is the practice of offshoring?

3. How do functionalists and conflict theorists view global offshoring?

DEFINITIONS OF KEY TERMS

Economic system: The social institution through which goods and services are produced, distributed, and consumed. (374)

Industrial society: A society that depends on mechanization to produce its goods and services. (375)

Capitalism: An economic system in which the means of production are held largely in private hands and the main incentive for economic activity is the accumulation of profits. (375)

Laissez-faire: A form of capitalism under which people compete freely, with minimal government intervention in the economy. (375)

Monopoly: Control of a market by a single business firm. (376)

Socialism: An economic system under which the means of production and distribution are collectively owned. (377)

Communism: As an ideal type, an economic system under which all property is communally owned and no social distinctions are made on the basis of people's ability to produce. (377)

Informal economy: Transfers of money, goods, or services that are not reported to the government. (378)

Alienation A condition of estrangement or dissociation from the surrounding society. (381)

Affirmative action: Positive efforts to recruit minority group members or women for jobs, promotions, and educational opportunities. (384)

Deindustrialization: The systematic, widespread withdrawal of investment in basic aspects of productivity such as factories and plants. (383)

Downsizing: Reductions taken in a company's workforce as part of deindustrialization. (385)

Off-shoring The transfer of work to foreign contractors. (385)

ANSWERS TO SELF-TEST

Modified True/False Questions

1. In Jeremy Rifkin's view, there will be inevitable dysfunctions and dislocations accompanying the major transformation of the global economic system. (374)
2. Monopolistic practices violate the ideal of free competition cherished by Adam Smith and other supporters of laissez-faire capitalism. (376)
3. True (377)
4. In Marx's view, communist societies will naturally evolve out of the stage of socialism. (377)
5. True (377)
6. The informal economy consists of transfers of money, goods, and services that are not reported to the government. (378)
7. True (379)
8. True (378)
9. Scholars are still waiting to see whether Chinese women will maintain the progress they began under Communism. (380)
10. Japan's unemployment rate is still low compared to European countries. (383)
11. True (383)
12. True (384)
13. While 60 percent of White women approved of affirmative action in college admissions in a 2004 survey, the approval rate for White men was only 49 percent. (384)
14. Viewed from a conflict perspective, the unprecedented attention given to downsizing in the mid-1990s reflected the continuing importance of social class in the United States. (385)
15. U.S. firms have been outsourcing certain types of work for generations. (385)

Multiple-Choice Questions

1. b (375)
2. a (375)
3. b (375)
4. b (376)
5. c (377)
6. d (381)
7. c (378)
8. d (379)
9. b (380)
10. b (382)
11. d (383)
12. b (384)
13. d (384)
14. a (383)
15. b (385)

Fill-In Questions

1. England (375)
2. industrial (375)
3. capitalism (375)
4. monopolies (376)
5. Conflict (376)
6. Communism (377)

7. ideal types (377)
8. anomie (381)
9. structural (381)
10. burnout (381)
11. George Ritzer (382)
12. quotas (384)
13. deindustrialization (385)
14. 50 (386)
15. 3.3 (386)

Understanding Social Policy: Global Offshoring

1. U.S. firms have been outsourcing certain types of work for generations. The new trend toward offshoring carries this practice further, by transferring new types of work to foreign contractors. Now, office and professional jobs are being transferred too. (385)

2. Today, when you call a toll-free number to reach a customer service representative, chances are that the person who answers the phone will not be speaking from the United States. Estimates are that by the year 2015, 3,3 million white-collar jobs worth an estimated annual payroll of $136.4 billion will have moved overseas from the United States alone. (385–386)

3. Because offshoring, and outsourcing in general, tend to improve the efficiency of business operations, they can be viewed as functional to society. But conflict theorists question whether this aspect of globalization furthers global inequality. (386)

CHAPTER 19
HEALTH AND MEDICINE

Culture and Health

Sociological Perspectives on Health and Illness
  Functionalist Approach
  Conflict Approach
  Interactionist Approach
  Labeling Approach

Social Epidemiology and Health
  Social Class
  Race and Ethnicity
  Gender
  Age

Health Care in the United States
  A Historical View
  Physicians, Nurses, and Patients
  Alternatives to Traditional Health Care
  The Role of Government

Mental Illness in the United States
  Theoretical Models of Mental Disorders
  Patterns of Care

Social Policy and Health: Financing Health Care Worldwide
  The Issue
  The Setting
  Sociological Insights
  Policy Initiatives

BOXES
  TAKING SOCIOLOGY TO WORK: *Jess Purmort, Research Assistant, New York Academy of Medicine*
  SOCIAL INEQUALITY: *To Inform or Not to Inform? How Race and Ethnicity Affect Views of Patient Autonomy*
  RESEARCH IN ACTION: *The Nun Study*

KEY POINTS

Functionalist Approach to Health and Illness: The **sick role** refers to societal expectations about the attitudes and behavior of a person viewed as being ill. Sociologist Talcott Parsons, well known for his contributions to functionalist theory, outlined the behavior required of people considered "sick." According to Parsons, physicians function as "gatekeepers" for the sick role, either verifying a patient's condition as "illness" or designating the patient as "recovered." (394)

Conflict Approach to Health and Illness: Conflict theorists use the term medicalization of society to refer to the growing role of medicine as a major institution of social control. Medicine serves as an agent of social control by retaining absolute jurisdiction over many health care procedures. Viewed from a conflict perspective, there are glaring inequities in health care delivery in the United States. For example, poor areas tend to be underserved because medical services concentrate where people are wealthy. Similarly, from a global perspective, there are obvious inequities in health care delivery. (394–395)

Interactionist Approach to Health and Illness: In examining health, illness, and medicine as a social institution, interactionists generally focus on micro-level study of the roles played by health care professionals and patients. They emphasize that the patient should not always be viewed as passive. Sometimes patients play an active role in health care by *failing* to follow a physician's advice. (395)

Labeling Approach to Health and Illness: Labeling theorists suggest that the designation "healthy" or "ill" generally involves social definition by others. Just as police officers, judges, and other regulators of social control have the power to define certain people as criminals, health care professionals (especially physicians) have the power to define certain people as "sick." Moreover, like labels that suggest nonconformity or criminality, labels that are associated with illness commonly reshape how others treat us and how we see ourselves. Our society attaches serious consequences to labels that suggest less than perfect physical or mental health. (396)

Social Epidemiology and Health: **Social epidemiology** is the study of the distribution of disease, impairment, and general health status across a population. Studies in the United States and other countries have consistently shown that people in the lower classes have higher rates of mortality and disability. The poor economic and environmental conditions of groups such as African Americans, Hispanics, and Native Americans are manifested in high morbidity and mortality rates for these groups. A large body of research indicates that in comparison with men, women experience a higher prevalence of many illnesses, though they tend to live longer. (397–400)

Physicians, Nurses, and Patients: Traditionally, physicians have a position of dominance in their dealings with both patients and nurses. Interactionists concur with Talcott Parsons's view that the relationship is generally asymmetrical, with doctors holding a position of dominance and controlling rewards. Despite their training and professional status, nurses commonly take orders from physicians. Traditionally, the relationship between doctors and nurses has paralleled the male dominance of the United States: Most physicians have been male, while virtually all nurses have been female. (401–402)

Mental Illness in the United States: **Mental illness** is a disorder of the brain that disrupts a person's thinking, feeling, and ability to interact with others. According to the medical model, mental illness is rooted in biological causes that can be treated through medical intervention. That is not to say that social factors do not contribute to mental illness. Just as culture affects the incidence and prevalence of illness in general, its treatment, and the expression of certain culture-bound syndromes, so too can it affect mental illness. (404–405)

Financing Health Care Worldwide: The focus of the policy section is on those industrialized (or developed) nations in which the availability of health care is not an issue. The question is more one of accessibility and affordability. The United States is now the only Western industrial democracy that does not treat health care as a basic right. Conflict theorists suggest that the health care system, like other social institutions, resists basic change. In general, those who receive substantial wealth and power through the workings of an existing institution will have a strong incentive to maintain the status quo. In this case, private insurance companies are benefiting financially from the current system, and have a clear interest in opposing certain forms of national health insurance. (407–408)

KEY TERMS

Briefly define or identify the following terms in the spaces provided below. The definitions of these terms can be found later in this chapter of the study guide.

Culture-bound syndrome	Brain drain
Health	Social epidemiology
Sick role	Incidence

Prevalence	Holistic medicine
Morbidity rate	Mental illness
Mortality rate	Health Maintenance Organization (HMO)
Curanderismo	

SELF-TEST

MODIFIED TRUE/FALSE QUESTIONS: If the statement below is true, write "true" in the space provided. If the statement is false, briefly correct the error.

1. The sick role is an interactionist concept developed by Talcott Parsons, which refers to societal expectations about the attitudes and behavior of a person viewed as being ill.

2. Conflict theorists use the term *medicalization of society* to refer to the growing role of medicine as a major institution of social control.

3. Today, the United States has about 256 physicians per 10,000 people, while African nations have fewer than 1 per 10,000. This situation is only worsened by "brain drain"—the immigration to the United States and other industrialized nations of skilled workers, professionals, and technicians who are desperately needed by their home countries.

4. The infant mortality rate of the United States is lower than that of any other nation.

5. Self-medication is extremely rare in the United States.

6. Labeling theorists argue that labels associated with illness commonly reshape how others treat us and how we see ourselves.

7. There are no racial or ethnic differences in attitudes toward patient autonomy.

8. Prevalence refers to the total number of cases of a specific disorder that exist at a given time.

9. Studies in the United States and in other countries have consistently shown that people in the lower classes have higher rates of mortality and disability than do more affluent people.

10. African Americans and Native Americans have infant mortality rates lower than Puerto Ricans but higher than Whites.

11. Researchers argue that women are much less likely than men to seek treatment, to be diagnosed as having diseases, and therefore to have their illnesses reflected in data examined by epidemiologists.

12. Women still have disproportionately low status within the medical profession.

13. Alternative medicine usually isn't covered by health insurance, and it is impossible to get a federal grant to do research on alternative medicine.

14. In the United States, about one out of every five Americans suffers from some form of mental illness.

15. The medical model suggests that mental illness is not really an "illness," since the individual's problems arise from living in society and not from physical maladies.

MULTIPLE-CHOICE QUESTIONS: In each of the following, select the phrase that best completes the statement.

1. In the United States, anorexia nervosa is an example of a(n)
    a. prevalence.
    b. culture-bound syndrome.
    c. incidence.
    d. medical model.

2. Which sociologist developed the concept of the sick role?
    a. Émile Durkheim
    b. Talcott Parsons
    c. C. Wright Mills
    d. Erving Goffman

3. Which of the following is a criticism of the sick role?
    a. Patients' judgments regarding their own state of health may be related to their gender, age, social class, and ethnic group.
    b. The sick role may be more applicable to people experiencing short-term illnesses than to those with recurring long-term illnesses.
    c. Even simple factors, such as whether a person is employed or not, seem to affect willingness to assume the sick role.
    d. all of the above

4. Which sociological perspective would note that poor sections of the United States tend to be underserved because medical services concentrate where people are numerous or wealthy?
    a. the functionalist perspective
    b. the conflict perspective
    c. the interactionist perspective
    d. the neo-Malthusian view

5. Regarding health care inequities, the conflict perspective would note that
    a. physicians serve as "gatekeepers" for the sick role, either verifying a patient's condition as "illness" or designating the patient as "recovered."
    b. patients play an active role in health care by failing to follow a physician's advice.
    c. emigration out of the Third World by physicians is yet another way that the world's core industrialized nations enhance their quality of life at the expense of developing countries.
    d. the designation "healthy" or "ill" generally involves social definition by others.

6. Which one of the following nations has the lowest infant mortality rate?
    a. the United States
    b. Mozambique
    c. Canada
    d. Sweden

7. Which sociological perspective emphasizes that a patient should not always be viewed as passive, but instead as someone who often plays an active role in his or her health care?
    a. the functionalist perspective
    b. the conflict perspective
    c. the interactionist perspective
    d. labeling theory

8. In examining health, illness, and medicine as a social institution, which sociological perspective generally focuses on micro-level study of the roles played by health care professionals and patients?
    a. the functionalist perspective
    b. the conflict perspective
    c. the interactionist perspective
    d. labeling theory

9. According to the _____ _____, a variety of life experiences can come to be viewed as illnesses or not.
   a. functionalist perspective
   b. conflict perspective
   c. interactionist perspective
   d. labeling theory

10. In 1974, members of the American Psychiatric Association voted to drop _____ from the standard manual of mental disorders.
    a. premenstrual syndrome
    b. homosexuality
    c. schizophrenia
    d. hyperactivity

11. Which theorist notes that capitalist societies, such as the United States, care more about maximizing profits than they do about the health and safety of industrial workers?
    a. Thomas Szasz
    b. Talcott Parsons
    c. Erving Goffman
    d. Karl Marx

12. Compared with Whites, Blacks have higher death rates from
    a. heart disease.
    b. diabetes.
    c. cancer.
    d. all of the above

13. Which sociological perspective suggests that established physicians and medical school professors serve as mentors or role models who transmit knowledge, skills, and values to the passive learner—the medical student?
    a. the functionalist perspective
    b. the conflict perspective
    c. the interactionist perspective
    d. labeling theory

14. Which program is essentially a compulsory health insurance plan for the elderly?
    a. Medicare
    b. Medicaid
    c. Blue Cross
    d. Healthpac

15. Health care costs are the highest in
    a. Poland.
    b. Canada.
    c. the United States.
    d. India.

FILL-IN QUESTIONS: Fill in the blank spaces in the sentences below with the correct words. Where two or more words are required, there will be a corresponding number of blank spaces.

1. _____ affects the way people interact with doctors and healers, the way they relate to their families when they are sick, and even the way they think about health.

2. As defined by the World Health Organization, _____ is the "state of complete physical, mental, and social well-being, and not merely the absence of disease and infirmity."

3. From a _____ perspective, "being sick" must be controlled so as to ensure that not too many people are released from their societal responsibilities at any one time.

4. According to Talcott Parsons, physicians function as "_____" for the sick role, either verifying a patient's condition as "illness" or designating the patient as "recovered."

5. The immigration to the United States and other industrialized nations of skilled workers, professionals, and technicians who are desperately needed by their home countries is known as the _____ _____.

6. _____ theorists suggest that the designation of a person as "healthy" or "ill" generally involves social definition by others.

7. Contemporary social _____ is concerned not only with epidemics but also with nonepidemic diseases, injuries, drug addiction and alcoholism, suicide, and mental illness.

8. Sociologists find it useful to consider _____ rates because they reveal that a specific disease occurs more frequently among one segment of a population compared with another.

9. In the view of Karl Marx and contemporary _____ theorists, capitalist societies such as the United States care more about maximizing profits than they do about the health and safety of industrial workers.

10. Traditionally, the relationship between doctors and nurses has paralleled the _____ dominance of the larger society.

11. In terms of the functionalist analysis of gender stratification offered by sociologists Talcott Parsons and Robert Bales, male medical residents took the _____, achievement-oriented role, while female medical residents took the expressive, interpersonal-oriented role.

12. The DRG system of reimbursement has contributed to the controversial practice of "_____," under which patients whose treatment may be unprofitable are transferred by private hospitals to public facilities.

13. According to the _____ model, mental illness is rooted in biological causes that can be treated through medical intervention.

14. Psychiatrist _____ _____, in his book *The Myth of Mental Illness*, which first appeared in 1961, advanced the view that numerous personality disorders are not diseases but simply patterns of conduct labeled as disorders by significant others.

15. The _____ _____ Association, one of Washington's most powerful lobbying groups, has been successfully fighting national health insurance since the 1930s.

UNDERSTANDING SOCIAL POLICY: All of the following questions are based on material that appears in the social policy section on Financing Health Care Worldwide. Write a brief answer to each question in the space provided below.

1. What is the view of conflict theorists concerning health care financing in the United States?

2. What is the "corporatization" of health care and what concerns does it raise?

3. What are the concerns about managed health care plans and the treatment of the elderly and minorities?

DEFINITIONS OF KEY TERMS

Culture-bound syndrome A disease or illness that cannot be understood apart from a specific social context. (393)

Health: As defined by the World Health Organization, a state of complete physical, mental, and social well-being, and not merely the absence of disease and infirmity. (393)

Sick role: Societal expectations about the attitudes and behavior of a person viewed as being ill. (394)

Brain drain: The immigration to the United States and other industrialized nations of skilled workers, professionals, and technicians who are desperately needed in their home countries. (395)

Social epidemiology: The study of the distribution of disease, impairment, and general health status across a population. (397)

Incidence: The number of new cases of a specific disorder that occur within a given population during a stated period. (398)

Prevalence: The total number of cases of a specific disorder that exist at a given time. (398)

Morbidity rate: The incidence of disease in a given population. (398)

Mortality rate: The incidence of death in a given population. (398)

Curanderismo: Latino folk medicine, a form of holistic health care and healing. (400)

Holistic medicine Therapies in which the health care practitioner considers the person's physical, mental, emotional, and spiritual characteristics. (403)

Mental illness A disorder of the brain that disrupts a person's thinking, feeling, and ability to interact with others. (404)

Health Maintenance Organization (HMO): An organization that provides comprehensive medical services for a preestablished fee. (408)

ANSWERS TO SELF-TEST

Modified True/False Questions
1. The sick role is a functionalist concept developed by Talcott Parsons, which refers to societal expectations about the attitudes and behavior of a person viewed as being ill. (394)
2. True (394)
3. True (395)
4. At least 31 nations have lower infant mortality rates than the United States. (395)
5. Self-medication is common in the United States. (395)
6. True (396)
7. Research has found marked racial and ethnic differences in attitudes toward patient autonomy. (396)
8. True (398)
9. True (399)
10. Puerto Ricans and Native Americans have infant mortality rates lower than African Americans but higher than Whites. (399)
11. Researchers argue that women are much more likely than men to seek treatment, to be diagnosed as having diseases, and therefore to have their illnesses reflected in data examined by epidemiologists. (400)
12. True (402)
13. Although alternative medicine usually isn't covered by health insurance, the Office of Alternative Medicine at the National Institutes of Health accepts grant requests for research on alternative medicine. (403)
14. True (404)
15. Labeling theory suggests that some behaviors that are viewed as mental illnesses are not really illnesses, since the individual's problems arise from living in society and not from physical maladies. (405)

Multiple-Choice Questions
1. b (393)
2. b (394)
3. d (394)
4. b (395)
5. c (395)
6. d (395)
7. c (395)
8. c (395)

Chapter 19 *Health and Medicine* | 281

9. c (397)
10. b (397)
11. d (399)
12. d (399)

13. c (402)
14. a (404)
15. c (407)

Fill-In Questions
1. Culture (392)
2. health (393)
3. functionalist (393)
4. gatekeepers (394)
5. brain drain (395)
6. Labeling (396)
7. epidemiology (397–398)
8. morbidity (398)

9. conflict (399)
10. male (402)
11. instrumental (403)
12. dumping (404)
13. medical (405)
14. Thomas Szasz (405)
15. American Medical (408)

Understanding Social Policy: Financing Health Care Worldwide

1. As conflict theorists suggest, the health care system, like other social institutions, resists basic change. In general, those who receive substantial wealth and power through the workings of an existing social institution will have a strong incentive to keep things as they are. In this case, private insurance companies benefit financially from the current system, and have a clear interest in opposing certain forms of national health insurance. (408)

2. The health care system is unquestionably undergoing "corporatization," as for-profit health care companies (often linking insurers, hospitals, and groups of physicians) are achieving increasing dominance. Conflict theorists have long argued that an underlying aspect of capitalism in the United States is that illness may be exploited for profit. Critics of the corporatization of health care worry that the growing pressures on physicians and other health care providers to make cost-effective decisions may lead to inadequate and even life-threatening patient care. (408)

3. Concern is growing about the quality of care people receive through managed care plans such as HMOs—especially the elderly and minorities, who are less likely to be able to afford private insurance plans. According to a national survey, people in managed care feel they spend less time with physicians, find it more difficult to see specialists, and generally sense that the overall quality of health care has deteriorated. (408)

CHAPTER 20
COMMUNITIES AND URBANIZATION

How Did Communities Originate?
- Early Communities
- Preindustrial Cities
- Industrial and Postindustrial Cities

Urbanization
- Functionalist View: Urban Ecology
- Conflict View: New Urban Sociology

Types of Communities
- Central Cities
- Suburbs
- Rural Communities

Social Policy and Communities: Seeking Shelter Worldwide
- The Issue
- The Setting
- Sociological Insights
- Policy Initiatives

BOXES
SOCIOLOGY IN THE GLOBAL COMMUNITY: Squatter Settlements
RESEARCH IN ACTION: Store Wars

KEY POINTS

Preindustrial, Industrial and Postindustrial Cities: The **preindustrial city**, as it is termed, generally had only a few thousand people living within its borders, and was characterized by a relatively closed class system and limited mobility. The factory system that developed during the industrial revolution led to a much more refined division of labor than was evident in early preindustrial cities. The many new occupations that were created produced a complex set of relationships among workers. Thus, the **industrial city** was not merely more populous than its preindustrial predecessors were, it was also based on very different principles of social organization. The **postindustrial city** is a city in which global finance and the electronic flow of information dominate the economy. (415–416)

Urbanization: The 1990 census was the first to demonstrate that more than half the population of the United States lived in urban areas of one million or more residents. During the nineteenth and early twentieth centuries, rapid urbanization occurred primarily in European and North American cities. Since World War II, however, there has been an urban "explosion" in the world's developing countries. (417)

Functionalist View—Urban Ecology: **Human ecology** is concerned with the interrelationships between people and their environment. **Urban ecology** focuses on such relationships as they emerge in urban areas. Early urban ecologists, such as Robert Park and Ernest Burgess, concentrated on city life but drew on the approaches used by ecologists who study plant and animal communities. Urban ecologists trace their work back to the **concentric-zone theory** devised in the 1920s by Burgess. Families and business firms compete for the most valuable land; those who possess the most wealth and power are generally the winners. Because of its functionalist orientation and its emphasis on stability, the concentric-zone theory tended to understate or ignore certain tensions that were apparent in metropolitan areas. As a response to the emergence of more than one focal point in some metropolitan areas, Chauncy D. Harris and Edward Ullman presented the **multiple-nuclei theory**. In their view, a metropolitan area may have many centers of development, each of which reflects a particular urban need or activity. In a refinement of the multiple-nuclei theory, contemporary urban ecologists have begun to study "edge cities," which have grown up on the outskirts of major metropolitan areas, and are economic and social centers with identities of their own. (417–419)

Conflict View—New Urban Sociology: Drawing on conflict theory, an approach that has come to be called the **new urban sociology** considers the interplay of local, national, and worldwide forces, and their effect on local space, with special emphasis on the impact of global economic activity. The new urban sociology also draws on Immanuel Wallerstein's **world systems theory**. Wallerstein argues that certain industrialized nations (among them the United States, Japan, and Germany) hold a dominant position at the core of the global economic system. They view cities not as independent and autonomous entities, but as the outcome of decision-making processes directed or influenced by a society's dominant classes, and by core industrialized nations. (419–420)

Central Cities: In 2000, some 226 million people—accounting for 80 percent of the nation's people—lived in metropolitan areas. Many urban residents are the descendants of European immigrants—Irish, Italians, Jews, Poles, and others—who came to the United States in the nineteenth and early twentieth centuries. In addition, a substantial number of low-income African Americans and Whites came to the cities from rural areas in the period following World War II. Even today, cities in the United States are the destinations of immigrants from around the world—including Mexico, Ireland, Cuba, Vietnam, and Haiti—as well as migrants from the U.S. commonwealth of Puerto Rico. (421–422)

Issues Facing Cities: Perhaps the single most dramatic reflection of the nation's urban ills has been the apparent "death" of entire neighborhoods. Such urban devastation has greatly contributed to the growing problem of homelessness. Another critical problem for the cities has been mass transportation. The federal government has traditionally given much more assistance to highway programs than to public transportation. Conflict theorists note that such a bias favors the relatively affluent (automobile owners), as well as corporations, such as auto manufacturers, tire makers, and oil companies. (422–423)

Suburban Expansion: Suburbanization was the most dramatic population trend in the United States throughout the twentieth century. The suburban boom has been especially evident since World War II. From the perspective of new urban sociology, suburban expansion is far from a natural ecological process; rather, it reflects the distinct priorities of powerful economic and political interests. (424)

Diversity in the Suburbs: The common assumption that suburbia includes only prosperous Whites is far from correct. By 2000, for example, 34 percent of the Black population, 46 percent Latinos, and 53 percent Asians in the United States lived in the suburbs. Again, in contrast to prevailing stereotypes, the suburbs include a significant number of low-income people from all backgrounds—White, Black, and Hispanic. (424–425)

Rural Communities: twenty-one percent of the population of the United States lives in rural areas. The postindustrial revolution has been far from kind to the rural communities of the United States. In desperation, residents of depressed rural areas have begun to encourage prison construction, to bring in badly needed economic development. But the construction of large businesses can create its own problems, as small communities that have experienced the arrival of large discount stores have discovered. (425)

Seeking Shelter Worldwide: For many people worldwide, the housing problem means finding shelter of any kind that they can afford, in a place where anyone would reasonably want to live. Homelessness is evident in both industrialized and developing countries. According to estimates, the number of homeless persons in the United States is at least 750,000 on any given night, and as many as 3.5 million Americans may experience homelessness for some period each year. Both in the United States and around the world, homelessness functions as a master status that largely defines a person's position within society. There has been a significant change in the profile of homelessness during the last 40 years. In the past, homeless people were primarily older White males living as alcoholics in skid row areas. However, today's homeless are comparatively younger, with an average age in the low 30s. An estimated 60 percent of homeless people in the United States are from racial and ethnic minority groups. (427)

KEY TERMS

Briefly define or identify the following terms in the spaces provided below. The definitions of these terms can be found later in this chapter of the study guide.

Community	Urban ecology
Preindustrial city	Urban ecology
Industrial city	Concentric-zone theory
Postindustrial city	Multiple-nuclei theory
Urbanism	New urban sociology
Megalopolis	World systems analysis
Human ecology	Squatter settlement

Defended neighborhood	Suburb
Asset-based community development (ABCD)	Gentrification

SELF-TEST

MODIFIED TRUE/FALSE QUESTIONS: If the statement below is true, write "true" in the space provided. If the statement is false, briefly correct the error.

1. Anthropologist George Murdock has observed that there are only two truly universal units of human social organization: the family and the school.

2. The transition from subsistence to surplus represented a critical step in the emergence of cities.

3. Louis Wirth identified three critical factors contributing to urbanism: the size of the population, population density, and technological advancements.

4. Wealth based on the ability to obtain and use information is the only trait that is characteristic of preindustrial, industrial, and postindustrial cities.

5. The industrial city is characterized by a relatively open class system in which social mobility is based significantly on ascribed characteristics.

6. The megalopolis is a phenomenon unique to the United States.

7. Because of its conflict orientation and its emphasis on stability, the concentric-zone theory tended to understate or ignore certain tensions apparent in metropolitan areas.

8. The rise of suburban shopping malls is a vivid example of the phenomenon of multiple nuclei within metropolitan areas.

9. Edge cities are communities that have been built on the edge of waterways, mountains, and other prominent geological features.

10. According to the world systems analysis, all nations prosper from a global economy.

11. The urban ecologists of the 1920s and 1930s were not ignorant of the role that the larger economy played in urbanization, but their theories emphasized the impact of local, rather than national or global forces.

12. Squatter settlements are disorganized collections of poor people living on the fringe of cities, particularly in the world's developing nations.

13. The approach of asset-based community development is to identify a community's weaknesses, and then to seek ways to strengthen them.

14. Despite suburban diversification, race and ethnicity remain the most important factors distinguishing cities from suburbs in the United States.

15. Today, many rural communities are facing problems that were first associated with central cities, like overdevelopment, gang warfare, and drug trafficking.

MULTIPLE-CHOICE QUESTIONS: In each of the following, select the phrase that best completes the statement.

1. Urbanization in preindustrial cities was restricted by
    a. reliance on animal power as a source of energy.
    b. the high levels of surplus produced by the agricultural sector.
    c. the ease of migration to the city.
    d. all of the above

2. Louis Wirth argued that a relatively large and permanent settlement leads to distinctive patterns of behavior, which he called
    a. squatting.
    b. linear development.
    c. urbanism.
    d. gentrification.

3. In comparison with industrial cities, preindustrial cities had
    a. relatively open class systems.
    b. extensive social mobility.
    c. a largely illiterate population.
    d. all of the above

4. In which type of city is there a greater openness to new religious faiths?
    a. preindustrial city
    b. industrial city
    c. postindustrial city
    d. edge city

5. Robert Park and Ernest Burgess are associated with
   a. the functionalist perspective.
   b. the conflict perspective.
   c. the linear-development model.
   d. multiple-nuclei theory.

6. The multiple-nuclei theory of urban growth was presented by
   a. Ernest Burgess.
   b. Homer Hoyt.
   c. Ferdinand Tönnies.
   d. C. D. Harris and Edward L. Ullman.

7. World systems analysis is closely aligned with
   a. the concentric-zone theory.
   b. the multiple-nuclei theory.
   c. new urban sociology.
   d. zone sector theory.

8. Which group of sociologists notes that developers, bankers, and other powerful real estate interests view housing as an investment, and are primarily concerned with maximizing profit, not with solving social problems?
   a. urban ecologists
   b. new urban sociologists
   c. functionalists
   d. human ecologists

9. According to Herbert Gans, residents who remain in the city to take advantage of the unique cultural and intellectual benefits of the city are called
   a. cosmopolites.
   b. ethnic villagers.
   c. urban villagers.
   d. the trapped.

10. Herbert Gans called urban residents who prefer to live in their own tight-knit communities
    a. cosmopolites.
    b. ethnic villagers.
    c. the trapped.
    d. gentrophiles.

11. The most dramatic population trend in the United States throughout the twentieth century was
    a. urbanization.
    b. suburbanization.
    c. the move to the sunbelt.
    d. the move to the "old homestead" in rural areas.

12. Proponents of new urban sociology contend that factories were initially moved from central cities to suburbs as a result of
    a. an attempt to reduce the power of labor unions.
    b. subsidies and tax incentives offered to companies to relocate.
    c. availability of favorable mortgages to military veterans.
    d. all of the above

13. What percentage of Americans currently live on farms?
    a. 1 percent
    b. 3 percent
    c. 5 percent
    d. 10 percent

14. On any given night, how many Americans are homeless?
    a. 750,000
    b. 3 million
    c. 10 million
    d. 12 million

15. Which of these results from gentrification, according to conflict theorists?
    a. low-income families receive tax breaks
    b. locally-owned businesses suffer
    c. poor people are displaced
    d. pollution increases

FILL-IN QUESTIONS: Fill in the blank spaces in the sentences below with the correct words. Where two or more words are required, there will be a corresponding number of blank spaces.

1. One of the reasons that preindustrial cities were small and few in number was that they relied on _____ power as a source of energy for economic production.

2. Louis Wirth distinguished three critical factors contributing to _____: the size of the population, population density, and the heterogeneity of the population.

3. The 500-mile corridor stretching from Boston south to Washington, D.C., which accounts for one-sixth of the total population of the United States, is an example of a _____.

4. _____ _____ is concerned with the interrelationships between people and their environment.

5. At the core of the city, according to the concentric-zone theory, is the _____ business district.

6. The urban ecology model is criticized by some for referring to the arrival of African Americans in white neighborhoods in the 1930s as an example of _____ and _____.

7. _____ _____ are communities that have grown up on the outskirts of major metropolitan areas, but are economic and social centers with identities of their own.

8. While some observers suggest that the growth of sun belt cities is due to a "good business climate," _____ theorists counter that this term is actually a euphemism for hefty government subsidies and antilabor policies.

9. Ferdinand Tönnies described close-knit communities where social interaction among people is intimate and familiar as a _____.

10. The emergence of squatter settlements often is accompanied by a thriving "_____ economy."

11. A less pejorative term for squatter settlements is _____ _____.

12. Many urban residents are the descendants of European _____—Irish, Italians, Jews, Poles, and others—who came to the United States in the nineteenth and early twentieth centuries.

13. A study of suburban residential patterns found that _____ Americans and _____ tend to reside in equivalent socioeconomic areas with Whites; however, _____ Americans are found in poorer suburbs than Whites.

14. Studies have shown that superstores, such as Wal-Mart, ultimately _____ employment.

15. Many cities and towns have started movements, known as "store wars" opposed to having _____ stores in their communities.

UNDERSTANDING SOCIAL POLICY: All of the following questions are based on material that appears in the social policy section on Seeking Shelter Worldwide. Write a brief answer to each question in the space provided below.

1. What is the extent of homelessness in the United States and globally?

2. How has the profile of the homeless changed in the last 40 years?

3. What are the causes of homelessness in the United States?

4. What did the report by the National Law Center on Homelessness and Poverty in 1996 indicate?

DEFINITIONS OF KEY TERMS

Community: A spatial or political unit of social organization that gives people a sense of belonging, based either on shared residence in a particular place or on a common identity. (414)

Preindustrial city: A city of only a few thousand people that is characterized by a relatively closed class system and limited mobility. (415)

Industrial city: A relatively large city characterized by open competition, an open class system, and elaborate specialization in the manufacturing of goods. (416)

Postindustrial city: A city in which global finance and the electronic flow of information dominate the economy. (416)

Urbanism: A term used by Louis Wirth to describe distinctive patterns of social behavior evident among city residents. (417)

Megalopolis: A densely populated area containing two or more cities and their suburbs. (417)

Human ecology: An area of study that is concerned with the interrelationships between people and their environment. (417)

Urban ecology: An area of study that focuses on the interrelationships between people and their environment in urban areas. (418)

Concentric-zone theory: A theory of urban growth devised by Ernest Burgess that sees growth in terms of a series of rings radiating from the central business district. (418)

Multiple-nuclei theory: A theory of urban growth developed by Harris and Ullman that views growth as emerging from many centers of development, each of which reflects a particular urban need or activity. (419)

New urban sociology: An approach to urbanization that considers the interplay of local, national, and worldwide forces and their effect on local space, with special emphasis on the impact of global economic activity. (419)

World systems analysis: Immanual Wallerstein's view of the global economic system as one divided between certain industrialized nations that control wealth and developing countries that are controlled and exploited. (420)

Squatter settlement: An area occupied by the very poor on the fringe of cities, in which housing is constructed by settlers themselves from discarded material. (421)

Defended neighborhood: A neighborhood that residents identify through defined community borders and a perception that adjacent areas are geographically separate and socially different. (422)

Asset-based community development (ABCD): An approach to community development in which planners first identify a community's strengths and then seek to mobilize those assets. (423)

Suburb: According to the Census Bureau, any territory within a metropolitan area that is not included in the central city. (423)

Gentrification: The resettlement of low-income city neighborhoods by prosperous families and business firms. (427)

ANSWERS TO SELF-TEST

Modified True/False Questions
1. Anthropologist George Murdock has observed that there are only two truly universal units of human social organization: the family and the community. (415)
2. True (415)
3. Louis Wirth identified three critical factors contributing to urbanism: the size of the population, population density, and heterogeneity. (417)
4. Wealth based on the ability to obtain and use information is only characteristic of postindustrial cities. (417)
5. The industrial city is characterized by a relatively open class system in which mobility is based significantly on achieved characteristics. (417)
6. The megalopolis is not evident solely in the United States; such areas are now seen in Great Britain, Germany, Italy, Egypt, India, Japan, and China. (417)
7. Because of its functionalist orientation and its emphasis on stability, the concentric-zone theory tended to understate or ignore certain tensions apparent in metropolitan areas. (418)
8. True (419)
9. Edge cities have grown up on the outskirts of major metropolitan areas and are economic and social centers with identities of their own. (419)
10. Rapidly growing cities of the world's developing countries are shaped by a global community controlled by core nations and multinational corporations. The outcome has not been beneficial to the poorest citizens. (420)
11. True (420)
12. True (421)
13. Squatter settlements often have well-developed social organizations. (421)
14. The approach of asset-based community development is to identify a community's strengths, and then to seek to mobilize those assets. (423)
15. True (425)

Multiple-Choice Questions
1. a (416)
2. c (417)
3. c (417)
4. c (417)
5. a (418)
6. d (419)
7. c (420)
8. b (420)
9. a (422)
10. b (422)
11. b (424)
12. a (424)
13. a (425)
14. a (427)
15. c (427)

Fill-In Questions
1. animal (416)
2. urbanism (417)
3. megalopolis (417)
4. Human ecology (417)
5. central (418)
6. invasion; succession (418)
7. Edge cities (419)
8. conflict (420)
9. *Gemeinschaft* (421)
10. informal (421)
11. autonomous settlements (421)
12. immigrants (471)
13. Asian; Hispanics; African (424–425)
14. reduce (426)
15. Wal-Mart (426)

Understanding Social Policy: Seeking Shelter Worldwide

1. According to estimates, the number of homeless persons in the United States is at least 750,000 on any given night and as many as 3.5 million Americans may experience homelessness for some period each year. In Third World countries, rapid population growth has outpaced the expansion of housing by a wide margin, leading to a rise in homelessness as well. (427)

2. There has been a significant change in the profile of homelessness during the last 40 years. In the past, homeless people were primarily older White males living as alcoholics in skid row areas. However, today's homeless are comparatively younger, with an average age in the low 30s. Overall, an estimated 60 percent of homeless people in the United States are from racial and ethnic minority groups. Moreover, a 25-city survey in 2004 found that the homeless population is growing faster than the increase in emergency food and shelter space. (427)

3. Changing economic and residential patterns account for much of the increase in homelessness. In recent decades, the process of urban renewal has included a noticeable boom in *gentrification* (the resettlement of low income city neighborhoods by prosperous families and businesses). Conflict theorists note that although the affluent may derive both financial and emotional benefits from gentrification and redevelopment, the poor often end up being thrown out on the street. (427)

4. According to a report by the National Law Center on Homelessness and Poverty (1996), there was a growing trend in the 1990s toward the adoption of anti-homeless public policies and the "criminalization" of homeless people. In 1995 alone, at least 29 cities enacted curbs on panhandling, sitting on sidewalks, standing near automated teller machines, or other behavior sometimes evident among the homeless. At the same time, more and more policymakers—especially conservative officials—have advocated cutbacks in government funding for the homeless and argued that voluntary associations and religious organizations should assume a more important role in addressing the problem. (427)

CHAPTER 21: POPULATION AND THE ENVIRONMENT

Demography: The Study of Population
- Malthus's Thesis and Marx's Response
- Studying Population Today
- Elements of Demography

World Population Patterns
- Demographic Transition
- The Population Explosion

Fertility Patterns in the United States
- The Baby Boom
- Stable Population Growth

Population and Migration
- International Migration
- Internal Migration

The Environment
- Environmental Problems: An Overview
- Functionalism and Human Ecology
- Conflict View of Environmental Issues
- Environmental Justice

Social Policy and Population: World Population Policy
- The Issue
- The Setting
- Sociological Insights
- Policy Initiatives

BOXES

TAKING SOCIOLOGY TO WORK: Kelsie Lenor Wilson-Dorsett, Deputy Director, Department of Statistics, Government of Bahamas

SOCIOLOGY IN THE GLOBAL COMMUNITY: Population Policy in China

KEY POINTS

Demography: **Demography** is the scientific study of population. It draws on several components of population, including size, composition, and territorial distribution, to understand the social consequences of population change. Demographers study geographical variations and historical trends in their effort to develop population forecasts. They also analyze the structure of a population—the age, gender, race, and ethnicity of its members. (433)

Malthus's Thesis and Marx's Response: The Reverend Thomas Robert Malthus suggested that the world's population was growing more rapidly than the available food supply. Malthus saw population control as an answer to this problem, and argued that couples must take responsibility for the number of children they choose to bear. Karl Marx strongly criticized Malthus's views on population. Marx believed that capitalism, rather than rising world population, was the cause of social ills. (433–344)

Studying Population Today: In the United States and most other countries, the census is the primary mechanism for collecting population information. A **census** is an enumeration, or counting, of a population. The Constitution of the United States requires that a census be held every 10 years to determine congressional representation. This periodic investigation is supplemented by **vital statistics**, or records of births, deaths, marriages, and divorces that are gathered through a registration system maintained by governmental units. (434–435)

Demographic Transition: Beginning in the late 1700s—and continuing until the mid-1900s—there was a gradual reduction in death rates in northern and western Europe. While death rates fell, birthrates remained high; as a result, this period of European history brought unprecedented population growth. By the late 1800s, birthrates in many European countries began to decline, and the rate of population growth also decreased. Such changes serve as an example of **demographic transition**, the term used to describe changes in birthrates and death rates that occur during a nation's development. The demographic transition should be regarded not as a "law of population growth" but rather as a generalization of the population history of industrial nations. (436)

The Population Explosion: Apart from war, rapid population growth has been perhaps the dominant international social problem of the past 40 years. Often this issue is referred to in emotional terms, such as the "population bomb" or the "population explosion." Such striking language is not surprising given the staggering increases in world population recorded during the twentieth century. The population of our planet rose from 1 billion around the year 1800 to 6.4 billion in 2004. (437)

The Baby Boom: The most recent period of high fertility in the United States has often been referred to as the baby boom. During World War II, large numbers of military personnel were separated from their spouses. When they returned, the annual number of births began to rise dramatically. The boom resulted from a striking decrease in the number of childless marriages and one-child families. Although a peak was reached in 1957, the nation maintained a relatively high birthrate of over 20 live births per 1,000 population until 1964. (439)

Stable Population Growth: In the 1980s and early 1990s, some analysts projected relatively low fertility levels and moderate net migration over the coming decades. As a result, it seemed possible that the United States might reach **zero population growth (ZPG)**. ZPG is the state of population where the number of births plus immigrants equals the number of deaths plus emigrants. A society with stable population growth would be quite different from the United States of the 1990s. There would be relatively equal numbers of people in each age group, and the median age of the population might be as high as 38. (439)

Migration: The term **migration** refers to the relatively permanent movement of people, with the purpose of changing their place of residence. Migration usually describes movement over a sizable distance, rather than from one side of a city to another. International migration—changes of residence across national boundaries—has been a significant force in redistributing the world's population during certain periods of history. Although nations typically have laws and policies governing movement across their borders, the same is not true of internal movement. (439–440)

Environmental Problems—An Overview: More than 1 billion people on the planet are exposed to potentially health-damaging levels of air pollution. Throughout the United States, streams, rivers, and lakes have been polluted by dumping of waste materials by both industries and local governments. Love Canal made it clear that land can be seriously contaminated by industrial dumping of hazardous wastes and chemicals. Paul Ehrlich and Anne Ehrlich see world population growth as the central factor in environmental deterioration. Barry Commoner, a biologist, counters that the primary cause of environmental ills is the increasing use of technological innovations that are destructive to the world's environment. (442–443)

Functionalism and Human Ecology: In an application of the human ecological perspective, sociologist Riley Dunlap suggests that the natural environment serves three basic purposes for humans, as it does for the many animal species: (1) the environment provides the resources essential for life; (2) the environment serves as a waste repository; and (3) the environment "houses" our species. Human use of the environment for one of these functions will often strain its ability to fulfill the other two. (443)

Conflict View of Environmental Issues: World systems analysis shows how a growing share of the human and natural resources of the developing countries is being redistributed to the core industrialized nations. This process only intensifies the destruction of natural resources in poorer regions of the world. From a conflict perspective, less affluent nations are being forced to exploit their mineral deposits, forests, and fisheries in order to meet their debt obligations. (444)

World Population Policy: Social policies that address population growth touch on the most sensitive aspects of people's lives: sexuality, childbearing, and family relationships. For this reason, reaching a global consensus on population issues has been difficult. In developing countries, the death rate has fallen because of the introduction of modern medicine. In many developing countries, the traditional culture places great value on large families, thus the birth rate remains high. Parents also see children as potential laborers, and ultimately, as a means of broadening the family's economic base through the children's marriage. Yet functionalists note that when a country is struggling to provide clean water, food, and shelter to its people, high population growth *is* dysfunctional. Feminists question the motives of workers in government-funded population control problems, which were distributing contraceptives without sufficient concern for health risks, and to meet government quotas. Conflict theorists have questioned why industrialized nations, such as the United States, are so concerned with controlling the population of developing countries. Conflict theorists note that population growth is not the cause of hunger and misery. (445–446)

KEY TERMS

Briefly define or identify the following terms in the spaces provided below. The definitions of these terms can be found later in this chapter of the study guide.

Fertility	Total fertility rate (TFR)
Demography	Death rate
Census	Infant mortality rate
Vital statistics	Life expectancy
Birthrate	Growth rate

Demographic transition	Migration
Population pyramid	Human ecology
Zero population growth (ZPG)	Environmental justice

SELF-TEST

MODIFIED TRUE/FALSE QUESTIONS: If the statement below is true, write "true" in the space provided. If the statement is false, briefly correct the error.

1. Fertility is influenced by people's age of entry into sexual unions, and by their use of contraceptives, which reflect the social and religious values that guide a particular culture.

2. According to Thomas Robert Malthus, the gap between the food supply and world population will diminish over time.

3. Almost 18 percent of the children in developing countries will die before age 5—a rate 11 times higher than in developed nations.

4. The Constitution of the United States requires that a census be held every 5 years in order to determine congressional representation.

5. The growth rate of a society is the difference between births and deaths.

6. In the demographic transition, the transition stage is when declining death rates, primarily the result of reductions in infant deaths, along with high to medium fertility, result in significant population growth.

7. Demographic transition in developing nations has involved a rapid increase in death rates without adjustments in birthrates.

8. While population growth is a major problem in developing nations, it is also a concern in all industrial societies.

9. Few displaced people want to migrate to developing nations in Asia and Africa.

10. Since 1990, while internal migration to the South has remained high, migration to the West has lessened as the job boom in that region has ended.

11. The World Health Organization estimates that up to 700,000 premature deaths per year could be prevented if pollutants were brought down to safer levels.

12. In an application of the human ecological perspective, sociologist Riley Dunlap suggests that the natural environment serves no sociological purpose.

13. Urban ecologists point out that Western industrialized nations account for only 25 percent of the world's population, but are responsible for 85 percent of worldwide consumption.

14. Environmental justice is a legal strategy based on claims that poor people are subjected disproportionately to environmental hazards.

15. Feminists charged that workers in government-funded population control programs were distributing contraceptives without sufficient concern for their health risks.

MULTIPLE-CHOICE QUESTIONS: In each of the following, select the phrase that best completes the statement.

1. In studying population, which of the following would most interest a sociologist?
    a. the impact of natural disasters on population trends
    b. the relationship between climate and fertility
    c. availability of natural resources, such as oil and arable land, and how this influences mortality rates
    d. social factors that influence population rates and trends

2. For Thomas Robert Malthus, the appropriate way to control population was to
    a. use artificial means of birth control.
    b. postpone marriage.
    c. pass legislation prohibiting families from having more than one child.
    d. all of the above

3. Karl Marx's work is important to the study of population because he linked overpopulation to
    a. migration.
    b. demographic transition.
    c. the sick role.
    d. the distribution of resources.

4. Paul Ehrlich's work is an example of the
    a. functionalist perspective.
    b. conflict perspective.
    c. interactionist perspective.
    d. neo-Malthusian view.

5. Of the following nations, life expectancy at birth is highest in
   a. Japan.
   b. the United States.
   c. Nigeria.
   d. all of the above

6. The first stage of the demographic transition is called the
   a. pretransition stage.
   b. transition stage.
   c. posttransition stage.
   d. initiation stage.

7. Which country is currently experiencing a negative birthrate in some areas?
   a. China
   b. Bangladesh
   c. Iran
   d. Tunisia

8. The final stage in demographic transition is marked by
   a. high birthrates and death rates.
   b. high birthrates and low death rates.
   c. low birthrates and high death rates.
   d. low birthrates and low death rates.

9. The most recent period of high fertility in the United States, which began after the end of World War II, has often been referred to as the
   a. baby boom.
   b. baby bust.
   c. population bomb.
   d. age of Aquarius.

10. Although the total fertility rate in the United States remains low, our population continues to grow, because
    a. we have the highest life expectancy in the world.
    b. of our high rates of immigration.
    c. much of our population is of childbearing age.
    d. both b and c are correct

11. Which is not true about international immigration?

a. Half of all asylum seekers and refugees come from Afghanistan and Palestine.

b. Immigrants are sometimes targets of violence in Germany and France.

c. Many displaced people seek asylum in Africa and Asia.

d. Immigration to the United States is at a historical low.

12. According to Riley Dunlop, which one of the following is not a basic function that the natural environment serves for humans?

   a. It provides the resources essential for life.

   b. It serves as a waste depository.

   c. It provides a natural setting for social inequalities.

   d. It "houses" our species.

13. Conflict theorists contend that blaming developing countries for the world's environmental deterioration contains an element of

   a. ethnocentrism.

   b. xenocentrism.

   c. separatism.

   d. goal displacement.

14. _____ further refined the conflict analysis by criticizing the focus on affluent consumers as the cause of environmental troubles.

   a. Karl Marx

   b. Max Weber

   c. Thomas Malthus

   d. Allan Schnaiberg

15. Which perspective would say that the cause of hunger in the world is the unjust economic domination of industrialized nations, which results in an unequal distribution of the world's resources, and in widespread poverty in developing nations?

   a. the functionalist perspective

   b. the conflict perspective

   c. the interactionist perspective

   d. none of the above

FILL-IN QUESTIONS: Fill in the blank spaces in the sentences below with the correct words. Where two or more words are required, there will be a corresponding number of blank spaces.

1. In their studies of population issues, sociologists are keenly aware that various elements of population, such as _____, _____, and _____ are profoundly affected by the norms, values, and social patterns of a society.

2. _____ is the scientific study of population.

3. Neo-Malthusians have a _____ flavor in their condemnation of developed nations, which, despite their low birthrates, consume a disproportionately large share of world resources.

4. In the United States and most other countries, the _____ is the primary mechanism for collecting population information.

5. In demography the letters TFR stand for: _____ _____ _____.

6. _____ _____ _____ is the average number of children born alive to any woman, assuming that she conforms to current fertility rates.

7. The TFR reported for the United States in 2004 was _____ live births per woman, as compared to over _____ births per woman in a developing country such as Niger.

8. The growth rate of a society is the difference between births and deaths, plus the difference between _____ and _____.

9. In 2001, the United States had a growth rate of _____.

10. Between 1700 and the mid-1900s there has been a gradual reduction in death rates. People were able to live longer because of _____ _____, _____, _____, and _____ _____.

11. Beginning in the 1960s, governments in certain developing nations, like _____ and _____, sponsored or supported campaigns to encourage family planning.

12. Since the 1970s there has been a significant internal migration in the United States from the "_____ _____" of the north central and northeastern states to the "_____ _____" in the South and West.

13. Regarding environmental problems, three broad areas of concern stand out: _____ pollution, _____ pollution, and contamination of _____.

14. In 1986, a series of explosions set off a catastrophic nuclear reactor accident at _____, a part of the Ukraine (in what was then the Soviet Union).

15. In an application of the _____ _____ perspective, one sociologist suggests that the natural environment serves three basic functions for humans and for many animal species.

UNDERSTANDING SOCIAL POLICY: All of the following questions are based on material that appears in the social policy section on World Population Policy. Write a brief answer to each question in the space provided below.

1. Why has it been so difficult to reach a global consensus on population issues?

2. Functionalists would note that the best course of action for a community might differ from the best course of action for a society. What do they mean?

3. What is the Mexico City policy? Is it still in existence and how has it affected public health care programs?

DEFINITIONS OF KEY TERMS

Fertility: The level of reproduction in a society. (433)
Demography: The scientific study of population. (433)
Census: An enumeration, or counting, of a population. (434)

Vital statistics: Records of births, deaths, marriages, and divorces gathered through a registration system maintained by governmental units. (435)

Birthrate: The number of live births per 1,000 population in a given year. Also known as the *crude birthrate*. (435)

Total fertility rate (TFR): The average number of children born alive to any woman, assuming that she conforms to current fertility rates. (435)

Death rate: The number of deaths per 1,000 population in a given year. Also known as the *crude death rate*. (435)

Infant mortality rate: The number of deaths of infants under one year old per 1,000 live births in a given year. (435)

Life expectancy: The median number of years a person can be expected to live under current mortality conditions. (435)

Growth rate: The difference between births and deaths, plus the difference between immigrants and emigrants per 1,000 population. (435)

Demographic transition: A term used to describe the change from high birthrates and death rates to low birthrates and death rates. (436)

Population pyramid: A special type of bar chart that shows the distribution of a population by gender and age. (437)

Zero population growth (ZPG): The state of a population in which the number of births plus immigrants equals the number of deaths plus emigrants. (439)

Migration: The relatively permanent movement of people, with the purpose of changing their place of residence. (439)

Human ecology: An area of study concerned with the interrelationships between people and their environment. (443)

Environmental justice: A legal strategy based on claims that racial minorities are subjected disproportionately to environmental hazards. (444)

ANSWERS TO SELF-TEST

Modified True/False Questions

1. True (433)
2. According to Malthus, the gap between the food supply and world population will increase over time. (433)
3. True (434)
4. The Constitution of the United States requires that a census be held every 10 years in order to determine congressional representation. (434–435)
5. The growth rate of a society is the difference between births and deaths, plus the difference between immigrants and emigrants. (435)
6. True (436)

7. Demographic transition in developing nations has involved a rapid decline in death rates without adjustments in birthrates. (437)
8. Population growth is not a problem in all industrialized nations. A handful of countries are adopting policies that encourage growth. (438)
9. Developing countries in Asia and Africa are also encountering difficulties as thousands of displaced people seek assistance and asylum there. (440)
10. True (440)
11. True (442)
12. In an application of the human ecological perspective, sociologist Riley Dunlap suggests that the natural environment serves three basic functions: provides resources essential for life, serves as a waste repository, and "houses" our species. (443)
13. Conflict theorists point out that Western industrialized nations account for only 25 percent of the world's population but are responsible for 85 percent of worldwide consumption. (444)
14. Environmental justice is a legal strategy based on claims that racial minorities are subjected disproportionately to environmental hazards. (444)
15. True (445)

Multiple-Choice Questions

1. d (433)
2. b (434)
3. d (434)
4. d (434)
5. a (435)
6. a (436)
7. a (437)
8. d (436)
9. a (439)
10. d (439)
11. d (440)
12. c (443)
13. a (444)
14. d (444)
15. b (444)

Fill-In Questions

1. fertility; mortality, migration (433)
2. Demography (433)
3. Marxist (434)
4. census (434)
5. total fertility rate (435)
6. Total fertility rate (435)
7. 2.0; 8 (435)
8. immigrants; emigrants (435)
9. 0.6 percent (435)
10. food production; sanitation; nutrition; public health care (436)
11. Thailand; China (437)
12. snow belt; sun belt (440)
13. air; water; land (442)
14. Chernobyl (442)
15. human ecological (443)

Understanding Social Policy: World Population Policy

1. Social policies that address population growth touch on the most sensitive aspects of people's lives: sexuality, childbearing, and family relationships. For this reason, reaching a global consensus on population issues has been difficult. (445)

2. In developing nations, parents see children as potential laborers, and ultimately as a means of broadening the family's economic base. Under such conditions, having fewer children may not appear to be a rational choice. Yet for a country that is struggling to provide clean water, food, and shelter to its people, high population growth is dysfunctional. (445)

3. In 1984, under President Ronald Reagan, U.S. delegates to the World Population Conference in Mexico City announced that the United States would no longer support international planning programs that provided abortion services. During President Clinton's administration, this policy was overturned, but was reinstated when President Bush came into office. Currently, there is a gag rule imposed on all health workers who receive U.S. government funding, which forbids them to discuss this option publicly or with their patients. This rule has polarized otherwise nonpartisan public health programs. (445–446)

CHAPTER 22
COLLECTIVE BEHAVIOR AND SOCIAL MOVEMENTS

Theories of Collective Behavior
  Emergent Norm Perspective
  Value-Added Perspective
  Assembling Perspective

Forms of Collective Behavior
  Crowds
  Disaster Behavior
  Fads and Fashions
  Panics and Crazes
  Rumors
  Publics and Public Opinions
  Social Movements

Communications and the Globalization of Collective Behavior

Social Policy and Social Movements: Disability Rights
  The Issue
  The Setting
  Sociological Insights
  Policy Initiatives

BOXES
  SOCIOLOGY ON CAMPUS: *Antiwar Protests*
  SOCIOLOGY IN THE GLOBAL COMMUNITY: *A New Social Movement in Rural India*

KEY POINTS

Emergent-Norm Perspective: The **emergent-norm perspective** offered by sociologists Ralph Turner and Lewis Killian notes that during an episode of collective behavior, a definition of what behavior is appropriate or not emerges from the crowd. Like other social norms, the emergent norm reflects shared convictions held by members of the group, and is enforced through sanctions. There is latitude for a wide range of acts within a general framework established by the emergent norms. (451)

Value-Added Perspective: Sociologist Neil Smelser uses the **value-added model** to explain how broad social conditions are transformed in a definite pattern into some form of collective behavior. This model outlines six important determinants of collective behavior: structural conduciveness, structural strain, a generalized belief, a precipitating factor, mobilization for action, and the exercise of social control. Smelser's perspective represents an advance over earlier theories that treated gatherings as being dominated by irrational, extreme impulses. (452)

Assembling Perspective: Building on the interactionist approach, McPhail and Miller introduced the concept of the assembling process. The **assembling perspective** sought for the first time to examine how and why people move from different points in space to a common location. A basic distinction has been made between two types of assemblies. **Periodic assemblies** include recurring, routine gatherings of people, and are characterized by advance scheduling and recurring attendance of the majority of participants. **Nonperiodic assemblies** result from casually transmitted information and are generally less formal than periodic assemblies. (452–453)

Crowds: A **crowd** is a temporary gathering of people in close proximity who share a common focus or interest. Like other forms of collective behavior, crowds are not totally lacking in structure. Even during riots, participants are governed by identifiable social norms and exhibit definite patterns of behavior. In effect, an emergent norm allows looters to take what they regard as properly theirs. (453)

Publics and Public Opinion: The public is the least organized and most individualized form of collective behavior. The term **public** refers to a dispersed group of people, not necessarily in contact with one another, who share an interest in an issue. By contrast, **public opinion** refers to expressions of attitudes on matters of public policy that are communicated to decision makers. Theorists of collective behavior see no public opinion without a public and a decision maker. (457)

Social Movements: Sociologists use the term **social movement** to refer to organized collective activities to bring about or resist fundamental change in an existing group or society. Social movements imply the existence of conflict, but we can also analyze their activities from a functionalist perspective, which views social movements as training grounds for leaders of the political establishment. (457)

Chapter 22 *Collective Behavior and Social Movements* | 313

Relative Deprivation: The term **relative deprivation** is defined as the conscious feeling of a negative discrepancy between legitimate expectations and present actualities. It may be characterized by scarcity rather than a complete lack of necessities. A relatively deprived person is dissatisfied because he or she feels downtrodden relative to some appropriate reference group. A group will not mobilize into a social movement unless there is a shared perception that members can end their relative deprivation only through collective action. (458)

Resource Mobilization: The term **resource mobilization** is used to refer to the ways in which a social movement utilizes such resources as money, political influence, access to the media, and personnel. Leadership is a central factor in the mobilization of the discontented into social movements. Karl Marx recognized the importance of recruitment when he called on workers to become aware of their oppressed status and to develop a class consciousness. (458)

New Social Movements: The term **new social movements** refers to organized collective activities that address values and social identities as well as improvements in the quality of life. Educated, middle-class people are significantly represented in some of these new social movements, such as the women's movement and the movement for lesbian and gay rights. (460)

Disability Rights: Since the 1960s, the effort to ensure not only the health, but also the rights of people with disabilities has been growing steadily. In 1990, working with a presidentially appointed council, organizations representing people with disabilities achieved passage of the Americans with Disabilities Act (ADA). From a labeling perspective, the ADA represents a significant framing of the issue of disability rights. Conflict theorists see the mobilization of resources of behalf of people with disabilities as part of a forty-year civil rights movement. (462–463)

KEY TERMS

Briefly define or identify the following terms in the spaces provided below. The definitions of these terms can be found later in this chapter of the study guide.

Collective behavior	Value-added model
Emergent norm perspective	Assembling perspective

Periodic assembly	Public
Non-periodic assembly	Public opinion
Crowd	Social movement
Disaster	Relative deprivation
Fad	Resource mobilization
Fashion	False consciousness
Craze	New social movement
Panic	Visitablity
Rumor	

SELF-TEST

MODIFIED TRUE/FALSE QUESTIONS: If the statement below is true, write "true" in the space provided. If the statement is false, briefly correct the error.

1. The emergent-norm perspective begins with the assumption that a large crowd, such as a group of rock fans, is basically ungovernable.

2. The value-added model appears to offer a more useful explanation of society-wide episodes of collective behavior, such as crazes and fashions, than the emergent-norm perspective.

3. Demonstrations, parades, and gatherings at the scenes of accidents are classified as periodic assemblies.

4. Even during riots, participants are governed by identifiable social norms, and exhibit definite patterns of behavior.

5. Natural disasters and technological disasters are two completely distinct types of events.

6. Disaster research has shown that even in natural calamities, maintaining and restoring communications is vital not just to directing relief efforts, but to reducing survivors' anxiety.

7. The key distinction between panics and crazes is that panics are movements to something whereas crazes are flights from something.

8. Poland's Lech Walesa, Russia's Boris Yeltsin, and the Czech Republic's Vaclav Havel led protest movements against Communist rule, and subsequently became leaders of their countries' governments.

9. A disadvantaged group will not mobilize into a social movement unless there is a shared perception that its relative deprivation can be ended only through collective action.

10. Since social movements tend to be progressive, women are often able to assume leadership positions in social movement organizations.

11. During the 1980s, many universities created "free speech zones" to contain political demonstrations. In effect, these zones limited the constitutional right to free speech to a few small areas of campus.

12. New social movements are usually focused on a single issue.

13. Whereas traditional views of social movements tended to emphasize resource mobilization on a broad global level, new social movements theory offers a local perspective on social and political activism.

14. India's SSKKMS social movement had a fairly typical leadership core comprised of middle-class men.

15. New technologies have little bearing on collective behavior.

Chapter 22 *Collective Behavior and Social Movements* | 317

MULTIPLE-CHOICE QUESTIONS: In each of the following, select the phrase that best completes the statement.

1. The early writings on collective behavior imply that crowds are basically
    a. functional.
    b. value-added.
    c. structured.
    d. ungovernable.

2. The emergent-norm perspective of collective behavior was developed by
    a. Neil Smelser.
    b. Clark McPhail.
    c. Ralph Turner and Lewis Killian.
    d. Sharon Barnartt.

3. The emergent-norm perspective has been criticized for being too vague in defining what constitutes a
    a. riot.
    b. crowd.
    c. belief.
    d. norm.

4. The demonstration at Gallaudet University in 1988 that forced the board of trustees to appoint the school's first deaf president is an example of
    a. a periodic assembly.
    b. a nonperiodic assembly.
    c. structural conduciveness.
    d. generalized belief.

5. In sociological terms, which of the following constitute a crowd?
    a. spectators at a baseball game
    b. participants at a college pep rally
    c. urban rioters
    d. all of the above

6. Disaster research has shown that even in natural calamities, maintaining and restoring communications is vital not just to _____, but to _____.
   a. structural normalization; awareness
   b. structural conduciveness: precipitating factors
   c. directing relief efforts; reducing survivors anxiety
   d. all of the above

7. _____ and _____ both represent responses to some generalized belief.
   a. Rumors; fads
   b. Rumors; panic
   c. Panic; crazes
   d. none of the above

8. Which sociological perspective would be most likely to emphasize that rumors serve a function by providing a group with a shared belief?
   a. the functionalist perspective
   b. the conflict perspective
   c. the interactionist perspective
   d. labeling theory

9. The least organized and most individualized form of collective behavior is represented by
   a. rumors.
   b. publics.
   c. fashions.
   d. panics.

10. From the point of view of theorists of collective behavior, there can be no public opinion unless there is both
    a. a public and mass media.
    b. a decision maker and mass media.
    c. a public and a decision maker.
    d. relative deprivation and resource mobilization.

11. From the point of view of social scientists, call-in telephone "polls" using 1-900 numbers are misleading because
    a. of the Hawthorne effect.
    b. the sample that emerges is hardly representative.
    c. they rely on improper resource mobilization.
    d. all of the above

12. The most all-encompassing type of collective behavior is
    a. public opinion.
    b. social movements.
    c. rumors.
    d. crowds.

13. "Collective enterprises to establish a new order of life" refers to
    a. public opinion.
    b. social movements.
    c. rumors.
    d. crowds.

14. Which sociological perspective emphasizes that social movements provide a training ground for leaders of the political establishment?
    a. the functionalist perspective
    b. the conflict perspective
    c. the interactionist perspective
    d. labeling theory

15. The resource mobilization perspective would be most interested in looking at the influence of _____ on social movements.
    a. tenacity
    b. desire
    c. emotion
    d. money

FILL-IN QUESTIONS: Fill in the blank spaces in the sentences below with the correct words. Where two or more words are required, there will be a corresponding number of blank spaces.

1. Like other social norms, the emergent norm reflects shared convictions held by members of a group, and is enforced through _____.

2. In the value-added model, the term _____ _____ is used to indicate that the organization of society can facilitate the emergence of conflicting interests.

3. Building on the _____ perspective, Clark McPhail and David Miller introduced the concept of the assembling process.

4. The term _____ refers to a sudden or disruptive event or set of events that overtaxes a community's resources, so that outside aid is necessary.

5. In the wake of many natural and technological disasters, decision making becomes more _____ than in normal times.

6. Punk haircuts would be considered a _____, whereas dancing to the Macarena is an example of a _____.

7. Members of a _____ may adopt a fad or fashion in order to break with tradition while remaining "in" with (accepted by) a significant reference group of peers.

8. One of the many _____ that emerged after the World Trade Center attacks was a false account that a police officer had "surfed" a steel beam down 86 floors as one of the towers collapsed.

9. "Collective enterprises to establish a new order of life" is the phrase used by Herbert Blumer to describe _____ _____.

10. The _____ perspective emphasizes that even when unsuccessful, social movements contribute to the formation of public opinion.

11. The term relative deprivation recognizes the importance of _____ in the emergence of social movements.

12. A relatively deprived person is dissatisfied because he or she feels deprived relative to some appropriate _____ group.

13. As Max Weber described it in 1904, _____ is the quality of an individual that sets him or her apart from ordinary people.

14. As Robert Michels pointed out, social movements often become more _____ over time.

15. The SSKKMS movement was unusual when compared to other social movements in the region in that about one-half of its participants, and many of its leaders, were _____.

UNDERSTANDING SOCIAL POLICY: All of the following questions are based on material that appears in the social policy section on Disability Rights. Write a brief answer to each question in the space provided below.

1. How did the movement for disability rights begin?

2. What is the difference between an organization *for* disabled people, and an organization *of* disabled people?

3. What is the Americans with Disabilities Act?

DEFINITIONS OF KEY TERMS

Collective behavior: In the view of sociologist Neil Smelser, the relatively spontaneous and unstructured behavior of a group of people who are reacting to a common influence in an ambiguous situation. (450)

Emergent-norm perspective: A theory of collective behavior proposed by Turner and Killian that holds that a collective definition of appropriate and inappropriate behavior emerges during episodes of collective behavior. (451)

Value-added model: A theory of collective behavior proposed by Neil Smelser to explain how broad social conditions are transformed in a definite pattern into some form of collective behavior. (452)

Assembling perspective: A theory of collective behavior introduced by McPhail and Miller that seeks to examine how and why people move from different points in space to a common location. (452)

Periodic assembly: A recurring, relatively routine gathering of people, such as a college class. (452)

Nonperiodic assembly: A nonrecurring gathering of people that often results from word-of-mouth information. (453)

Crowd: A temporary gathering of people in close proximity who share a common focus or interest. (453)

Disaster: A sudden or disruptive event or set of events that overtaxes a community's resources, so that outside aid is necessary. (453)

Fad: A temporary pattern of behavior that involves large numbers of people and is independent of preceding trends. (455)

Fashion: A pleasurable mass involvement that has a line of historical continuity. (455)

Craze: An exciting mass involvement that lasts for a relatively long period. (455)

Panic: A fearful arousal or collective flight based on a generalized belief that may or may not be accurate. (455)

Rumor: A piece of information gathered informally that is used to interpret an ambiguous situation. (456)

Public: A dispersed group of people, not necessarily in contact with one another, who share an interest in an issue. (457)

Public opinion: Expressions of attitudes on matters of public policy that are communicated to decision makers. (457)

Social movement: An organized collective activity to bring about or resist fundamental change in an existing group or society. (457)

Relative deprivation: The conscious feeling of a negative discrepancy between legitimate expectations and present actualities. (458)

Resource mobilization: The ways in which a social movement utilizes such resources as money, political influence, access to the media, and personnel. (458)

False consciousness: A term used by Karl Marx to describe an attitude held by members of a class that does not accurately reflect their objective position. (459)

New social movement: An organized collective activity that addresses values and social identities, as well as improvements in the quality of life. (460)

Visitablity: The accessibility of private homes to visitors with disabilities. (463)

ANSWERS TO SELF-TEST

Modified True/False Questions

1. The emergent-norm perspective begins with the assumption that a large crowd, such as a group of rock fans, is governed by expectations of proper behavior just as much as is four people playing doubles tennis. (451)
2. The emergent-norm perspective appears to offer a more useful explanation of society-wide episodes of collective behavior, such as crazes and fashions, than the value-added approach. (452)
3. Demonstrations, parades, and gatherings at the scenes of accidents are classified as nonperiodic assemblies. (453)
4. True (453)

5. The distinction between these two types of disaster is not clear-cut. As environmentalists have observed, many human practices either contribute to, or trigger natural disasters. (454)
6. True (454)
7. The key distinction between panics and crazes is that crazes are movements to something whereas panics are flights from something. (455)
8. True (457)
9. True (458)
10. In our male-dominated society, women find it more difficult than men to assume leadership positions in social movement organizations. (459)
11. True (460)
12. Many new social movements have complex agendas that go beyond a single issue. (460)
13. Whereas traditional views of social movements tended to emphasize resource mobilization on a local level, new social movements theory offers a broad global perspective on social and political activism. (460)
14. The leadership core of the SSKKMS social movement contained a number of women. (461)
15. New technologies can have a big impact on various forms of collective behavior. For example, the Internet can allow rumors to spread very quickly. (461)

Multiple-Choice Questions

1. d (451)
2. c (451)
3. d (452)
4. b (453)
5. d (453)
6. c (454)
7. c (455)
8. a (456)
9. b (457)
10. c (457)
11. b (457)
12. b (457)
13. b (457)
14. a (457)
15. d (458)

Fill-In Questions

1. sanctions (451)
2. structural conduciveness (452)
3. interactionist (452)
4. disaster (453–454)
5. centralized (454)
6. fashion; fad (455)
7. subculture (455)
8. rumors (457)
9. social movements (457)
10. functionalist (457)
11. perception (458)
12. reference (458)
13. charisma (458)
14. bureaucratic (458)
15. women (461)

Understanding Social Policy: Disability Rights

1. In the early 1960s, a group of young adults with disabilities organized to be allowed admission at the University of California at Berkeley. The university, reluctant to admit them at first, finally agreed, and found living quarters for them in the infirmary. Dubbed the Rolling Quads, these students proved that they could succeed in college despite the extraordinary challenges they faced. Eventually the group turned their attention to the surrounding community. Their activism marked the beginning of advocacy for people with disabilities. (462)

2. According to disability rights activists, there is an important distinction between organizations *for* disabled people, and organizations *of* disabled people. Because people with disabilities do not control the service providers, charitable associations, and parents' groups that work for their welfare, those organizations do not stress the goals of independence and self-help that are important to people with disabilities. (462)

3. In 1990, working with a presidentially appointed council, organizations representing people with disabilities achieved passage of the Americans with Disabilities Act (ADA). The act defines disability as a condition that substantially limits a major life activity, such as walking to seeing. It prohibits bias against people with disabilities in employment, transportation, public accommodations, and telecommunications. Businesses with more than 25 employees cannot refuse to hire a qualified applicant with a disability. Instead, they must make reasonable accommodations that will allow workers with disabilities to do their jobs. (462–463)

CHAPTER 23: GLOBALIZATION, TECHNOLOGY, AND SOCIAL CHANGE

Theories of Social Change
  Evolutionary Theory
  Functionalist Theory
  Conflict Theory

Resistance to Social Change
  Economic and Cultural Factors
  Resistance to Technology

Global Social Change

Technology and the Future
  Computer Technology
  Privacy and Censorship in a Global Village
  Biotechnology

Social Policy and Globalization: Transnationals
  The Issue
  The Setting
  Sociological Insights
  Policy Initiatives

BOXES
  SOCIOLOGY IN THE GLOBAL COMMUNITY: Social Change in South Africa
  RESEARCH IN ACTION: The Human Genome Project

KEY POINTS

Evolutionary Theory: **Evolutionary theory** views society as moving in a definite direction. Early evolutionary theorists generally agreed that society was inevitably progressing to a higher state. August Comte saw human societies as moving forward in their thinking from mythology to the scientific method. Émile Durkheim maintained that society progressed from simple to more complex forms of social organization. (469)

The Functionalist View of Change: Talcott Parsons, a leading proponent of functionalist theory, viewed society as being in a natural state of equilibrium. According to his equilibrium model, as changes occur in one part of society, adjustments must be made in other parts. Though Parsons's approach explicitly incorporates the evolutionary notion of continuing progress, the dominant theme in this model is balance and stability. (469)

The Conflict View of Change: Conflict theorists contend that social institutions and practices persist because powerful groups have the ability to maintain the status quo. Change has crucial significance, since it is needed to correct social injustices and inequalities. In contrast to functionalists' emphasis on stability, Karl Marx argues that conflict is a normal and desirable aspect of social change. In fact, change must be encouraged as a means of eliminating social inequality. (470)

Resistance to Social Change: Efforts to promote social change are likely to meet with resistance. Social economist Thorstein Veblen coined the term **vested interests** to refer to those people or groups who will suffer in the event of social change. In general, those with a disproportionate share of society's wealth, status, and power have a vested interest in preserving the status quo. (470)

Global Social Change: In this era of massive social, political, and economic change on a global scale, is it possible to predict change? In her presidential address to the American Sociological Association, Maureen Hallinan cautioned that we need to move beyond the restrictive models of social change—the linear view of evolutionary theory and the assumptions about equilibrium in functionalist theory. (472)

Computer Technology: The Internet is the world's largest computer network. Until recently, it was difficult to gain access to the Internet without holding a position at a university or a government research laboratory. Today, however, virtually anyone can reach the Internet with a phone line, a computer, and a modem. However, it is much more difficult for the less affluent to get onto the information highway. (473)

Privacy and Censorship in a Global Village: The complex issue of privacy and censorship in this technological age can be considered an illustration of culture lag, in which the material culture (the technology) is changing faster than the nonmaterial culture (norms controlling the technology). Functionalists point to the manifest function of the Internet in its ability to facilitate communications. They also identify the latent function of providing a forum for groups with few resources to communicate with the masses. Conflict theorists note that there is ever-present danger that a society's most powerful groups will use technological advances to invade the privacy of the less powerful. (474-475)

Biotechnology: George Ritzer's concept of McDonaldization applies to the entire area of biotechnology. Just as the fast-food concept has permeated society, no phase of life now seems exempt from therapeutic or medical intervention. Today's biotechnology holds itself out as totally beneficial to human beings, but it is in constant need of monitoring, (475)

Transnationals: The labor market has become an increasingly global one. Sociologists are finding that new technologies which facilitate international travel and communications are accelerating the transnational movement of workers. Functionalists see the free flow of immigrants as one way for economies to maximize their use of human labor. Conflict theorists charge that globalization and international migration have increased the economic gulf between developed and developing nations. (477-478)

KEY TERMS

Briefly define or identify the following terms in the spaces provided below. The definitions of these terms can be found later in this chapter of the study guide.

Social change	Luddites
Evolutionary theory	Apartheid
Vested interests	Technology
Culture lag	Transnational

Technology	

SELF-TEST

MODIFIED TRUE/FALSE QUESTIONS: If the statement below is true, write "true" in the space provided. If the statement is false, briefly correct the error.

1. Early evolutionary theorists generally agreed that society was inevitably progressing to a higher state.

2. Talcott Parsons' approach to social change explicitly rejects the evolutionary notion of continuing progress.

3. As noted by critics, the functionalist approach places substantial emphasis on the use of coercion by the powerful to maintain the illusion of a stable, well-integrated society.

4. The Marxist view of social change restricts people to a passive role in responding to inevitable cycles or changes in material culture.

5. Those with a disproportionate share of society's wealth, status, and power generally have a vested interest in preserving the status quo.

6. Conflict theorists argue that, in a capitalistic economic system, many companies are not willing to pay the price to meet strict safety standards.

7. Nonmaterial culture encompasses ideas, norms, communication, and social organization.

8. In England beginning in 1811, masked craft workers known as neo-Luddites mounted nighttime raids on factories and destroyed some of the new machinery.

9. In 1997 scientists in Scotland cloned a sheep.

10. Biotechnology has generally been seen as a benefit to society; critics have been concerned mostly with the possibility of unintended negative consequences.

11. Between 1975 and August 2000, terrorists created 342 incidents involving biological or chemical agents.

12. One concern about bioterrorism is that biological and chemical weapons are not difficult or expensive to make.

13. One concern raised by the Human Genome Project is that not everyone who donates their genes to the project will do so voluntarily, after being informed of the risks and benefits.

14. From a functionalist perspective there is the ever-present danger that a society's most powerful groups will use technological advances to invade the privacy of the less powerful, and thereby maintain or intensify various forms of inequality and injustice.

15. Today's immigrants rely primarily on foreign-language newspapers to keep up with events at home.

MULTIPLE-CHOICE QUESTIONS: In each of the following, select the phrase that best completes the statement.

1. Nineteenth-century theories of social change reflect the pioneering work in biological evolution done by
    a. Albert Einstein.
    b. Charles Darwin.
    c. Harriet Martineau.
    d. Benjamin Franklin.

2. The writings of Auguste Comte and Émile Durkheim are examples of
    a. cyclical theory.
    b. evolutionary theory.
    c. interactionist theory.
    d. conflict theory.

3. Which term was used by Talcott Parsons in asserting that society tends toward a state of stability or balance?
    a. charisma
    b. magnetism
    c. equilibrium
    d. status quo

4. The acceptance of preventative medicine is an example of the process that Parsons called
    a. differentiation.
    b. value generalization.
    c. inclusion.
    d. adaptive upgrading.

5. Which of the following theorists argued that conflict is a normal and desirable aspect of social change?
   a. Karl Marx
   b. Talcott Parsons
   c. Émile Durkheim
   d. all of the above

6. The term *vested interests* was coined by social economist
   a. William F. Ogburn.
   b. Talcott Parsons.
   c. Auguste Comte.
   d. Thorstein Veblen.

7. The abbreviation "NIMBY" stands for "not in my backyard," a cry often heard when people protest
   a. landfills.
   b. prisons.
   c. nuclear power facilities.
   d. all of the above

8. Which sociologist introduced the concept of culture lag?
   a. William F. Ogburn
   b. Talcott Parsons
   c. Auguste Comte
   d. Thorstein Veblen

9. An example of global inequality is evident in Immanual Wallerstein's world system analysis, which states that
   a. core nations have a virtual monopoly on information technology.
   b. developing nations like Africa, Asia, and Latin America are on the periphery.
   c. periphery nations must rely on industrial giants for technology, and the information it provides.
   d. all of the above

10. Which term was introduced by Charles Perrow to refer to failures that are inevitable, given the manner in which human and technological systems are organized?
    a. the Perrow principle
    b. the Peter principle
    c. standard accidents
    d. normal accidents

11. In 1994 South Africa held its first universal election and chose as its president
    a. F. W. DeKlerk.
    b. Steven Biko.
    c. Nelson Mandela.
    d. Chinua Achebe.

12. Internationally, which language is most common on the Internet?
    a. English
    b. Russian
    c. German
    d. Japanese

13. Which sociological perspective would be especially interested in studying how people communicate with each other and develop relationships through MUDS (multi-user domains) and electronic chat rooms?
    a. the functionalist perspective
    b. the conflict perspective
    c. the interactionist perspective
    d. labeling theory

14. Which term refers to an immigrant who sustains multiple social replationships that link his or her society of origin with the society of settlement?
    a. transnational
    b. transglobal
    c. global citizen
    d. none of the above

Chapter 23 *Globalization, Technology, and Social Change* | 333

15. Which sociological perspective sees transnationals as a way for economies to maximize their use of human labor?
    a. functionalist
    b. conflict
    c. interactionist
    d. feminist

FILL-IN QUESTIONS: Fill in the blank spaces in the sentences below with the correct words. Where two or more words are required, there will be a corresponding number of blank spaces.

1. Early evolutionary theorists concluded in a(n) _____ fashion that their own behavior and culture were more advanced than those of earlier civilizations.

2. Talcott Parsons used the term _____ to refer to the increasing complexity of social organization.

3. As the work of Talcott Parsons demonstrates, the _____ perspective has made a distinctive contribution to the study of social change.

4. _____ argued that conflict is a normal and desirable aspect of social change.

5. Social economist _____ _____ coined the term vested interests to refer to those people or groups who will suffer in the event of social change, and who have a stake in maintaining the status quo.

6. William Ogburn introduced the concept of culture lag to refer to the period of maladjustment during which the _____ culture is still adapting to new _____ conditions.

7. The term _____ refers to those who are wary of technological innovations, and who question the incessant expansion of industrialization, the increasing destruction of the natural and agrarian world, and the "throw it away" mentality of contemporary capitalism.

8. _____ is information about how to use the material resources of the environment to satisfy human needs and desires.

9. The _____ is the world's largest computer network.

10. North America and Europe, and a few other industrialized nations, have almost all the world's _____ _____.

11. From a _____ perspective, sex selection can be viewed as an adaptation of the basic family function of regulating reproduction.

12. "Today we stand at the brink of becoming two societies, one largely white and plugged in and the other black and unplugged." This is how Black historian Henry Lewis Gates, Jr., starkly describes today's "_____ _____."

13. _____ note that just as we may disapprove of some associations that relatives or friends have with other people, we also express concern over controversial websites.

14. The _____ perspective would stress the danger that the most powerful groups in a society will use technology to violate the privacy of the less powerful.

15. Regarding privacy on the Internet, young people who have grown up browsing the Internet seem to accept the existence of _____ and _____ they may pick up while surfing.

UNDERSTANDING SOCIAL POLICY: All of the following questions are based on material that appears in the social policy section on Transnationals. Write a brief answer to each question in the space provided below.

1. How has globalization impacted the world labor market?

2. What is the conflict view of transnationals?

3. What voting rights do transnationals typically have?

DEFINITIONS OF KEY TERMS

Social change: Significant alteration over time in behavior patterns and culture, including norms and values. (468)

Evolutionary theory: A theory of social change that holds that society is moving in a definite direction. (469)

Equilibrium model: The functionalist view that society tends toward a state of stability or balance. (469)

Vested interests: Those people or groups who will suffer in the event of social change, and who have a stake in maintaining the status quo. (470)

Culture lag: A period of maladjustment when the nonmaterial culture is still struggling to adapt to new material conditions. (471)

Luddites: Rebellious craft workers in 19th-century England who destroyed new factory machinery as part of their resistance to the industrial revolution. (471)

Apartheid: A former policy of the South African government, designed to maintain the separation of Blacks and other non-Whites from the dominant Whites. (473)

Technology: Information about how to use the material resources of the environment to satisfy human needs and desires. (472)

Transnational: An immigrant who sustains multiple social relationships that link his or her society of origin with the society of settlement. (477)

ANSWERS TO SELF-TEST

Modified True/False Questions
1. True (469)
2. Talcott Parsons's approach to social change explicitly incorporates the evolutionary notion of continuing progress. (469)
3. As noted by critics, the functionalist approach virtually disregards the use of coercion by the powerful to maintain the illusion of a stable, well-integrated society. (469–470)
4. The Marxist view of social change does not restrict people to a passive role in responding to inevitable cycles or changes in material culture. (470)
5. True (470)
6. True (471)
7. True (471)
8. In England beginning in 1811, masked craft workers known as Luddites mounted nighttime raids on factories and destroyed some of the new machinery. (471)
9. True (475)
10. True (477)
11. True (477)

12. True (477)
13. True (476)
14. From a conflict perspective there is the ever-present danger that a society's most powerful groups will use technological advances to invade the privacy of the less powerful. (475)
15. In generations past immigrants read foreign-language newspapers to keep in touch with events in their home countries. Today, the Internet gives immigrants immediate access to their countries and kinfolk. (477)

Multiple-Choice Questions

1. b (469)
2. b (469)
3. c (469)
4. b (469)
5. a (470)
6. d (470)
7. d (471)
8. a (471)
9. d (474)
10. d (474)
11. c (473)
12. a (474)
13. c (474)
14. a (477)
15. a (478)

Fill-In Questions

1. ethnocentric (469)
2. differentiation (469)
3. functionalist (469)
4. Marx (470)
5. Thorstein Veblen (470)
6. nonmaterial; material (471)
7. neo-Luddites (471)
8. Technology (472)
9. Internet (473)
10. Internet hosts (474)
11. functionalist (475)
12. digital divide (474)
13. Interactionists (475)
14. conflict (475)
15. cookies; spyware (475)

Understanding Social Policy: Transnationals

1. Despite legal restrictions, the labor market has become an increasingly global one. Just as globalization has integrated government policies, cultures, social movements, and financial markets, it has unified what once were discrete national labor markets. (477)

2. Conflict theorists charge that globalization and international migration have increased the economic gulf between developed and developing nations. In addition, through tourism and the global reach of the mass media, people in poorer countries have become aware of the affluent lifestyle common in developed nations—and, of course, many of them now aspire to it. Sociologists who follow the world systems analysis suggest that the global flow of people, not just goods and resources, should be factored into the theoretical relationship between core and periphery nations. (478)

3. Voter eligibility is an unresolved transnational issue. Not all nations allow dual citizenship, and even those countries that do may not allow absent nationals to vote. The United States and Great Britain are rather liberal in this regard, permitting dual

citizenship and allowing émigrés to continue to vote. Mexico, in contrast, has been reluctant to allow citizens who have emigrated to vote. (479)